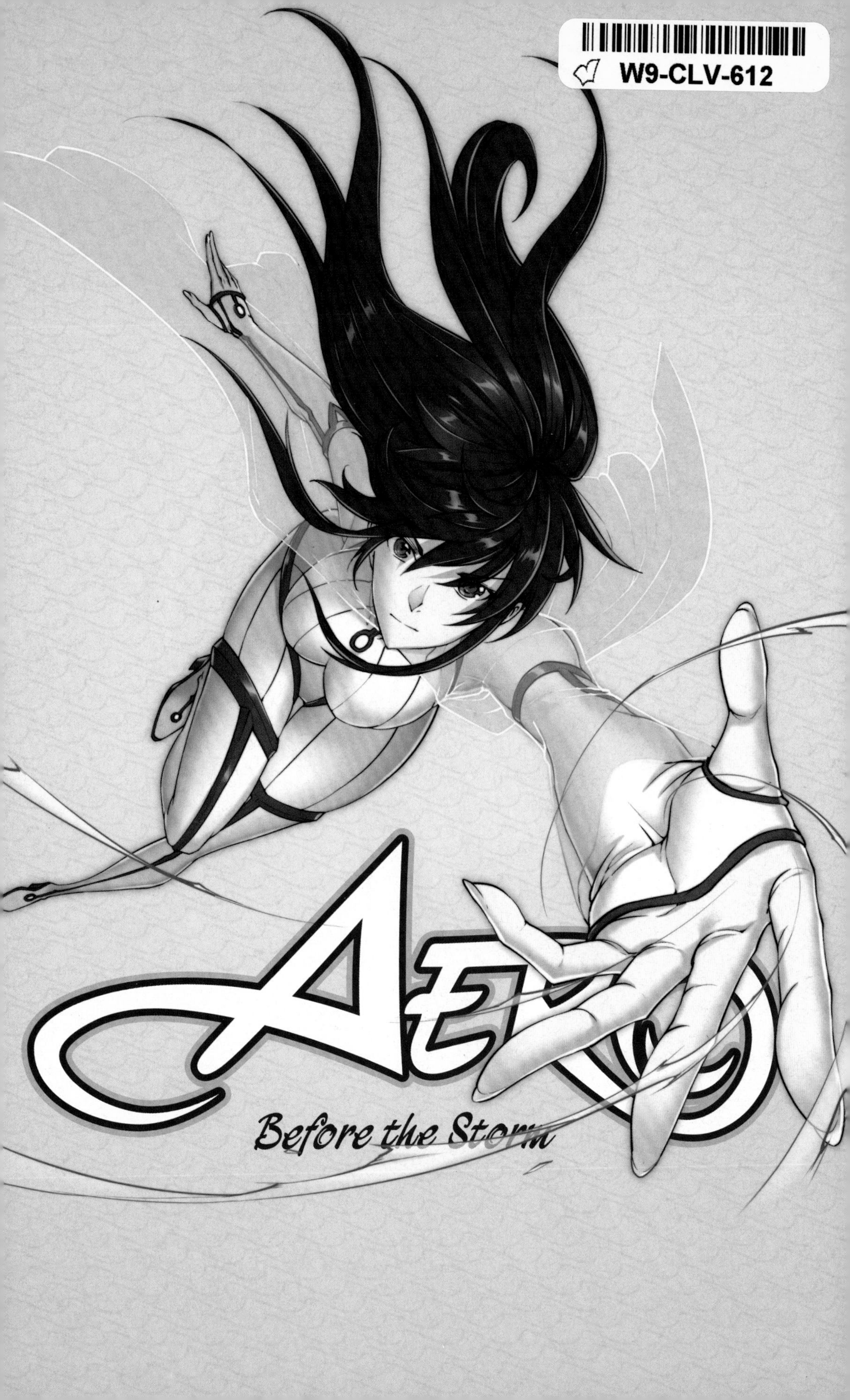
Before the Storm

Lei Ling wants to build a better, balanced and more beautiful Shanghai. As a brilliant architect and rising young elite, she's worked incredibly hard to achieve an unprecedented level of success for herself and her city. The key? For Lei, it's all about balance. But balancing her career as well as her second life as a super hero and new Agent of Atlas is getting more and more difficult.

And now, everything that Lei's built — in both of her lives — may be crumbling.
And Aero doesn't do failure...

With the power of the wind at her command, Lei Ling is the master of the sky! She is the astonishing, awe-inspiring...

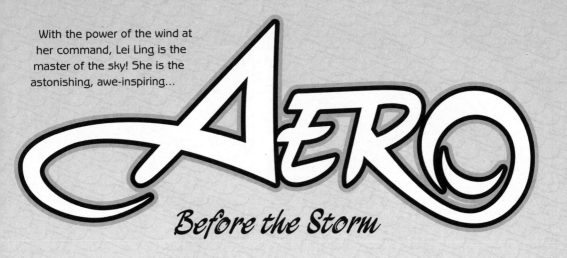

AERO

Before the Storm

Zhou Liefen
Writer

Keng
Artist

Greg Pak
Adaptation

VC's Joe Caramagna
Letterer

Keng
Cover Art

Carlos Lao
Logo Design

Tom Groneman, Lindsey Cohick & Martin Biro
Assistant Editors

Mark Paniccia
Editor

Special Thanks to
Winni Woo & Yifan Jiang

Collection Editor **Jennifer Grünwald**
Assistant Managing Editor **Maia Loy**
Assistant Editor **Caitlin O'Connell**
Editor, Special Projects **Mark D. Beazley**

VP Production & Special Projects **Jeff Youngquist**
Book Designer **Adam Del Re**
SVP Print, Sales & Marketing **David Gabriel**
Editor in Chief **C.B. Cebulski**

AERO VOL. 1: BEFORE THE STORM. Contains material originally published in magazine form as AERO (2019) #1-6. First printing 2019. ISBN 978-1-302-91944-3. Published by MARVEL WORLDWIDE, INC., a subsidiary of MARVEL ENTERTAINMENT, LLC. OFFICE OF PUBLICATION: 1290 Avenue of the Americas, New York, NY 10104. © 2019 MARVEL No similarity between any of the names, characters, persons, and/or institutions in this magazine with those of any living or dead person or institution is intended, and any such similarity which may exist is purely coincidental. **Printed in Canada.** KEVIN FEIGE, Chief Creative Officer; DAN BUCKLEY, President, Marvel Entertainment; JOHN NEE, Publisher; JOE QUESADA, EVP & Creative Director; TOM BREVOORT, SVP of Publishing; DAVID BOGART, Associate Publisher & SVP of Talent Affairs; Publishing & Partnership; DAVID GABRIEL, VP of Print & Digital Publishing; JEFF YOUNGQUIST, VP of Production & Special Projects; DAN CARR, Executive Director of Publishing Technology; ALEX MORALES, Director of Publishing Operations; DAN EDINGTON, Managing Editor; SUSAN CRESPI, Production Manager; STAN LEE, Chairman Emeritus. For information regarding advertising in Marvel Comics or on Marvel.com, please contact Vit DeBellis, Custom Solutions & Integrated Advertising Manager, at vdebellis@marvel.com. For Marvel subscription inquiries, please call 888-511-5480. **Manufactured between 12/20/2019 and 1/21/2020 by SOLISCO PRINTERS, SCOTT, QC, CANADA.**

10 9 8 7 6 5 4 3 2 1

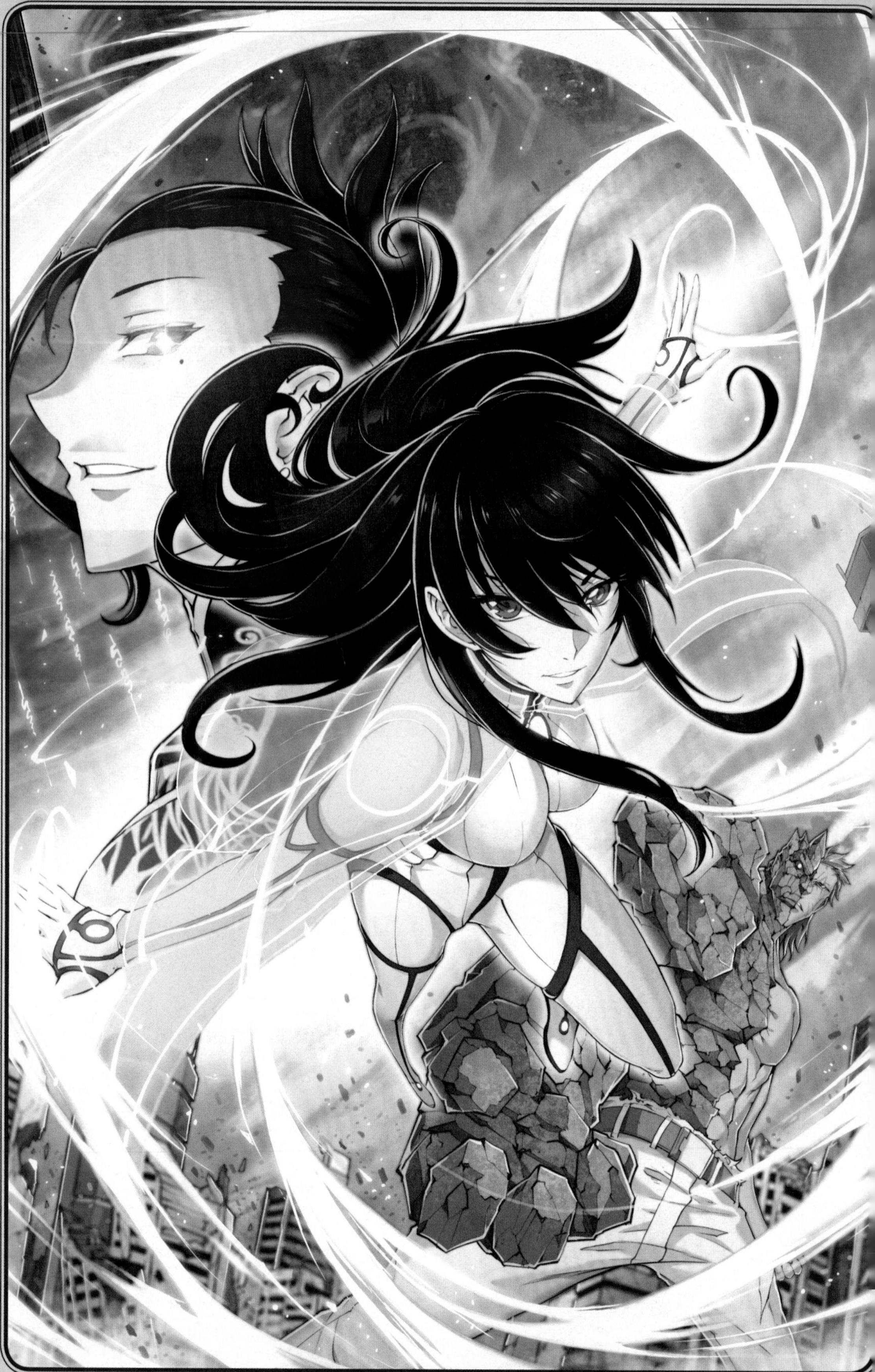

1 Protector of the City

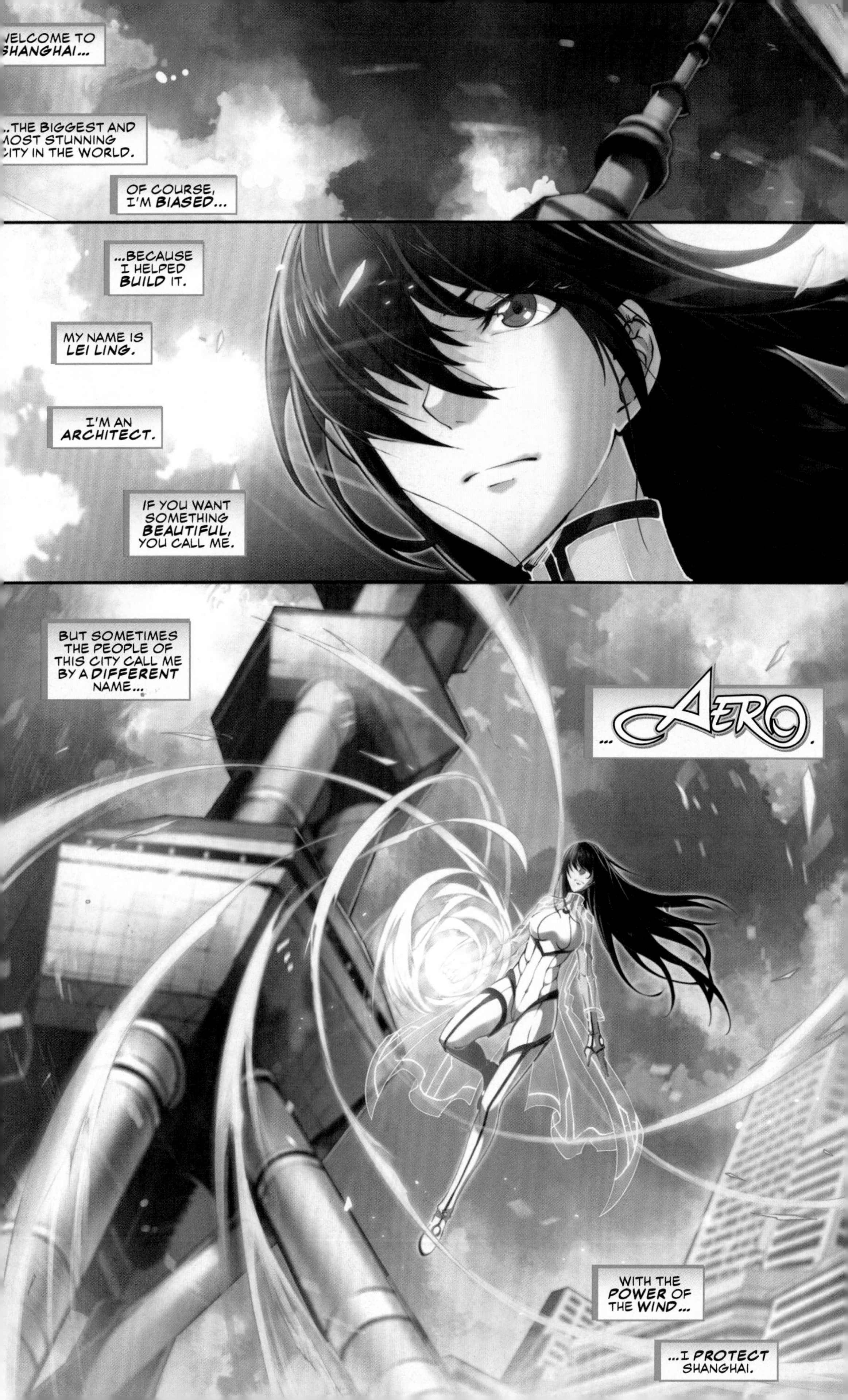
WELCOME TO SHANGHAI...
...THE BIGGEST AND MOST STUNNING CITY IN THE WORLD.
OF COURSE, I'M BIASED...
...BECAUSE I HELPED BUILD IT.
MY NAME IS LEI LING.
I'M AN ARCHITECT.
IF YOU WANT SOMETHING BEAUTIFUL, YOU CALL ME.
BUT SOMETIMES THE PEOPLE OF THIS CITY CALL ME BY A DIFFERENT NAME...
...AERO.
WITH THE POWER OF THE WIND...
...I PROTECT SHANGHAI.

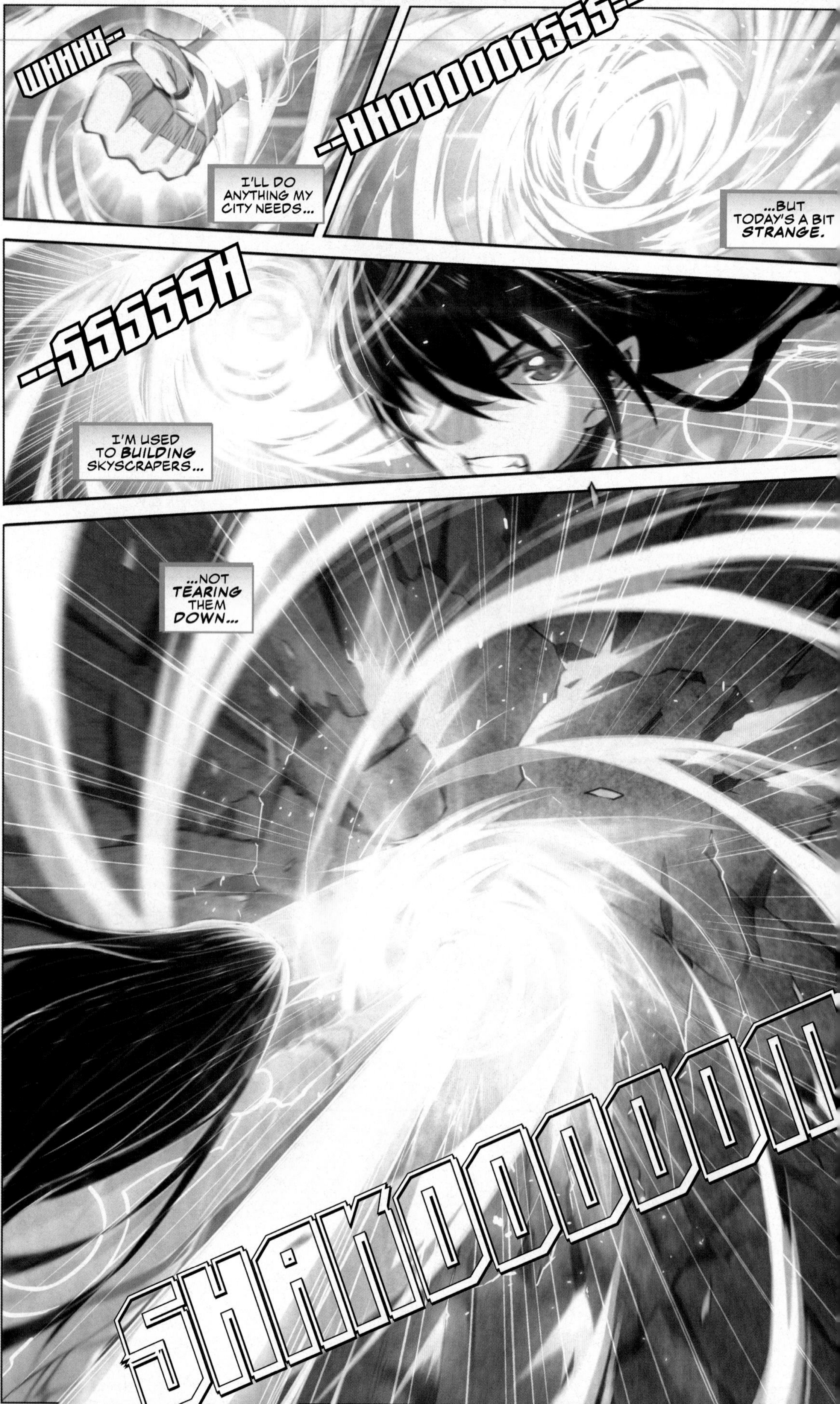
WHHHH--
I'LL DO ANYTHING MY CITY NEEDS...
--HHOOOOOOSSS--
...BUT TODAY'S A BIT STRANGE.
--SSSSSH
I'M USED TO BUILDING SKYSCRAPERS...
...NOT TEARING THEM DOWN...
SHAKOOOOOOM

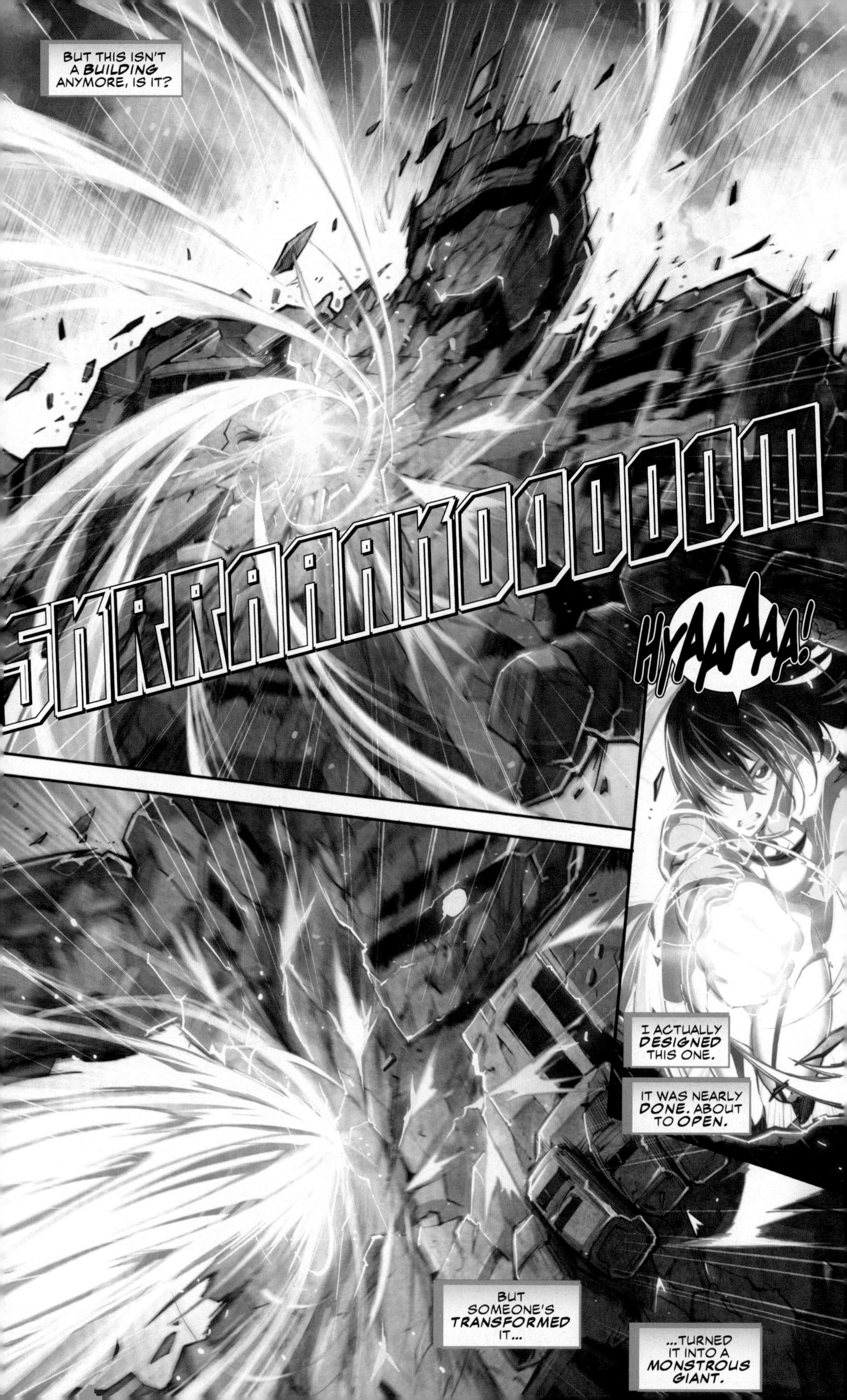
BUT THIS ISN'T A BUILDING ANYMORE, IS IT?
SKRRAAAKOOOOOM
HYAAAAA!
I ACTUALLY DESIGNED THIS ONE.
IT WAS NEARLY DONE. ABOUT TO OPEN.
BUT SOMEONE'S TRANSFORMED IT...
...TURNED IT INTO A MONSTROUS GIANT.

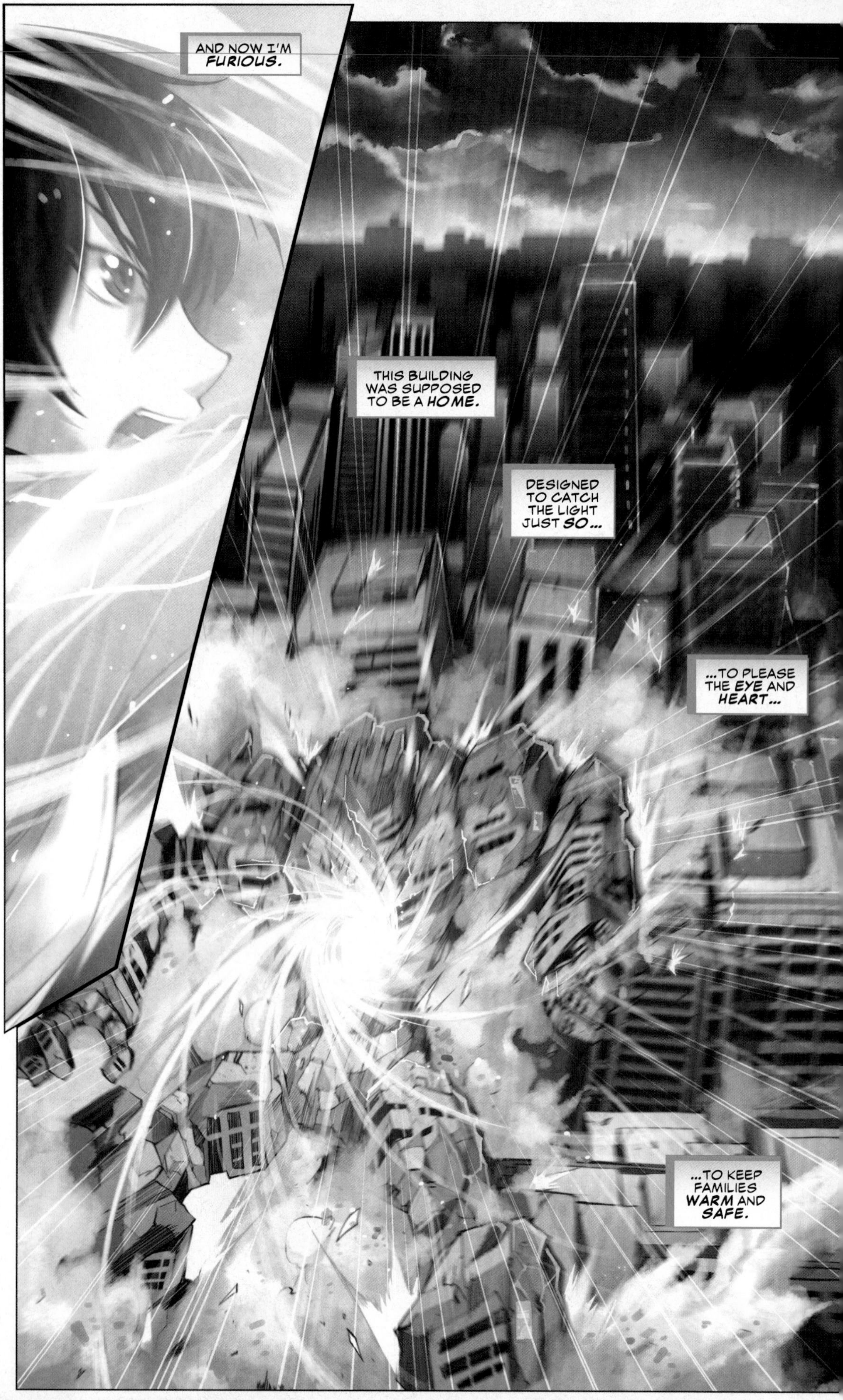
AND NOW I'M FURIOUS.
THIS BUILDING WAS SUPPOSED TO BE A HOME.
DESIGNED TO CATCH THE LIGHT JUST SO...
...TO PLEASE THE EYE AND HEART...
...TO KEEP FAMILIES WARM AND SAFE.

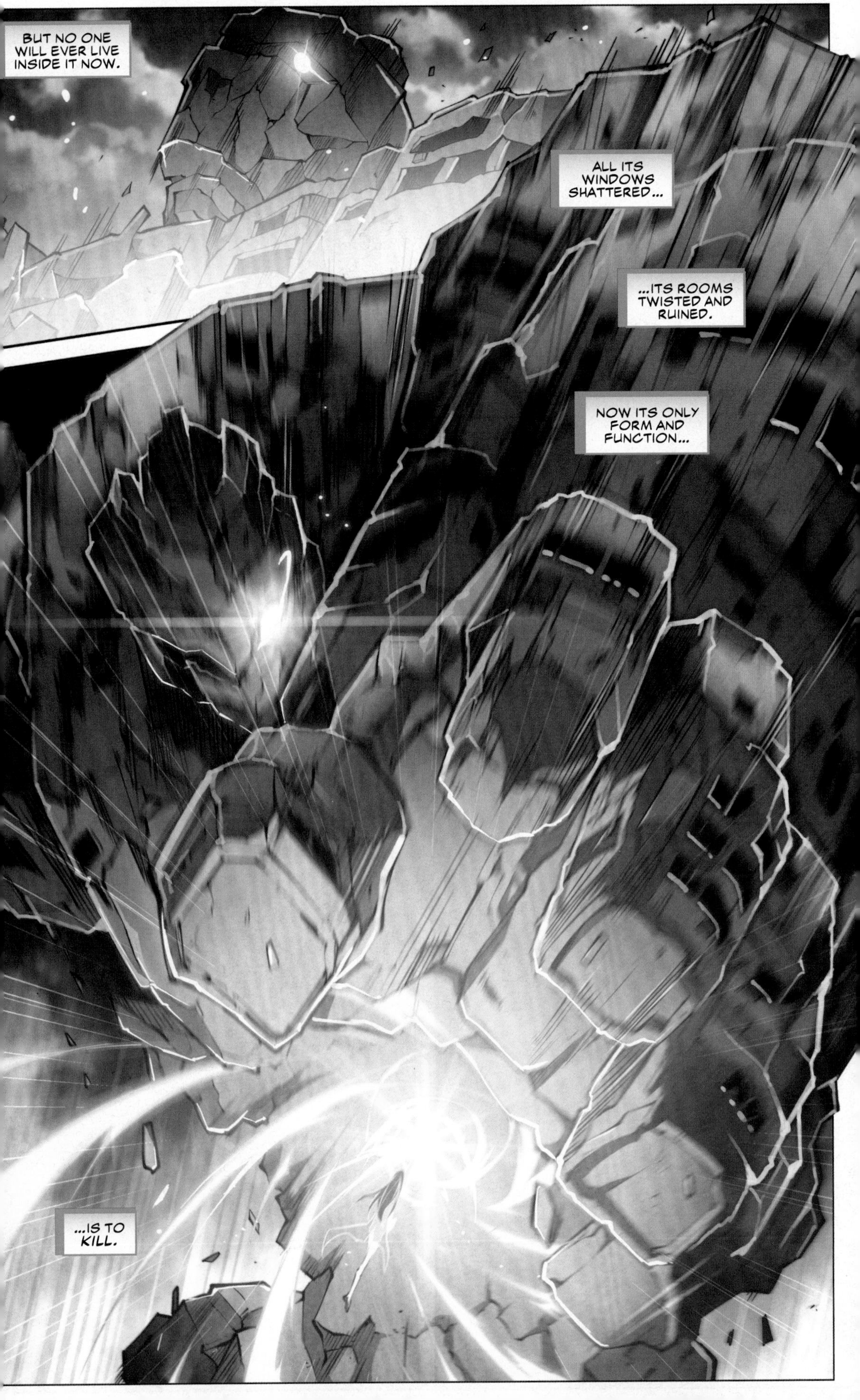
BUT NO ONE WILL EVER LIVE INSIDE IT NOW.
ALL ITS WINDOWS SHATTERED...
...ITS ROOMS TWISTED AND RUINED.
NOW ITS ONLY FORM AND FUNCTION...
...IS TO KILL.

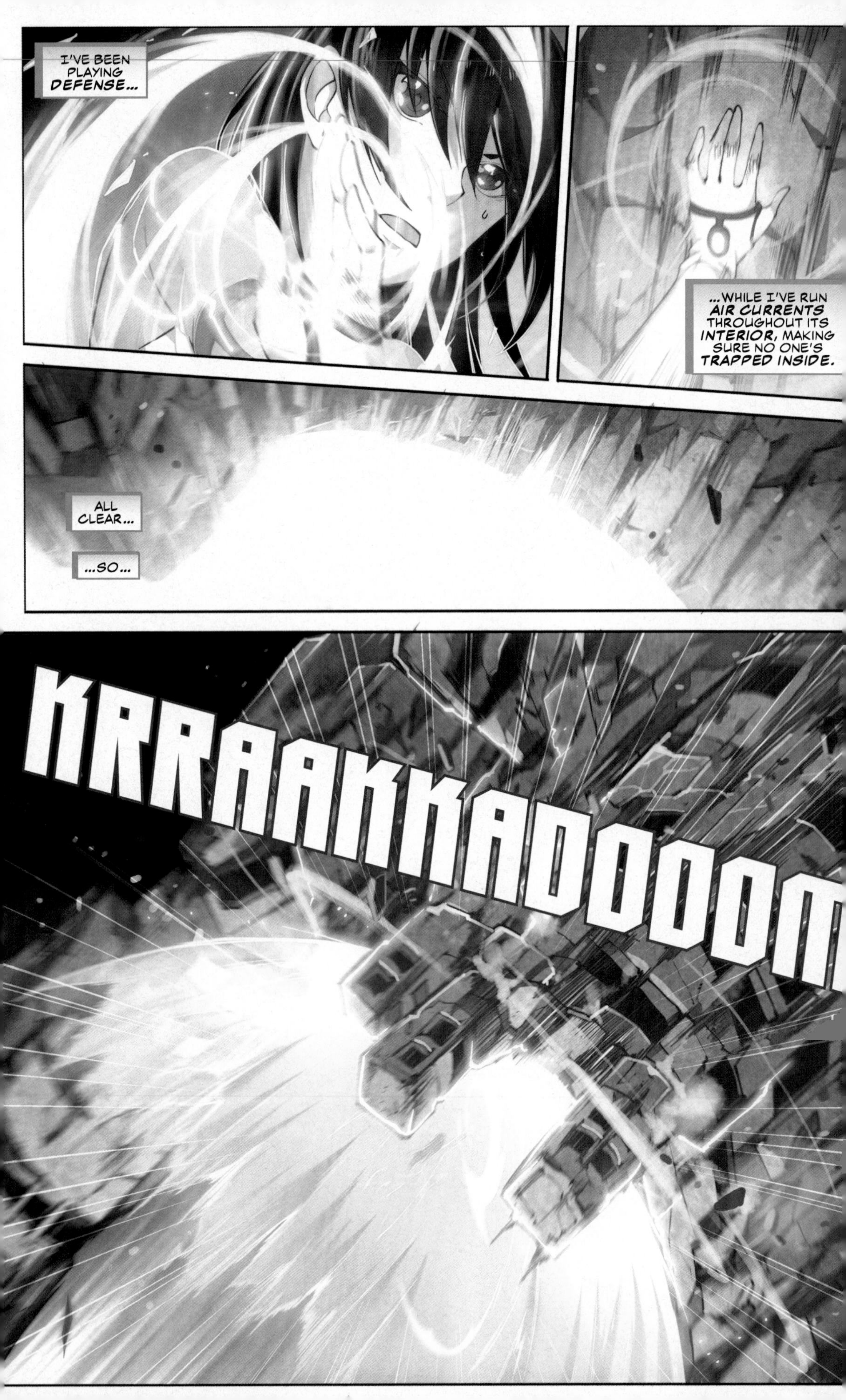
I'VE BEEN PLAYING DEFENSE...
...WHILE I'VE RUN AIR CURRENTS THROUGHOUT ITS INTERIOR, MAKING SURE NO ONE'S TRAPPED INSIDE.
ALL CLEAR...
...SO...
KRRAAKKADOOOOM

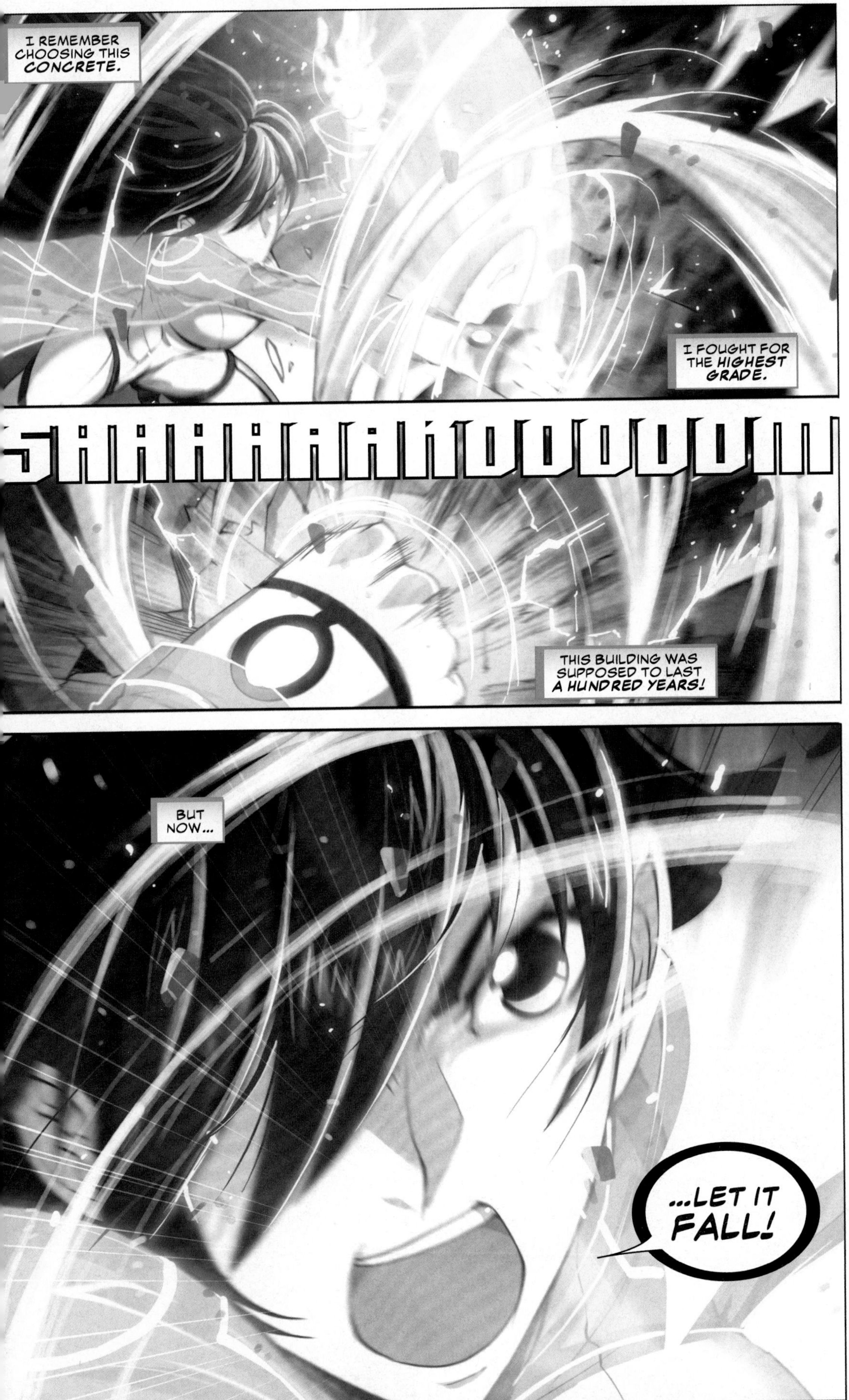
I REMEMBER CHOOSING THIS CONCRETE.
I FOUGHT FOR THE HIGHEST GRADE.
SAAAAAAKOOOOOM
THIS BUILDING WAS SUPPOSED TO LAST A HUNDRED YEARS!
BUT NOW...
...LET IT FALL!

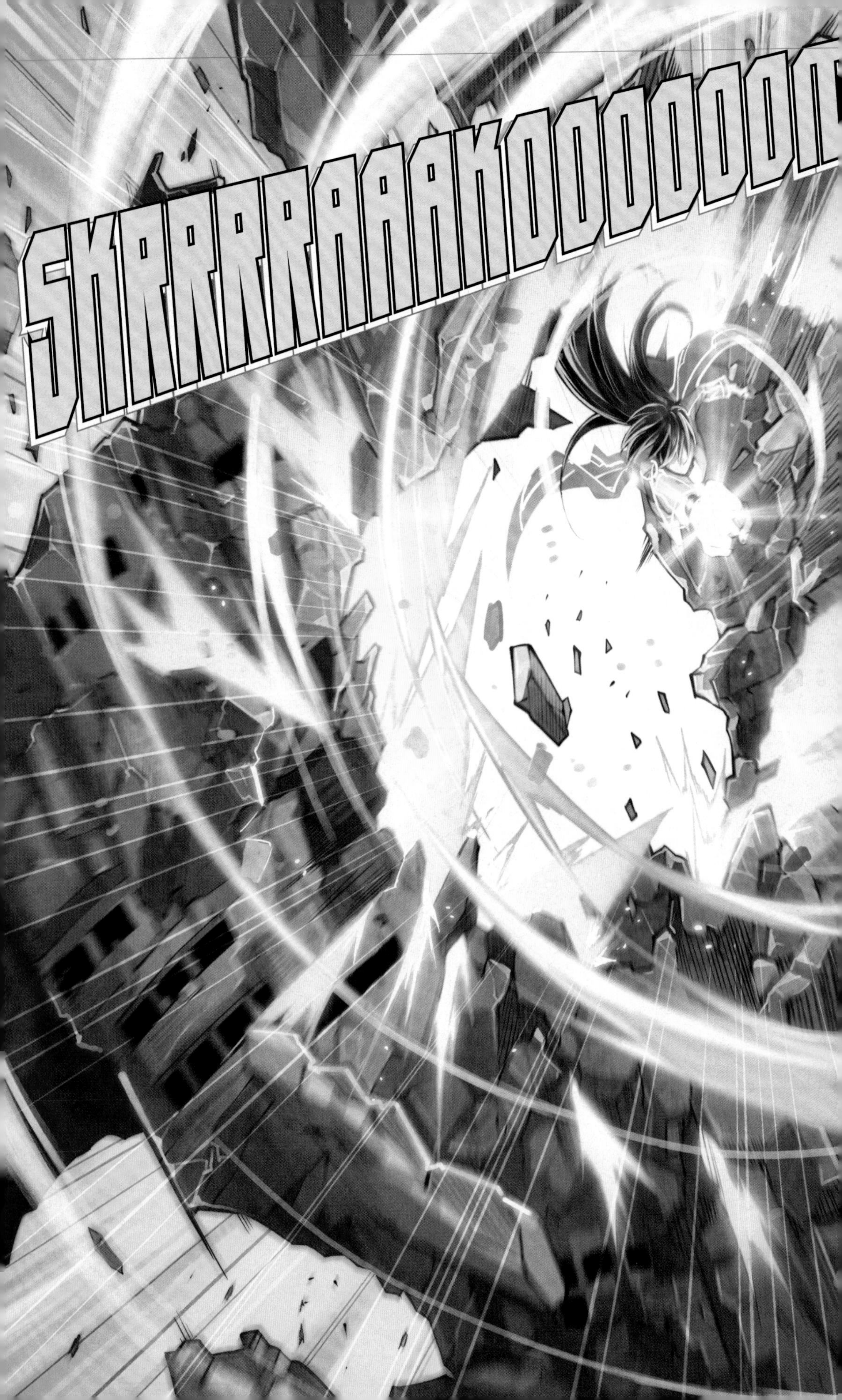
SKRRRRAAAKOOOOOO

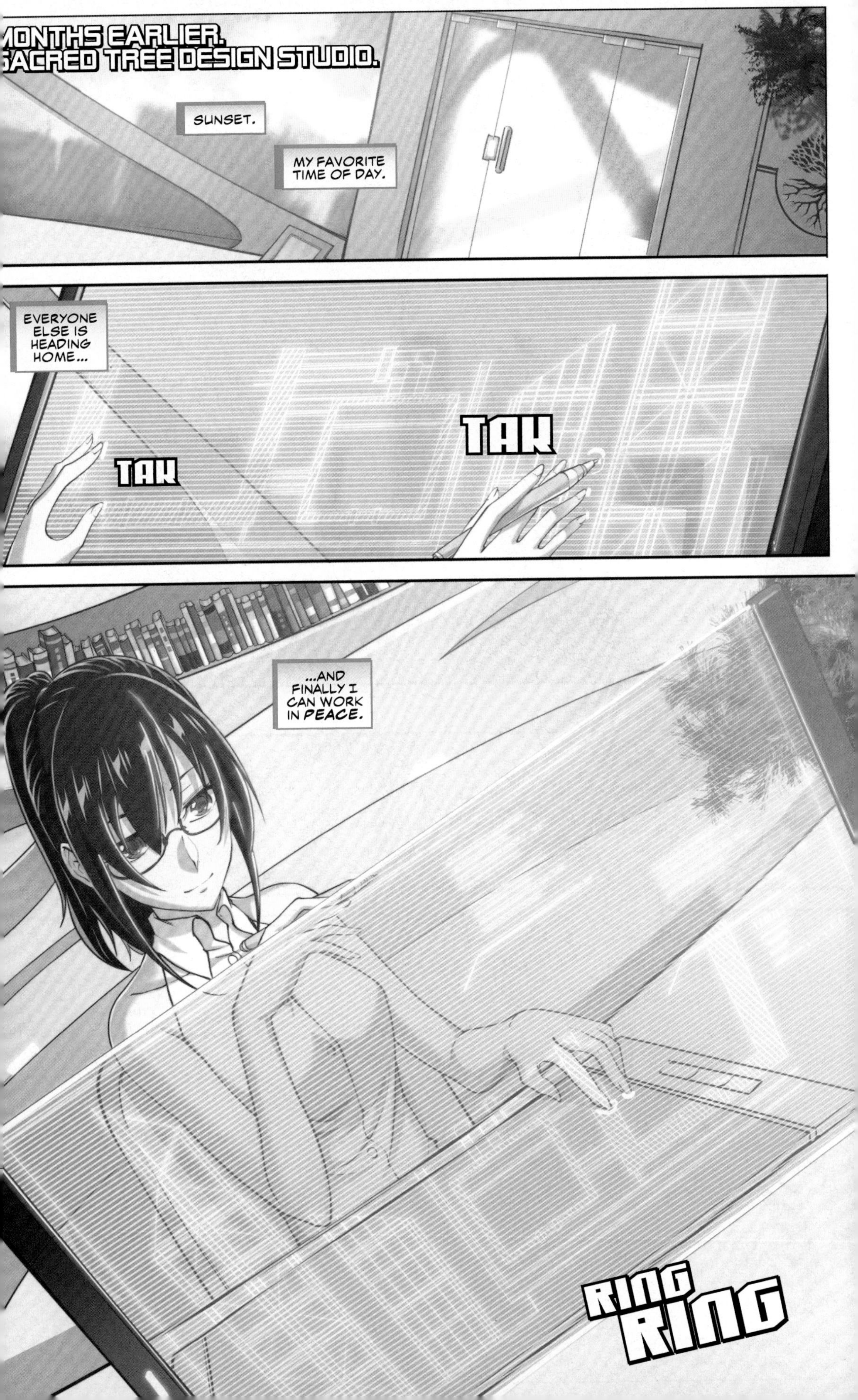
MONTHS EARLIER.
SACRED TREE DESIGN STUDIO.
SUNSET.
MY FAVORITE TIME OF DAY.
EVERYONE ELSE IS HEADING HOME...
TAK
TAK
...AND FINALLY I CAN WORK IN PEACE.
RING
RING

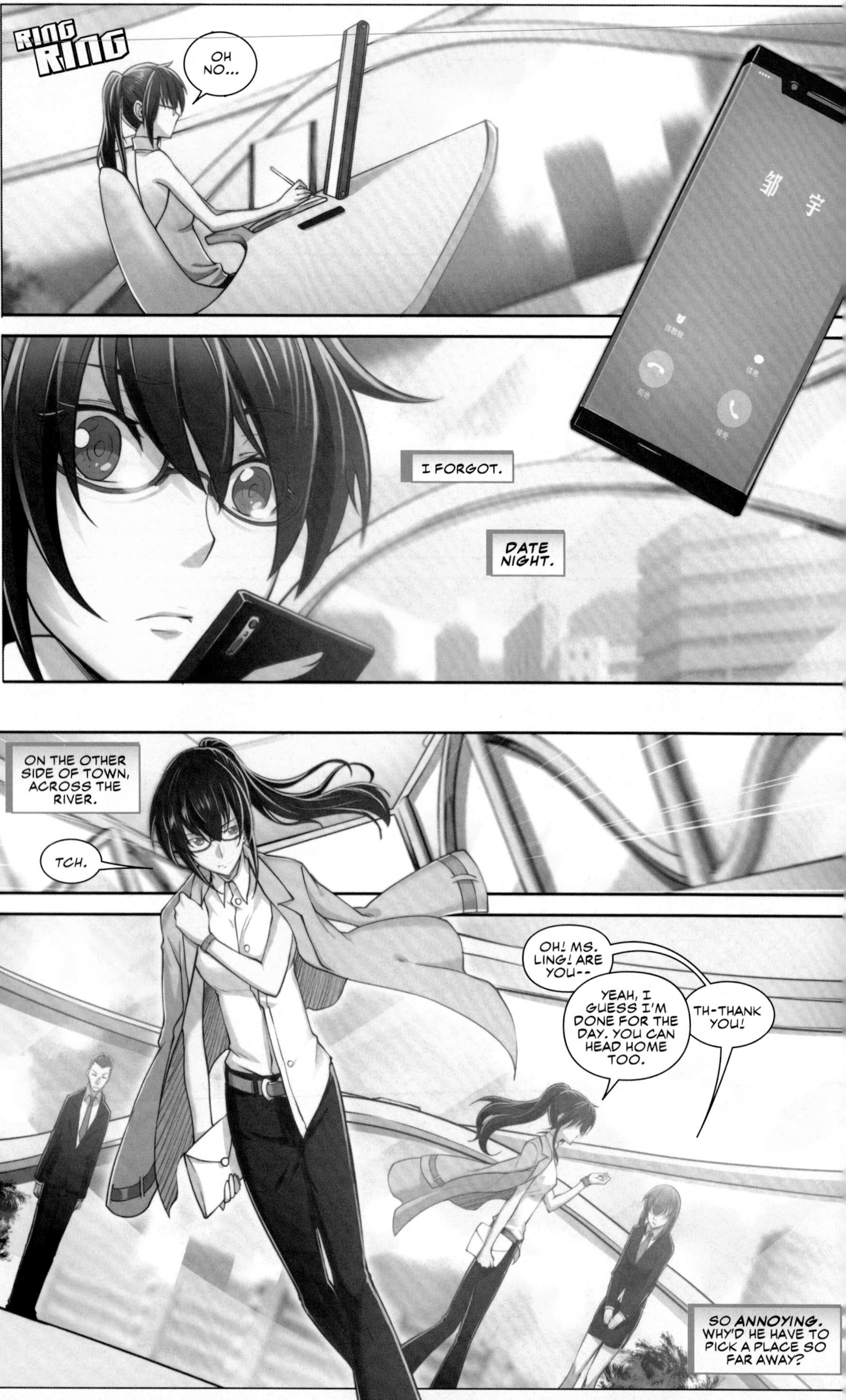
RING RING
OH NO...
邹宇
I FORGOT.
DATE NIGHT.
ON THE OTHER SIDE OF TOWN, ACROSS THE RIVER.
TCH.
OH! MS. LING! ARE YOU--
YEAH, I GUESS I'M DONE FOR THE DAY. YOU CAN HEAD HOME TOO.
TH-THANK YOU!
SO ANNOYING. WHY'D HE HAVE TO PICK A PLACE SO FAR AWAY?

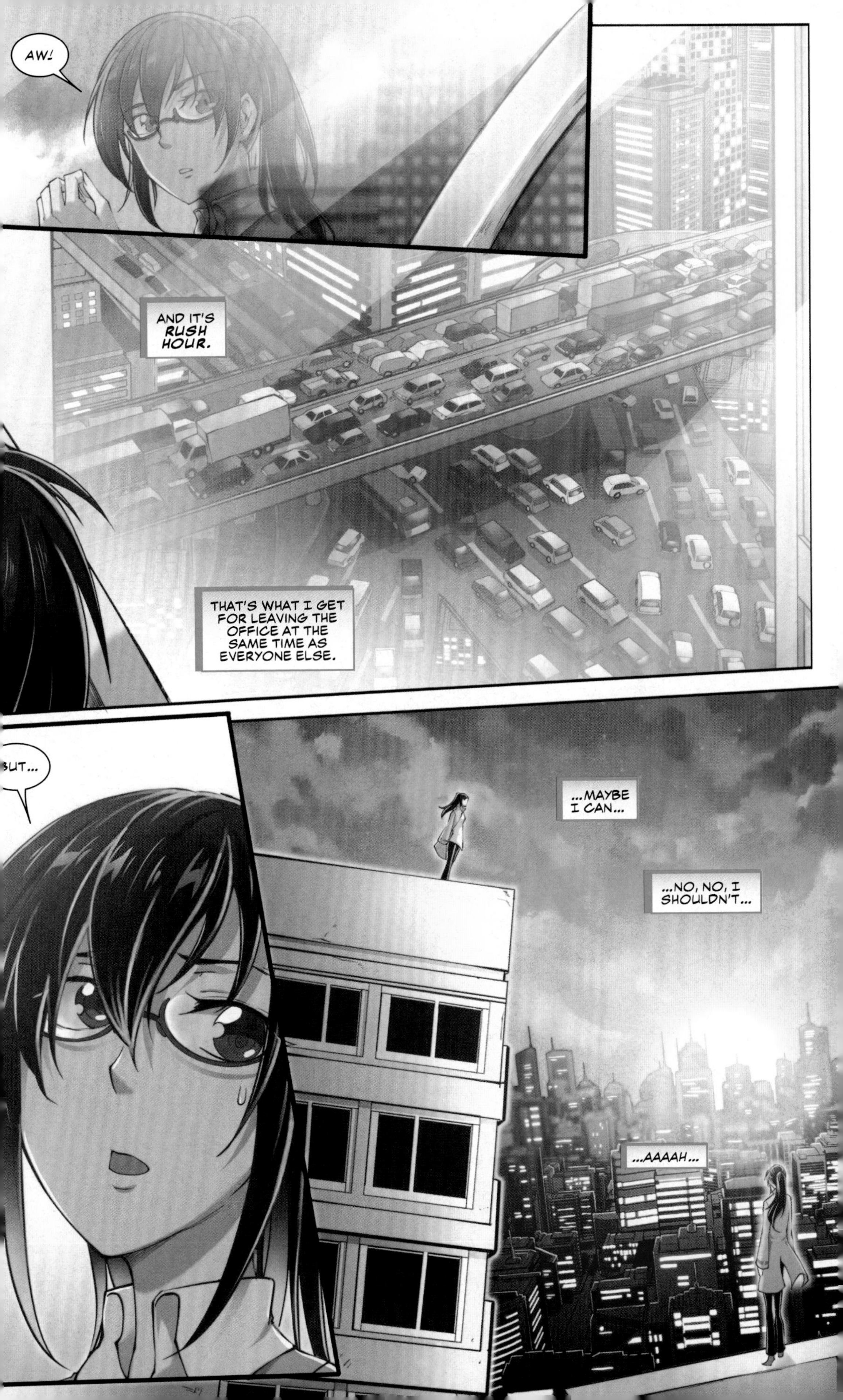
AW!
AND IT'S RUSH HOUR.
THAT'S WHAT I GET FOR LEAVING THE OFFICE AT THE SAME TIME AS EVERYONE ELSE.
BUT...
...MAYBE I CAN...
...NO, NO, I SHOULDN'T...
...AAAAH...

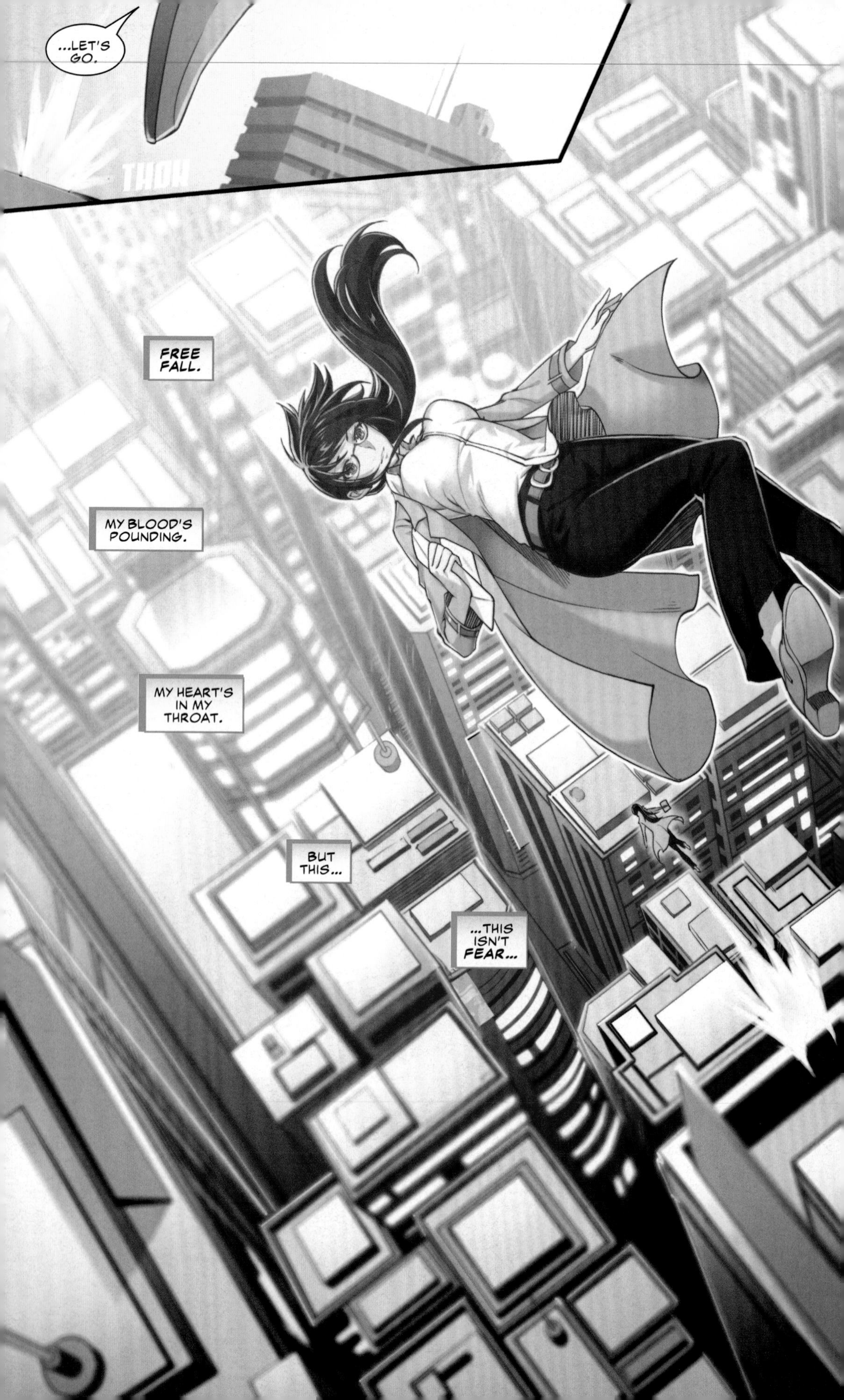
...LET'S GO.
THOK
FREE FALL.
MY BLOOD'S POUNDING.
MY HEART'S IN MY THROAT.
BUT THIS...
...THIS ISN'T FEAR...

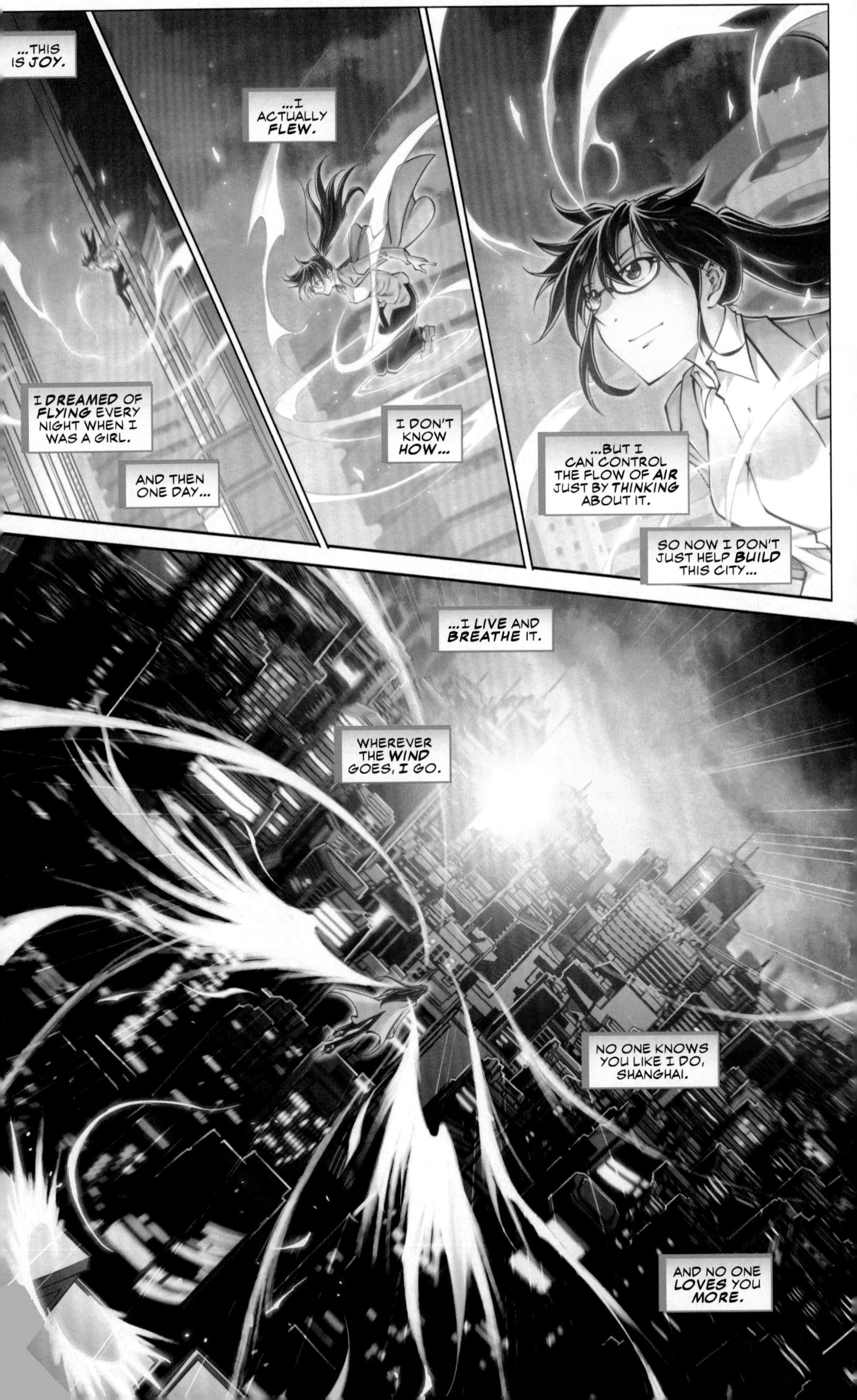
...THIS IS JOY.
I DREAMED OF FLYING EVERY NIGHT WHEN I WAS A GIRL.
AND THEN ONE DAY...
...I ACTUALLY FLEW.
I DON'T KNOW HOW...
...BUT I CAN CONTROL THE FLOW OF AIR JUST BY THINKING ABOUT IT.
SO NOW I DON'T JUST HELP BUILD THIS CITY...
...I LIVE AND BREATHE IT.
WHEREVER THE WIND GOES, I GO.
NO ONE KNOWS YOU LIKE I DO, SHANGHAI.
AND NO ONE LOVES YOU MORE.

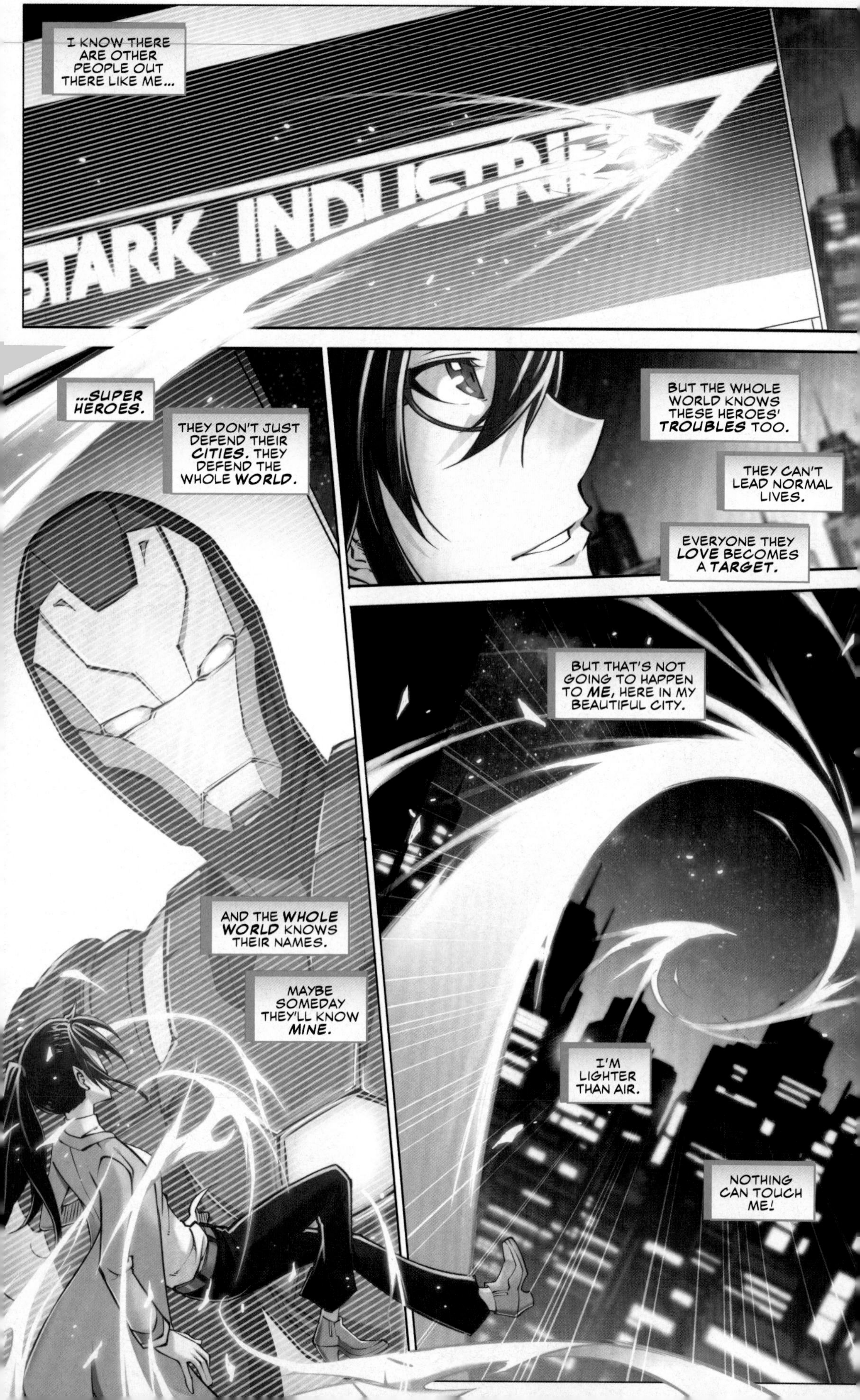
I KNOW THERE ARE OTHER PEOPLE OUT THERE LIKE ME...
STARK INDUSTRIES
...SUPER HEROES.
THEY DON'T JUST DEFEND THEIR CITIES. THEY DEFEND THE WHOLE WORLD.
AND THE WHOLE WORLD KNOWS THEIR NAMES.
MAYBE SOMEDAY THEY'LL KNOW MINE.
BUT THE WHOLE WORLD KNOWS THESE HEROES' TROUBLES TOO.
THEY CAN'T LEAD NORMAL LIVES.
EVERYONE THEY LOVE BECOMES A TARGET.
BUT THAT'S NOT GOING TO HAPPEN TO ME, HERE IN MY BEAUTIFUL CITY.
I'M LIGHTER THAN AIR.
NOTHING CAN TOUCH ME!

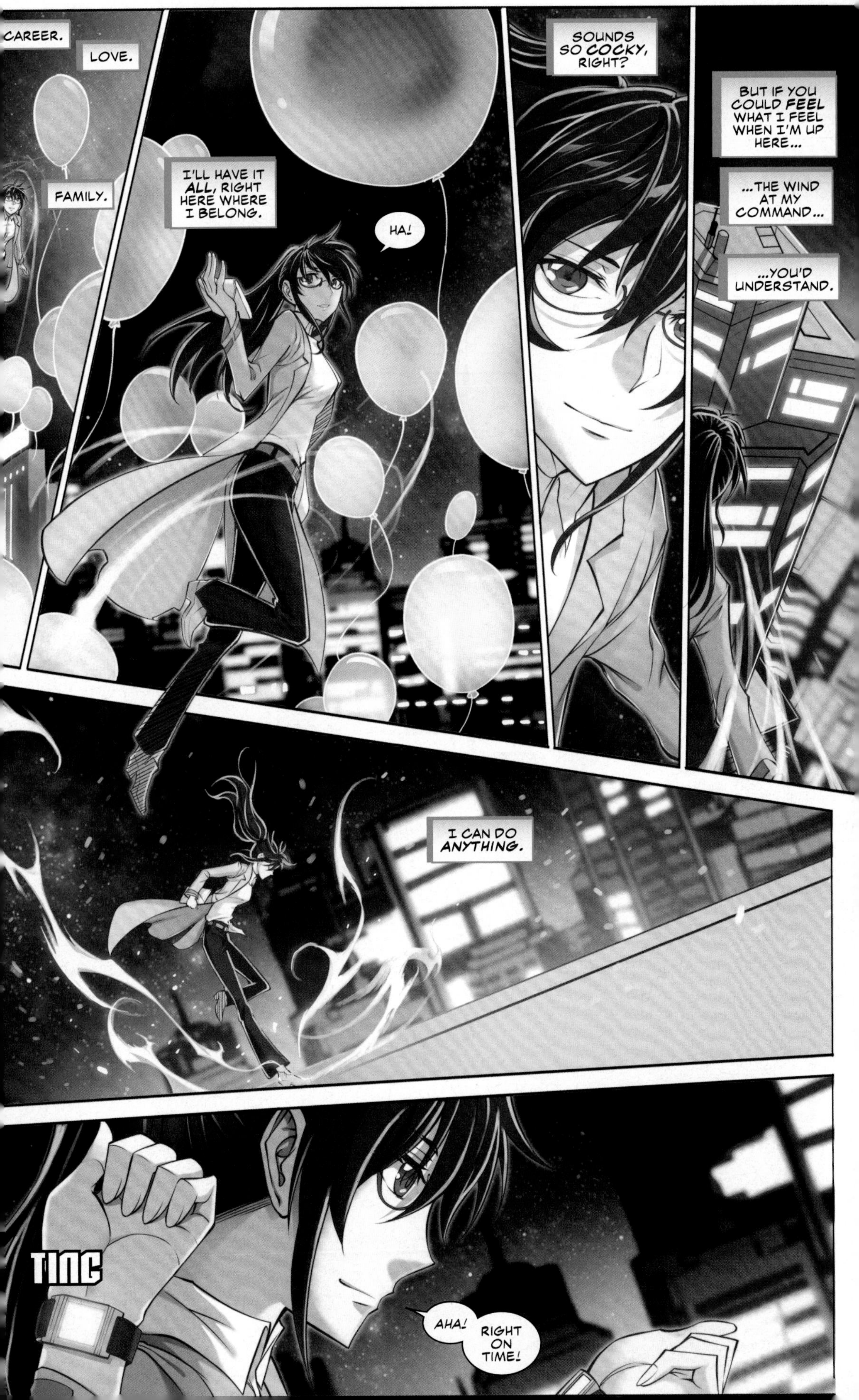
CAREER.
LOVE.
FAMILY.
I'LL HAVE IT ALL, RIGHT HERE WHERE I BELONG.
HA!
SOUNDS SO COCKY, RIGHT?
BUT IF YOU COULD FEEL WHAT I FEEL WHEN I'M UP HERE...
...THE WIND AT MY COMMAND...
...YOU'D UNDERSTAND.
I CAN DO ANYTHING.
TING
AHA! RIGHT ON TIME!

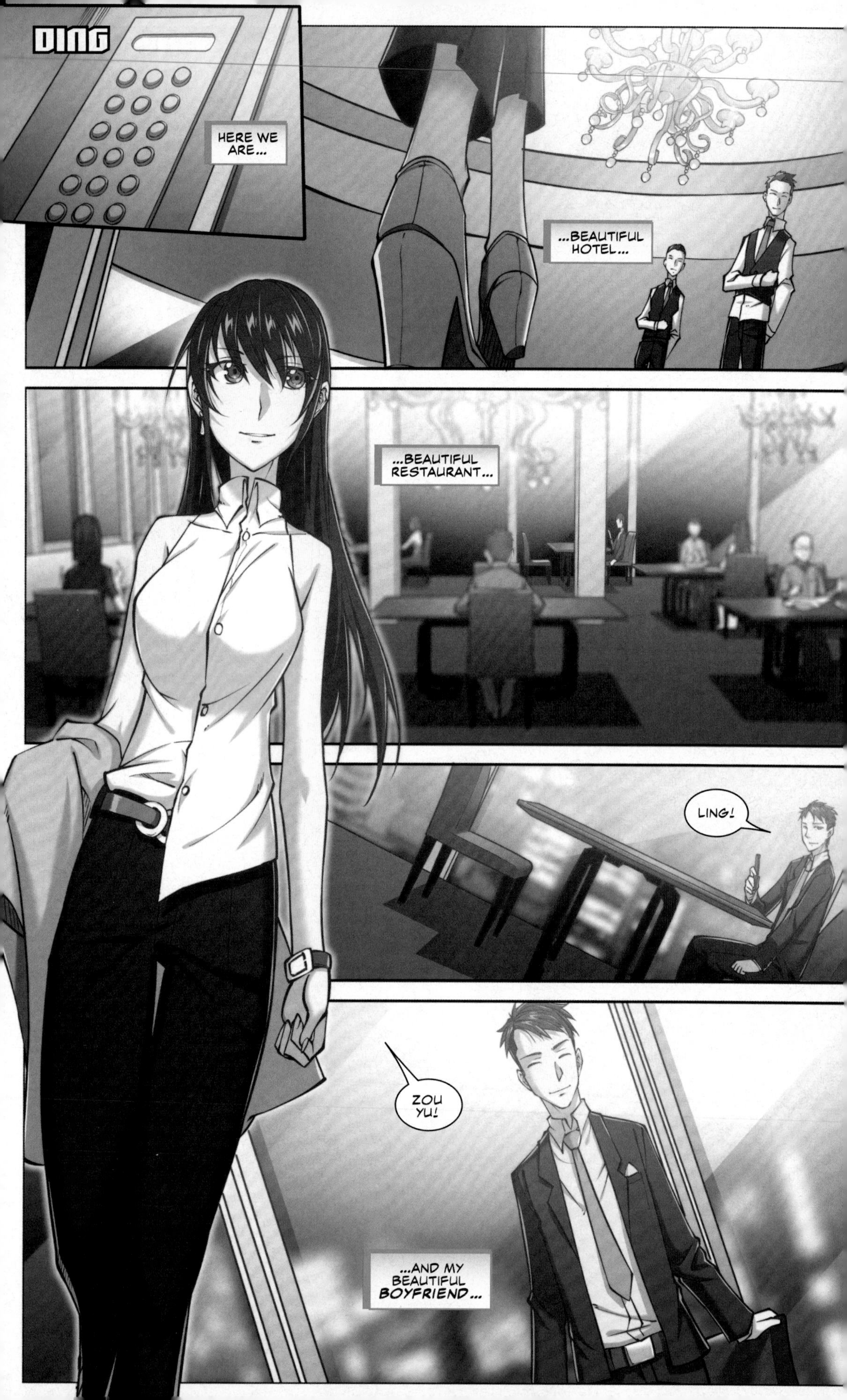
DING
HERE WE ARE...
...BEAUTIFUL HOTEL...
...BEAUTIFUL RESTAURANT...
LING!
ZOU YU!
...AND MY BEAUTIFUL BOYFRIEND...

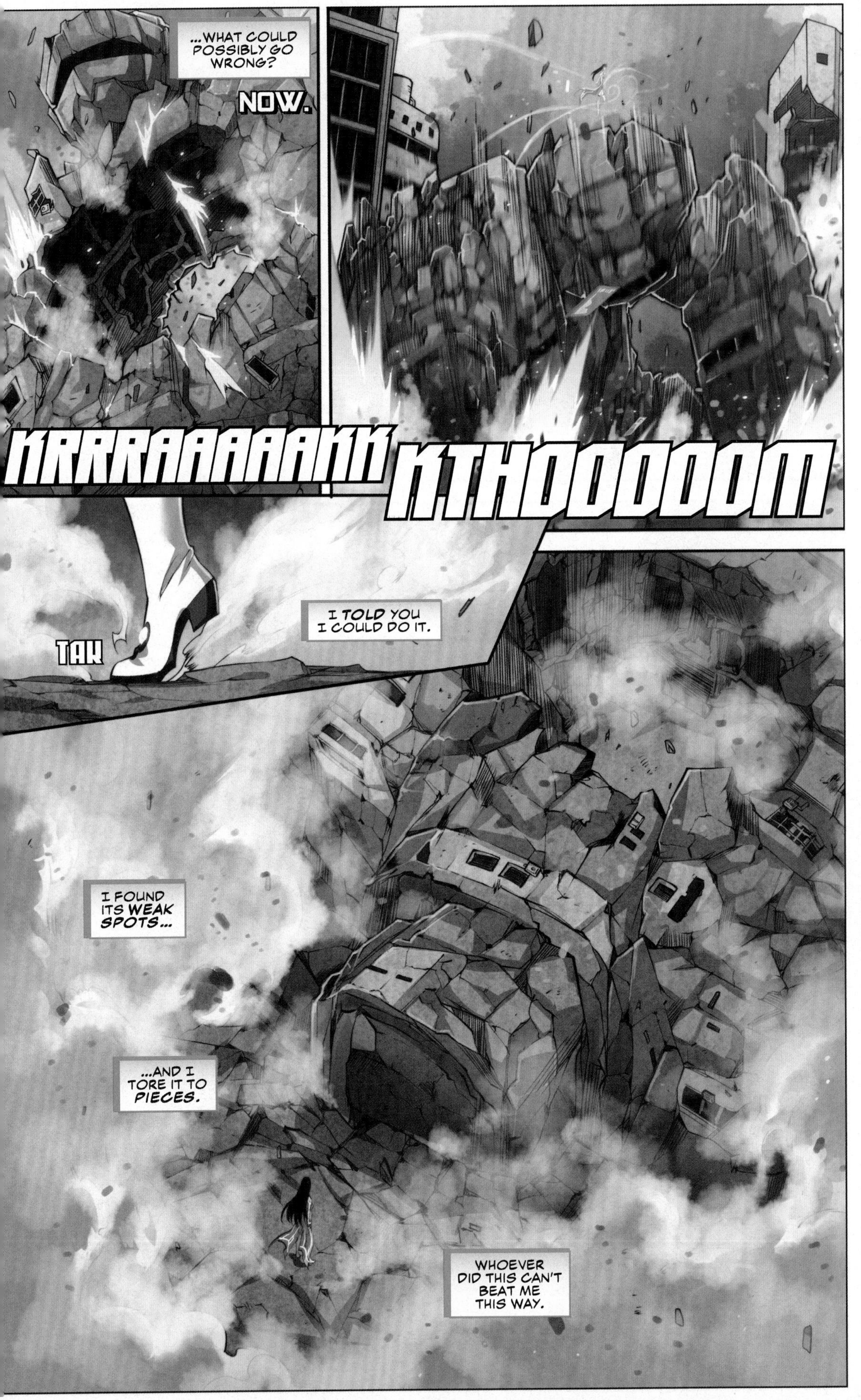
...WHAT COULD POSSIBLY GO WRONG?
NOW.
KRRRAAAAAAKK
KTHOOOOOM
TAK
I TOLD YOU I COULD DO IT.
I FOUND ITS WEAK SPOTS...
...AND I TORE IT TO PIECES.
WHOEVER DID THIS CAN'T BEAT ME THIS WAY.

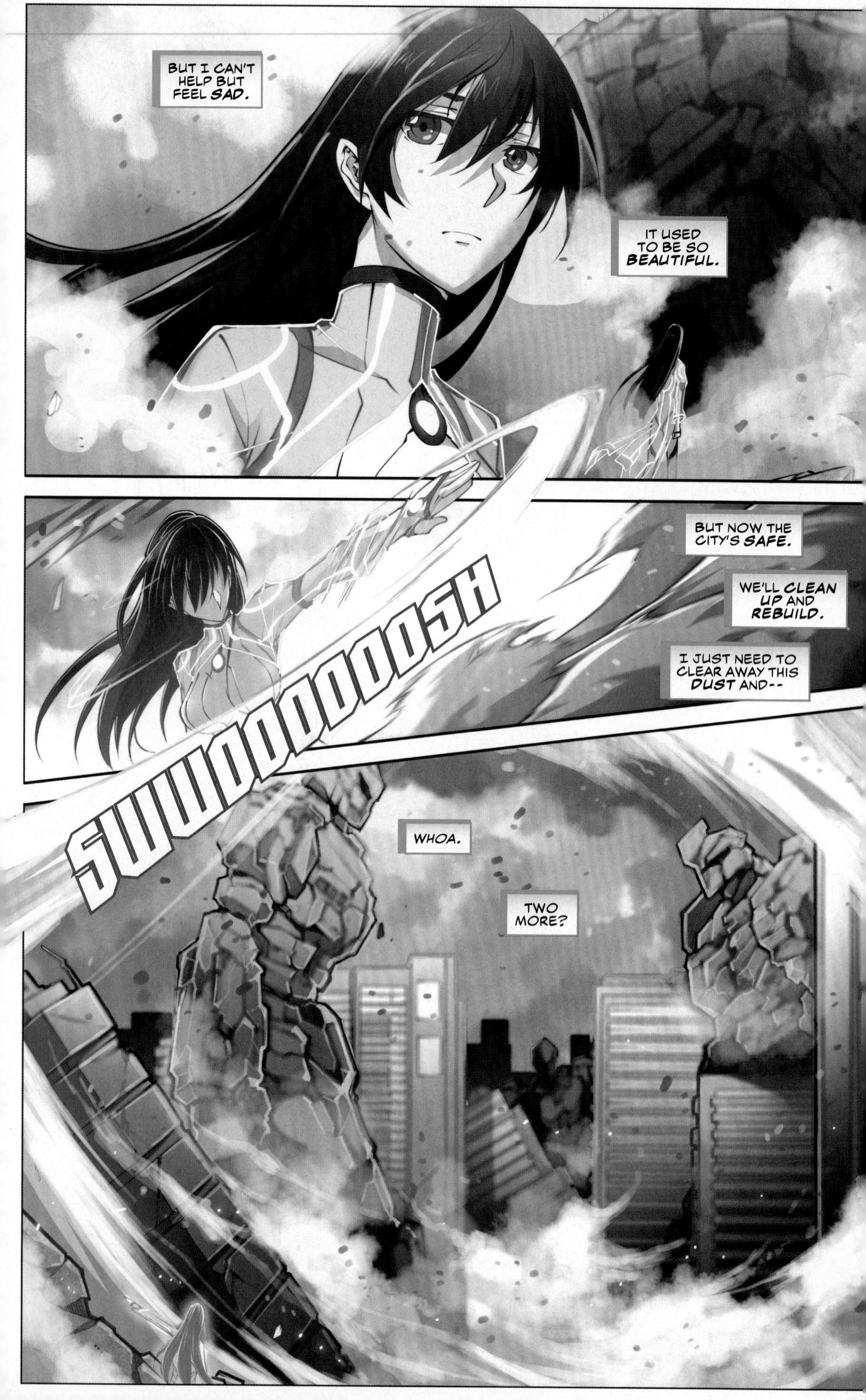
BUT I CAN'T HELP BUT FEEL SAD.
IT USED TO BE SO BEAUTIFUL.
BUT NOW THE CITY'S SAFE.
WE'LL CLEAN UP AND REBUILD.
I JUST NEED TO CLEAR AWAY THIS DUST AND--
SWWOOOOOOOSH
WHOA.
TWO MORE?

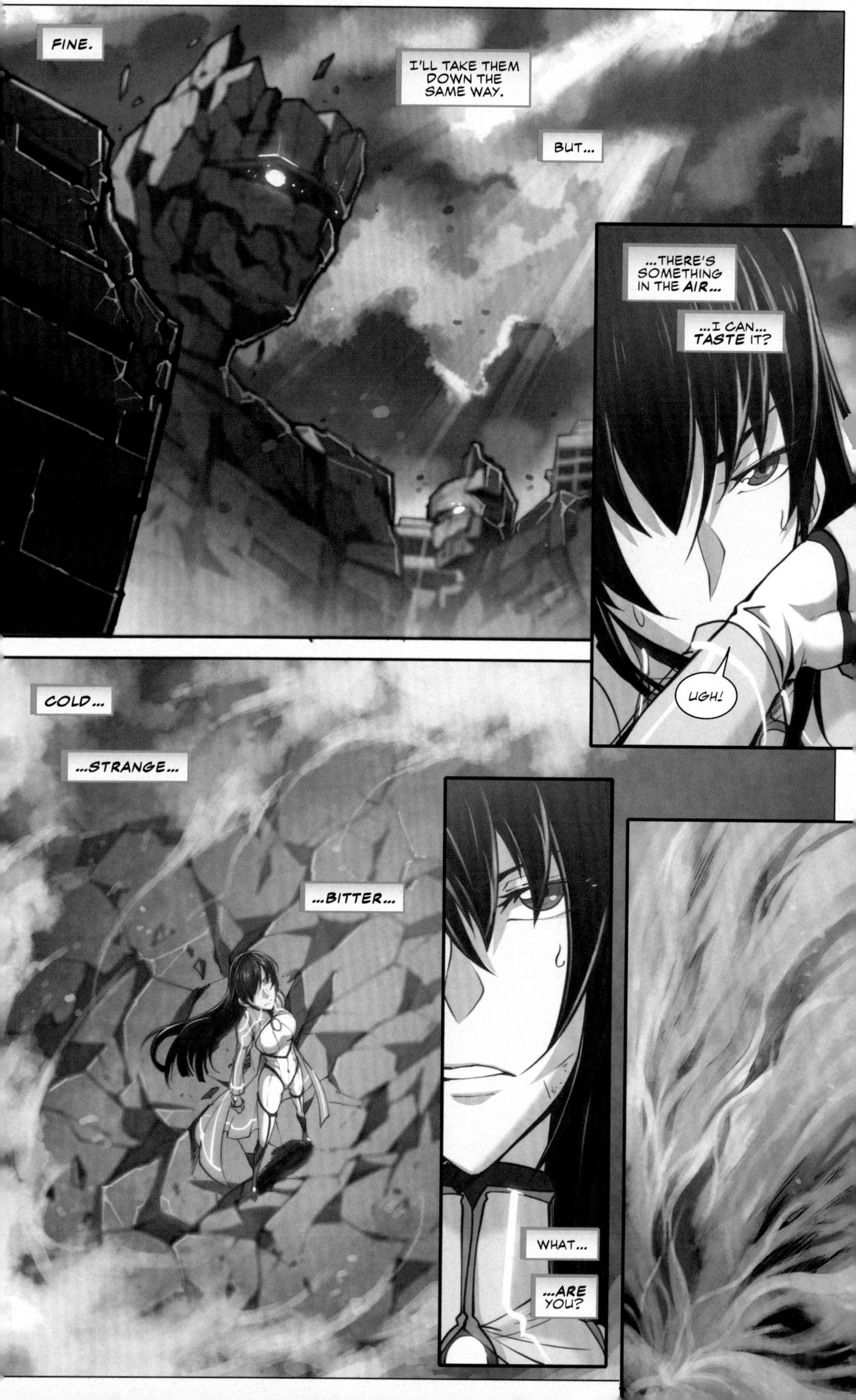
FINE.
I'LL TAKE THEM DOWN THE SAME WAY.
BUT...
...THERE'S SOMETHING IN THE AIR...
...I CAN... TASTE IT?
UGH!
COLD...
...STRANGE...
...BITTER...
WHAT...
...ARE YOU?

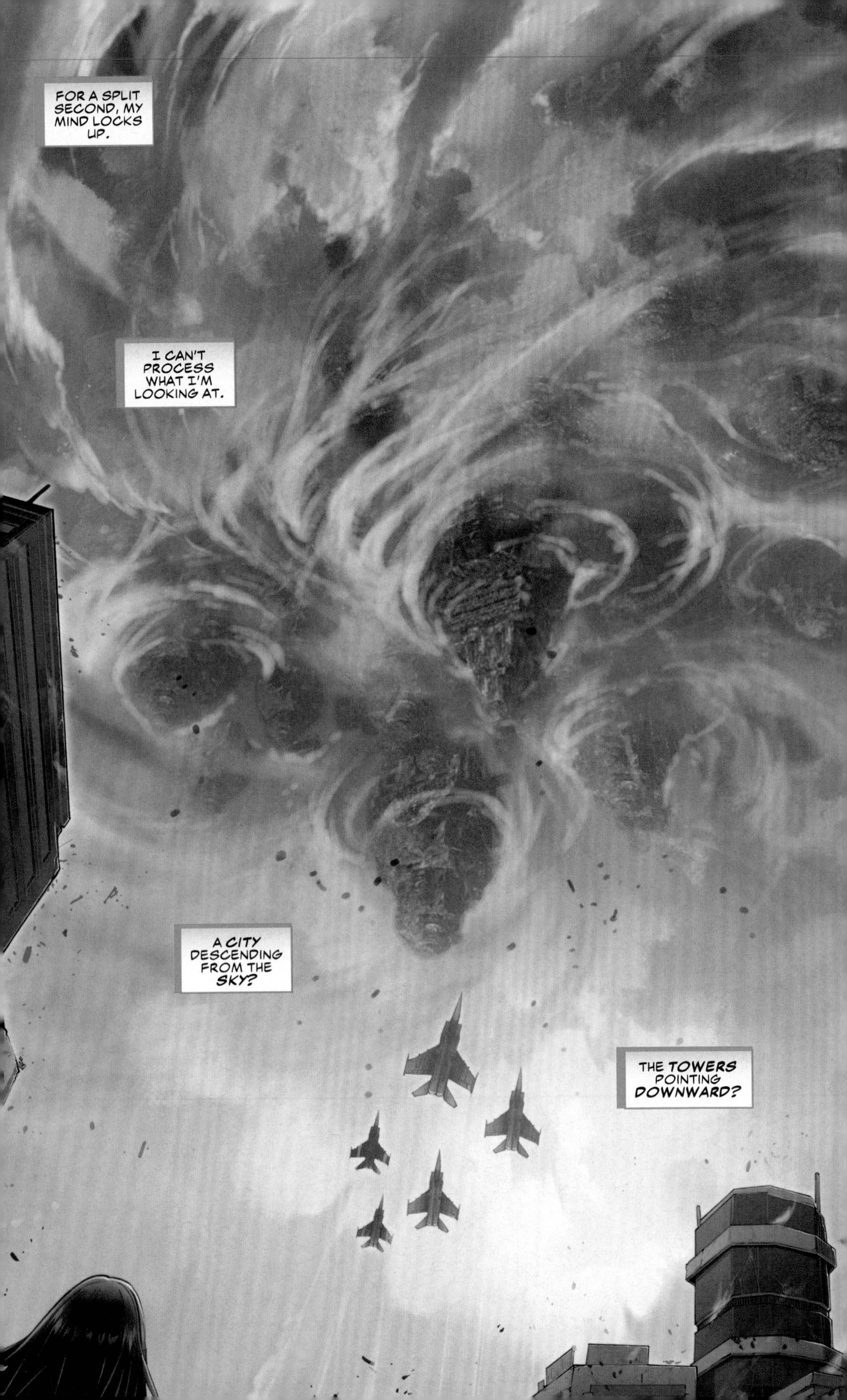
FOR A SPLIT SECOND, MY MIND LOCKS UP.
I CAN'T PROCESS WHAT I'M LOOKING AT.
A *CITY* DESCENDING FROM THE *SKY?*
THE *TOWERS* POINTING *DOWNWARD?*

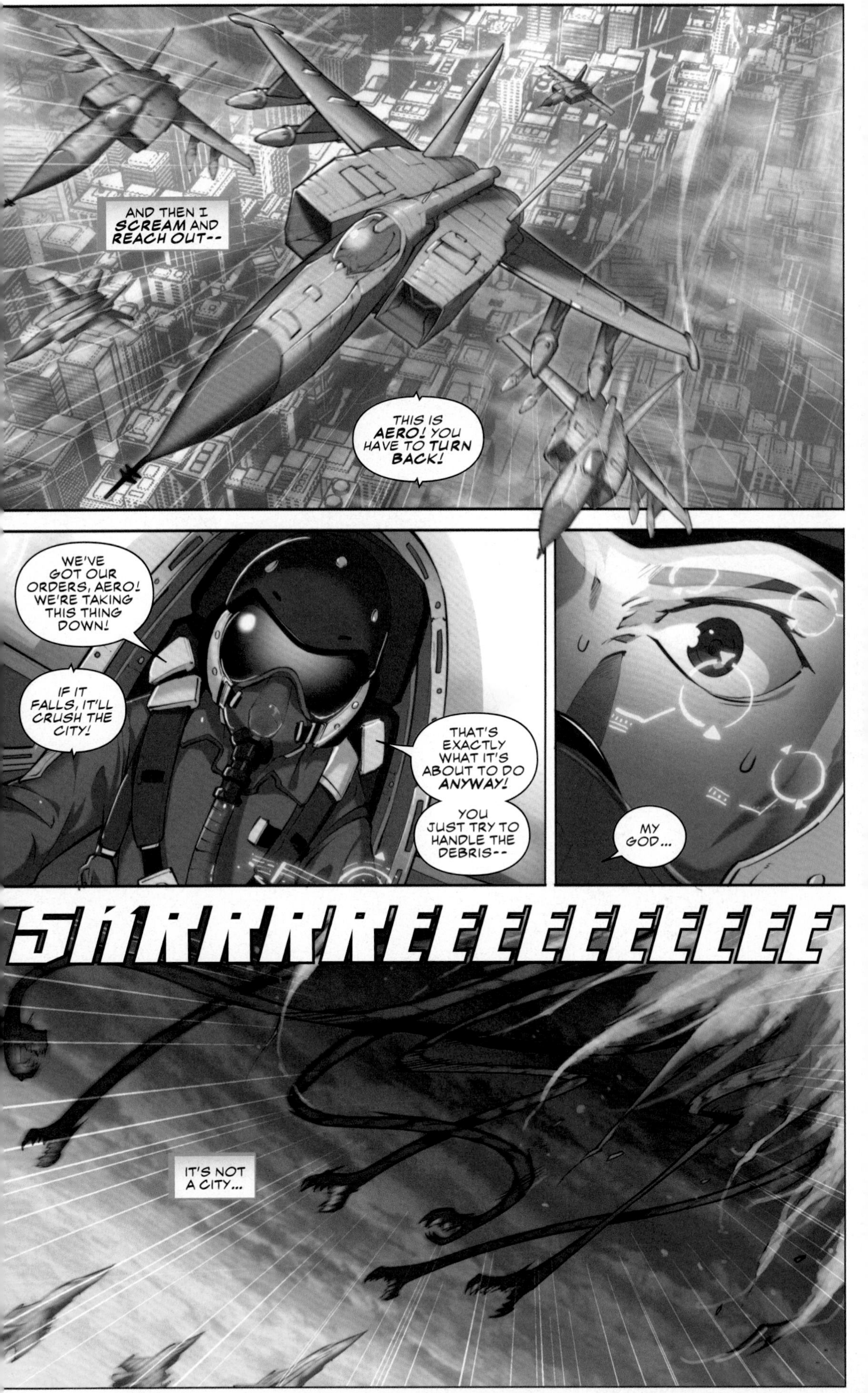
AND THEN I SCREAM AND REACH OUT--
THIS IS AERO! YOU HAVE TO TURN BACK!
WE'VE GOT OUR ORDERS, AERO! WE'RE TAKING THIS THING DOWN!
IF IT FALLS, IT'LL CRUSH THE CITY!
THAT'S EXACTLY WHAT IT'S ABOUT TO DO ANYWAY!
YOU JUST TRY TO HANDLE THE DEBRIS--
MY GOD...
SHRRRREEEEEEEEEE
IT'S NOT A CITY...

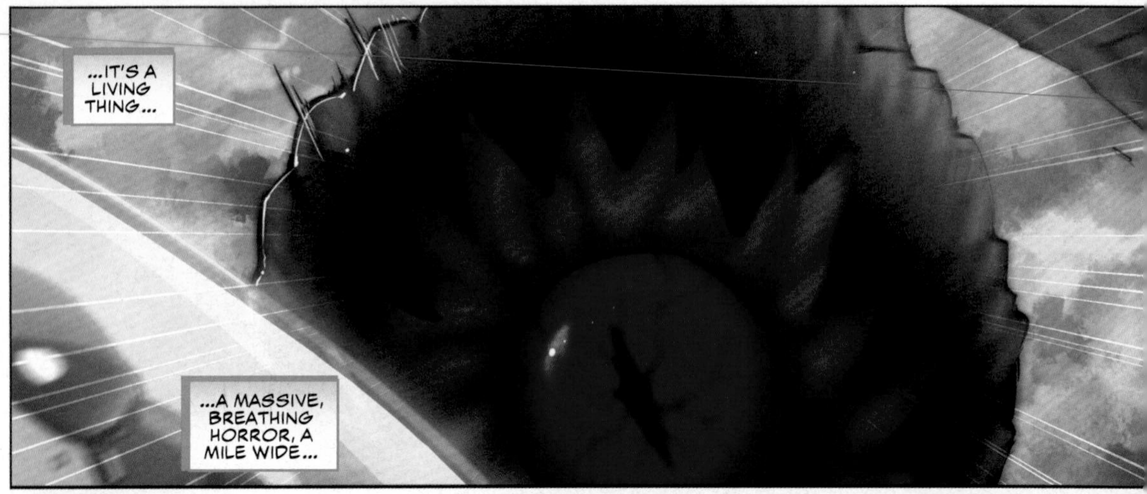
...IT'S A LIVING THING...
...A MASSIVE, BREATHING HORROR, A MILE WIDE...

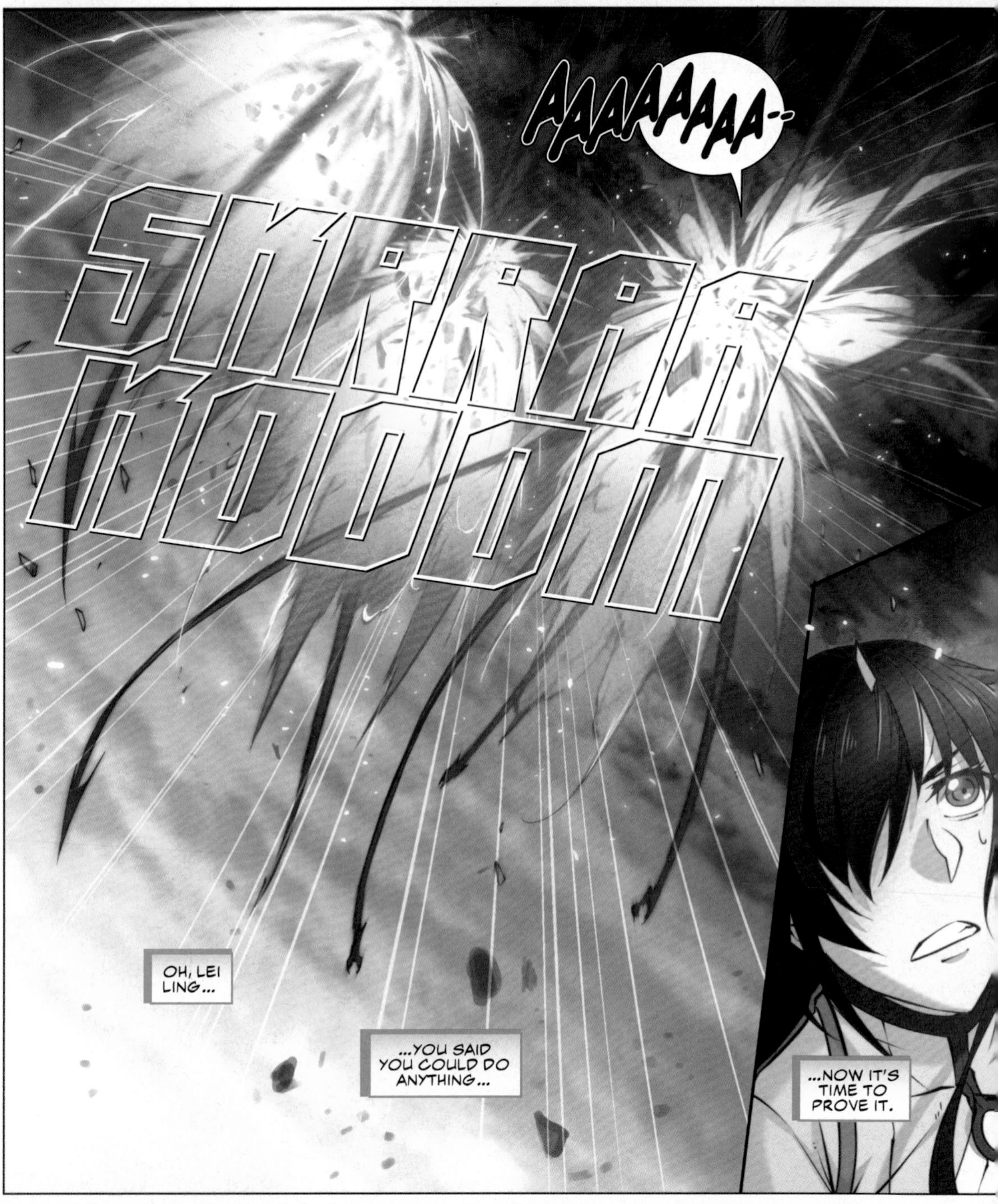
AAAAAAAAA--
SKRAA BOOOM
OH, LEI LING...
...YOU SAID YOU COULD DO ANYTHING...
...NOW IT'S TIME TO PROVE IT.

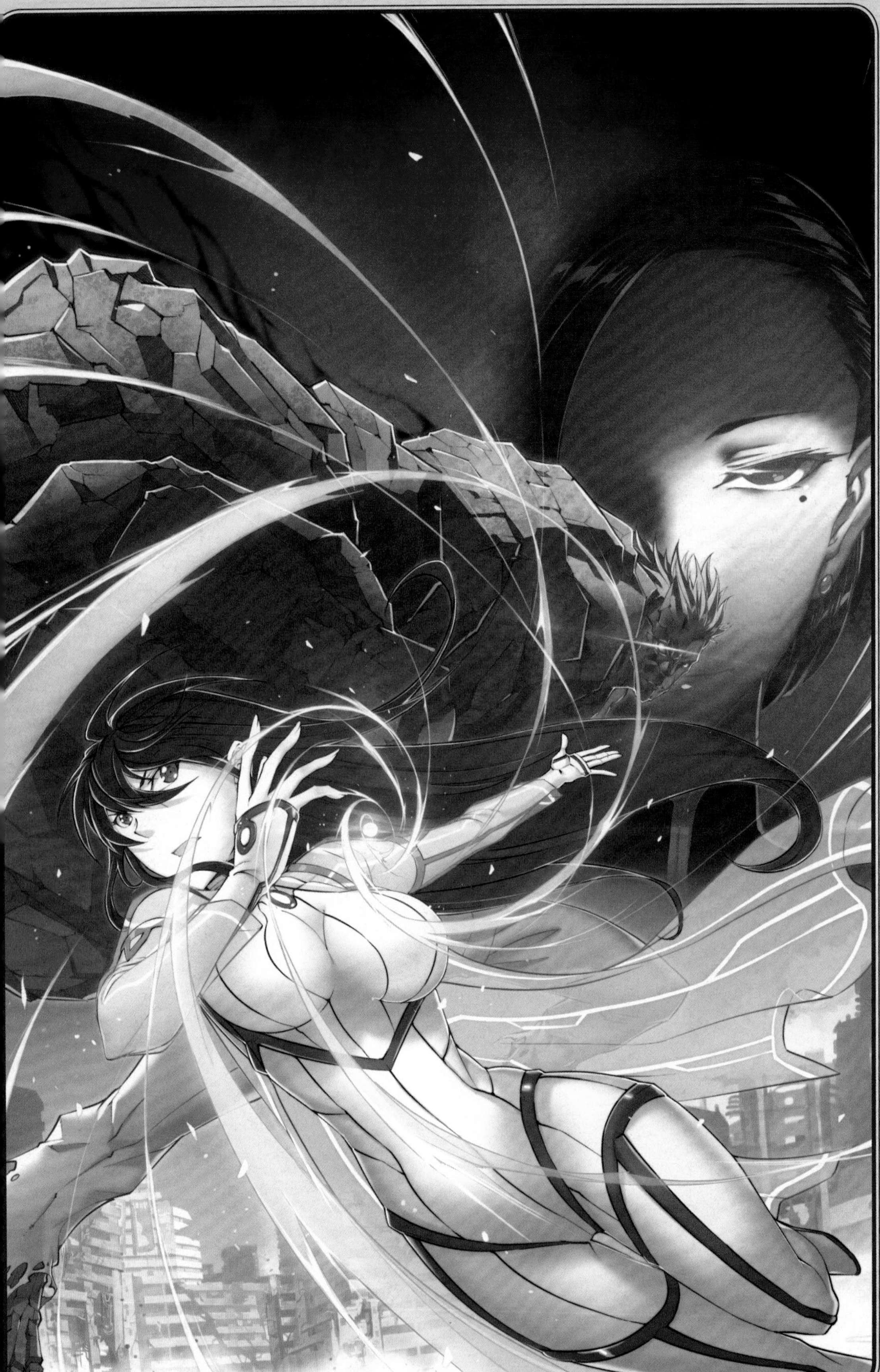

2 Foreshadowing

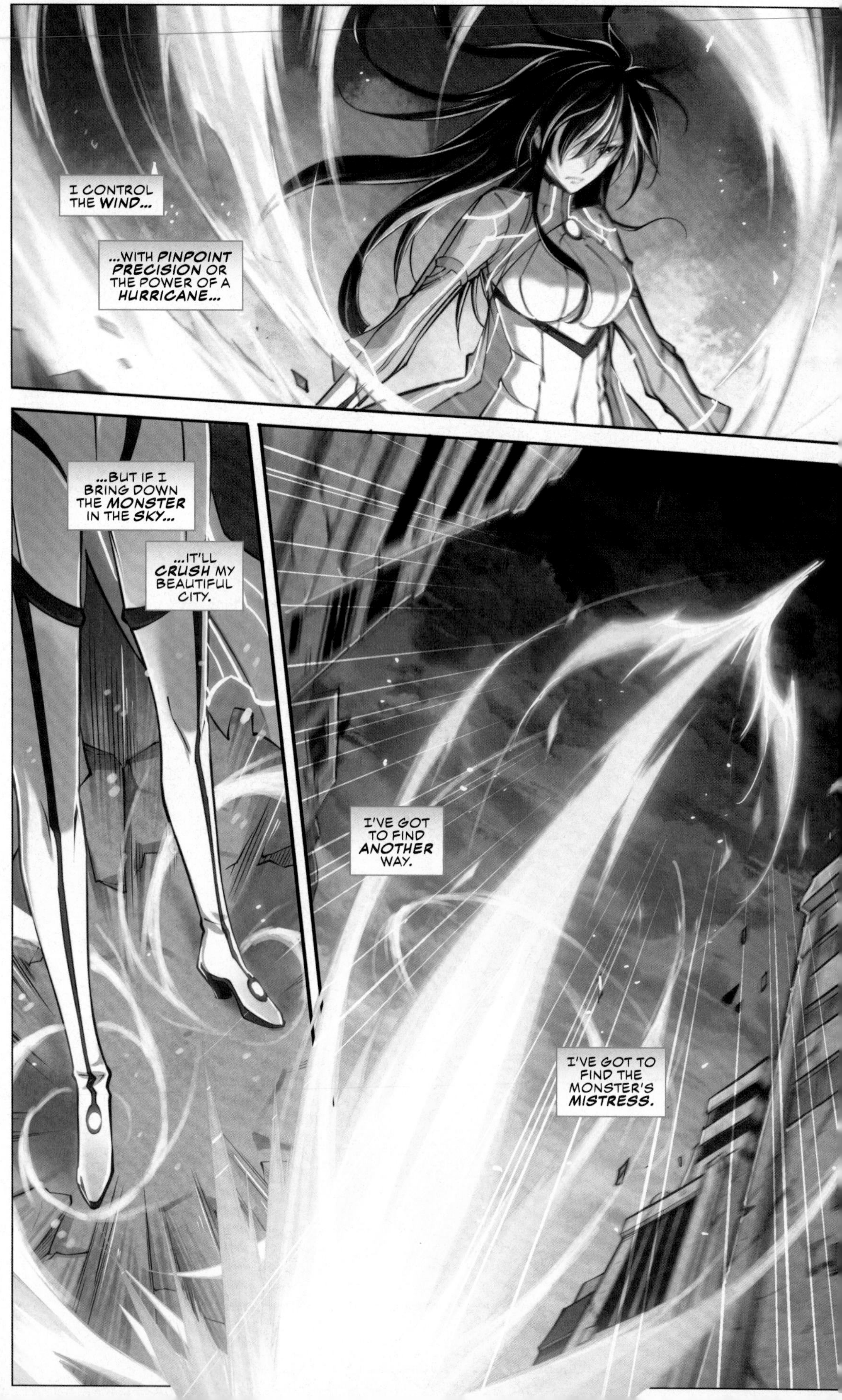
I CONTROL THE WIND...
...WITH PINPOINT PRECISION OR THE POWER OF A HURRICANE...
...BUT IF I BRING DOWN THE MONSTER IN THE SKY...
...IT'LL CRUSH MY BEAUTIFUL CITY.
I'VE GOT TO FIND ANOTHER WAY.
I'VE GOT TO FIND THE MONSTER'S MISTRESS.

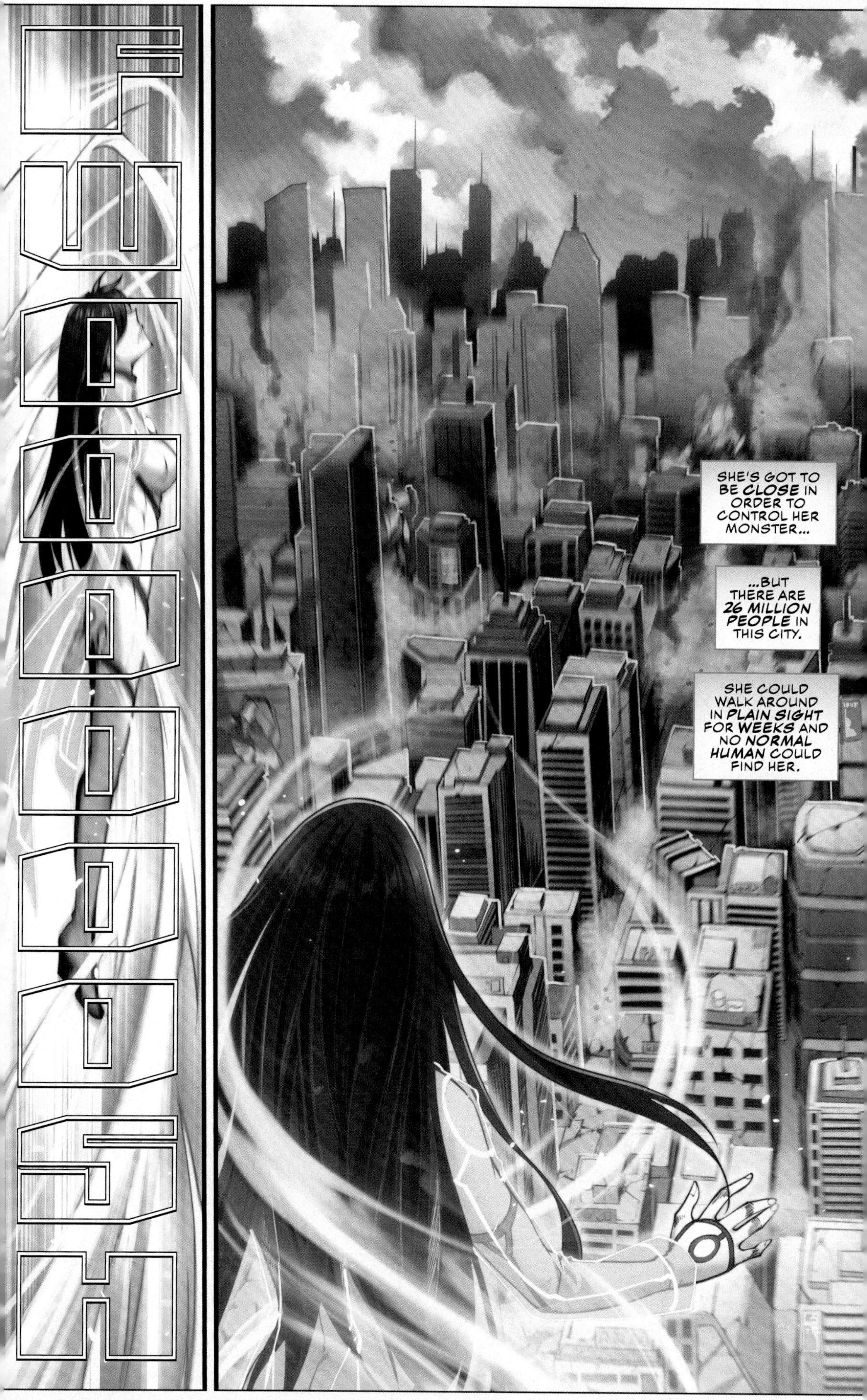
FWOOOOOOSH
SHE'S GOT TO BE CLOSE IN ORDER TO CONTROL HER MONSTER...
...BUT THERE ARE 26 MILLION PEOPLE IN THIS CITY.
SHE COULD WALK AROUND IN PLAIN SIGHT FOR WEEKS AND NO NORMAL HUMAN COULD FIND HER.

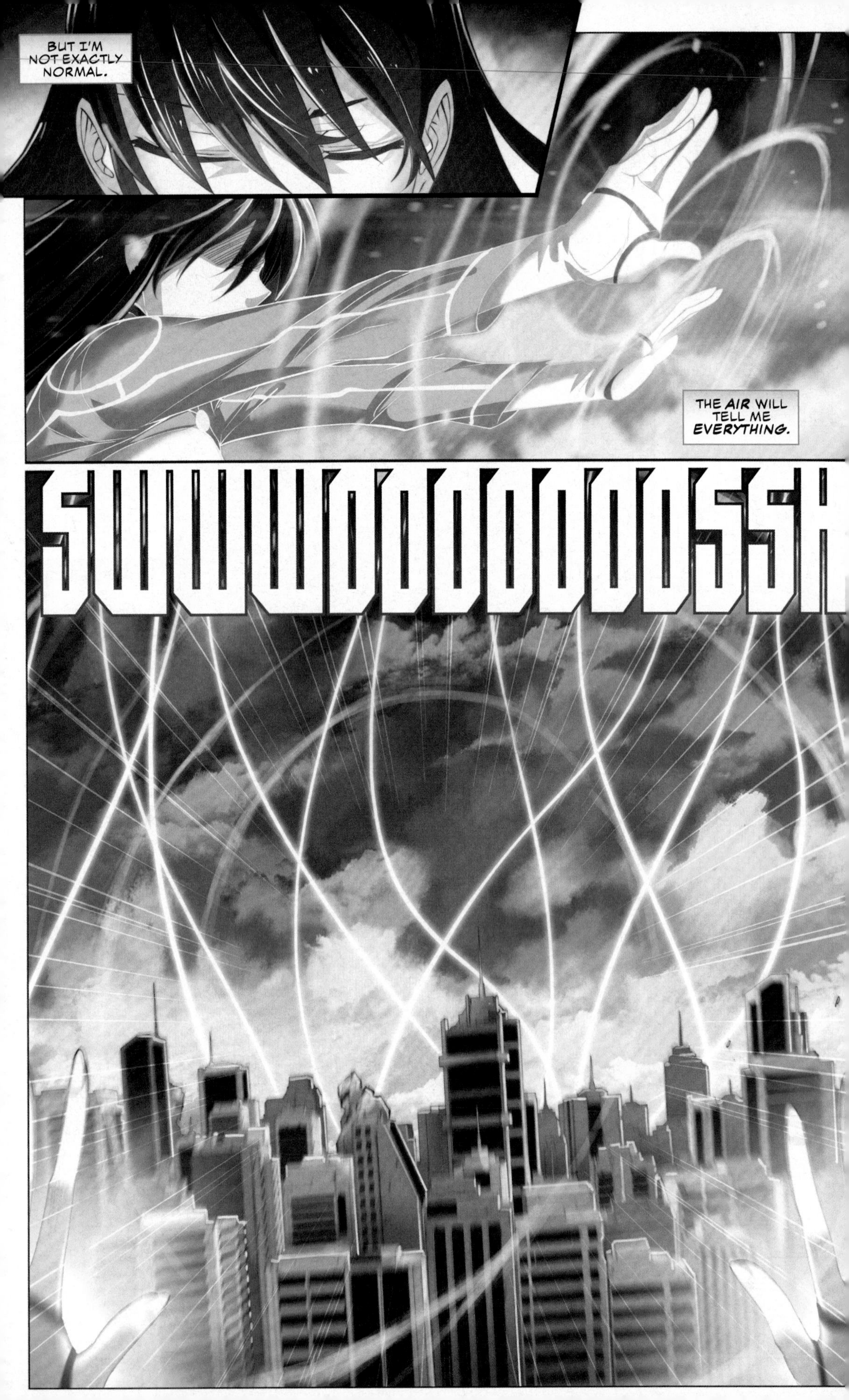

BUT I'M NOT EXACTLY NORMAL.
THE *AIR* WILL TELL ME *EVERYTHING.*
SWWOOOOOOOOSSH

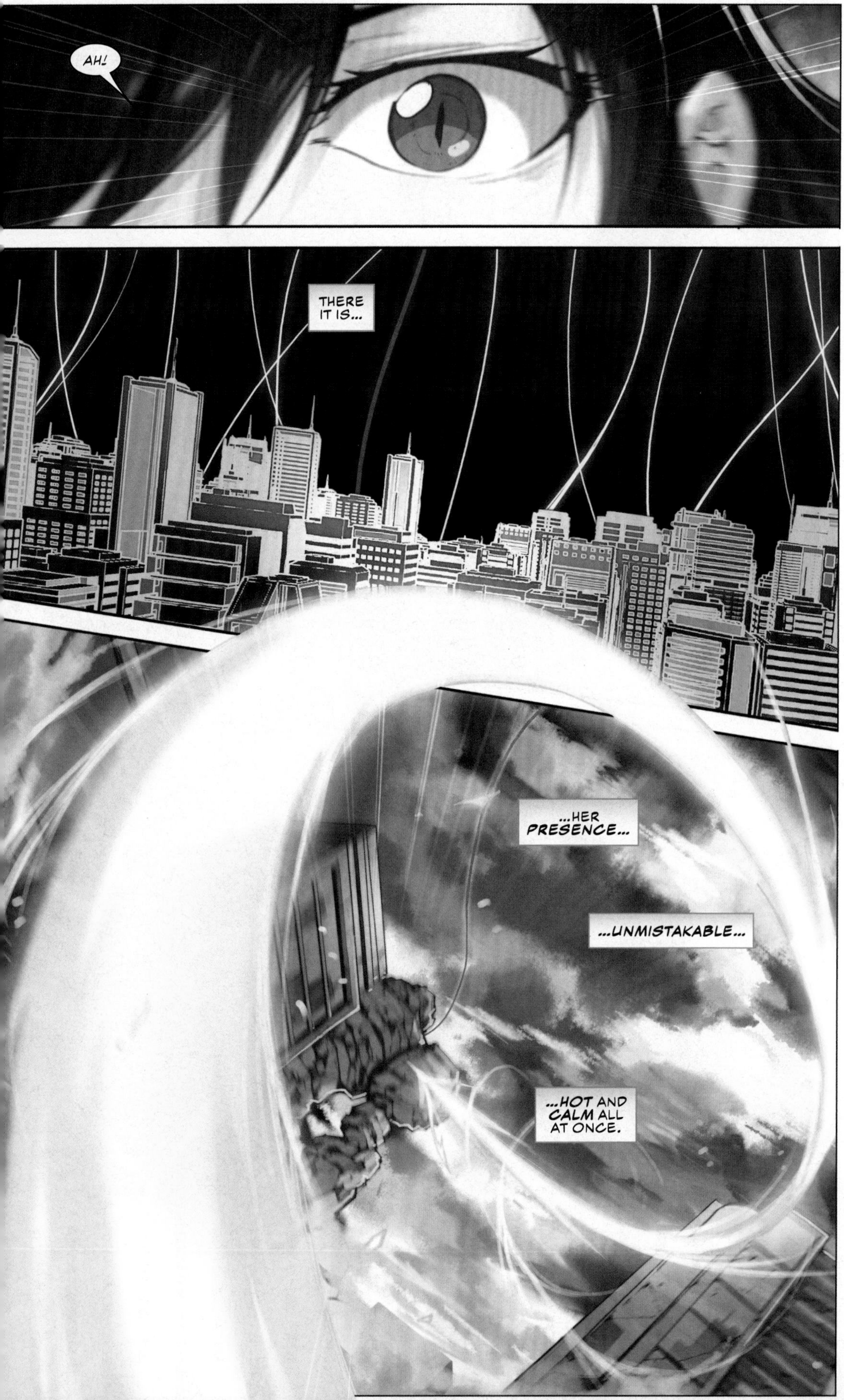
AH!
THERE IT IS...
...HER PRESENCE...
...UNMISTAKABLE...
...HOT AND CALM ALL AT ONCE.

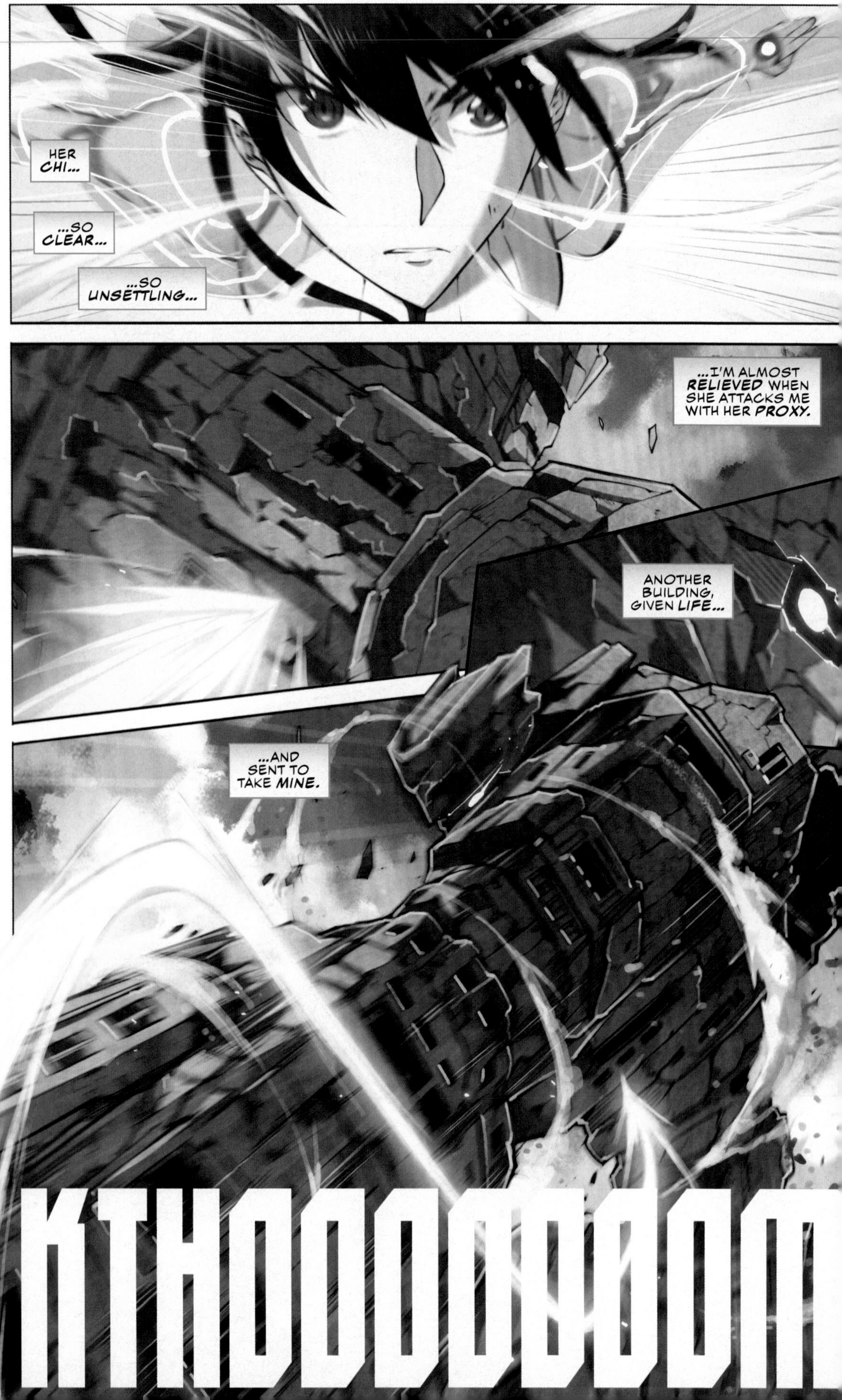
HER CHI...
...SO CLEAR...
...SO UNSETTLING...
...I'M ALMOST RELIEVED WHEN SHE ATTACKS ME WITH HER PROXY.
ANOTHER BUILDING, GIVEN LIFE...
...AND SENT TO TAKE MINE.
KTHOOOOOOOOM

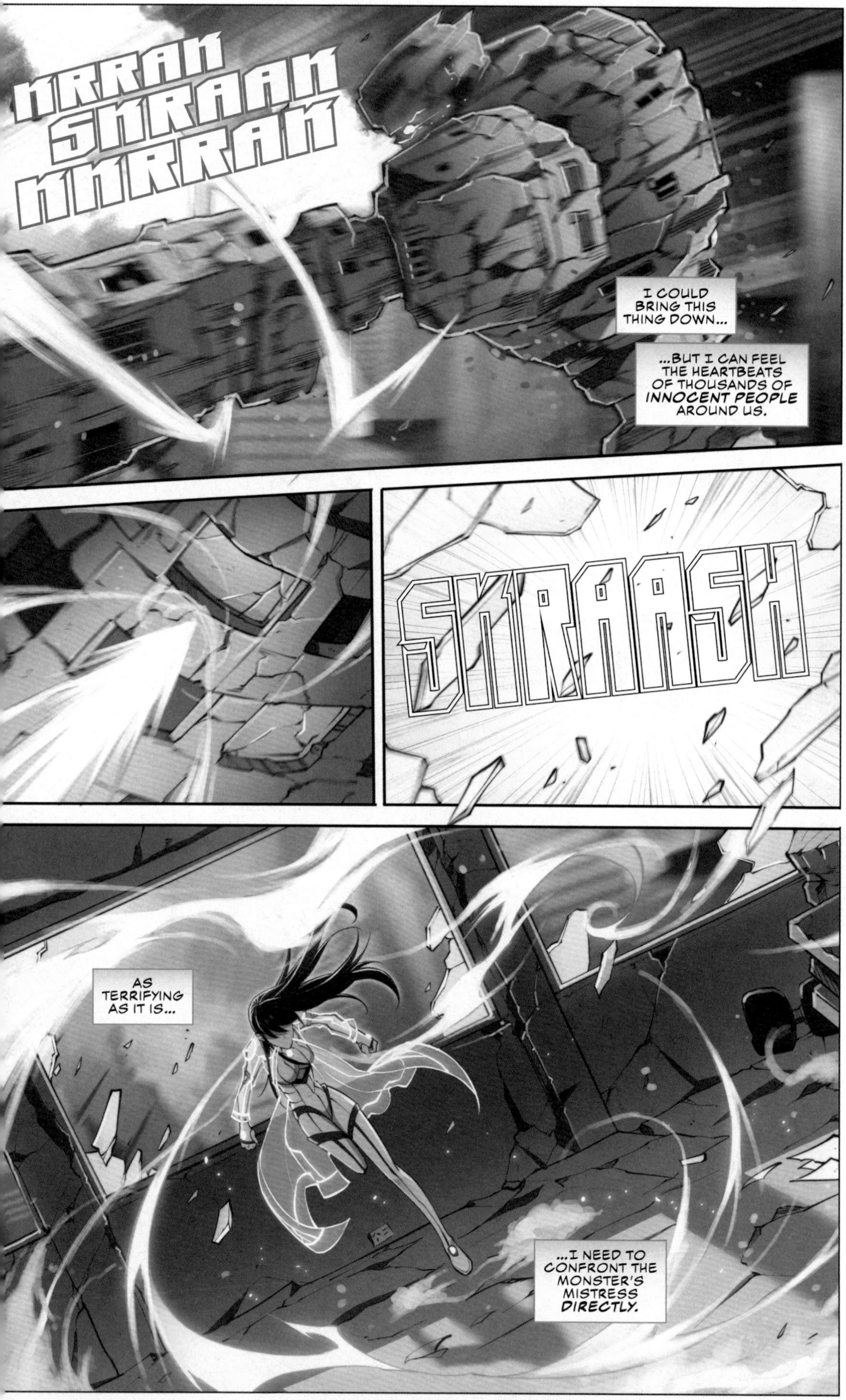
KRRAK
SHRAAK
KHRRAK
I COULD BRING THIS THING DOWN...
...BUT I CAN FEEL THE HEARTBEATS OF THOUSANDS OF INNOCENT PEOPLE AROUND US.
SKRAASH
AS TERRIFYING AS IT IS...
...I NEED TO CONFRONT THE MONSTER'S MISTRESS DIRECTLY.

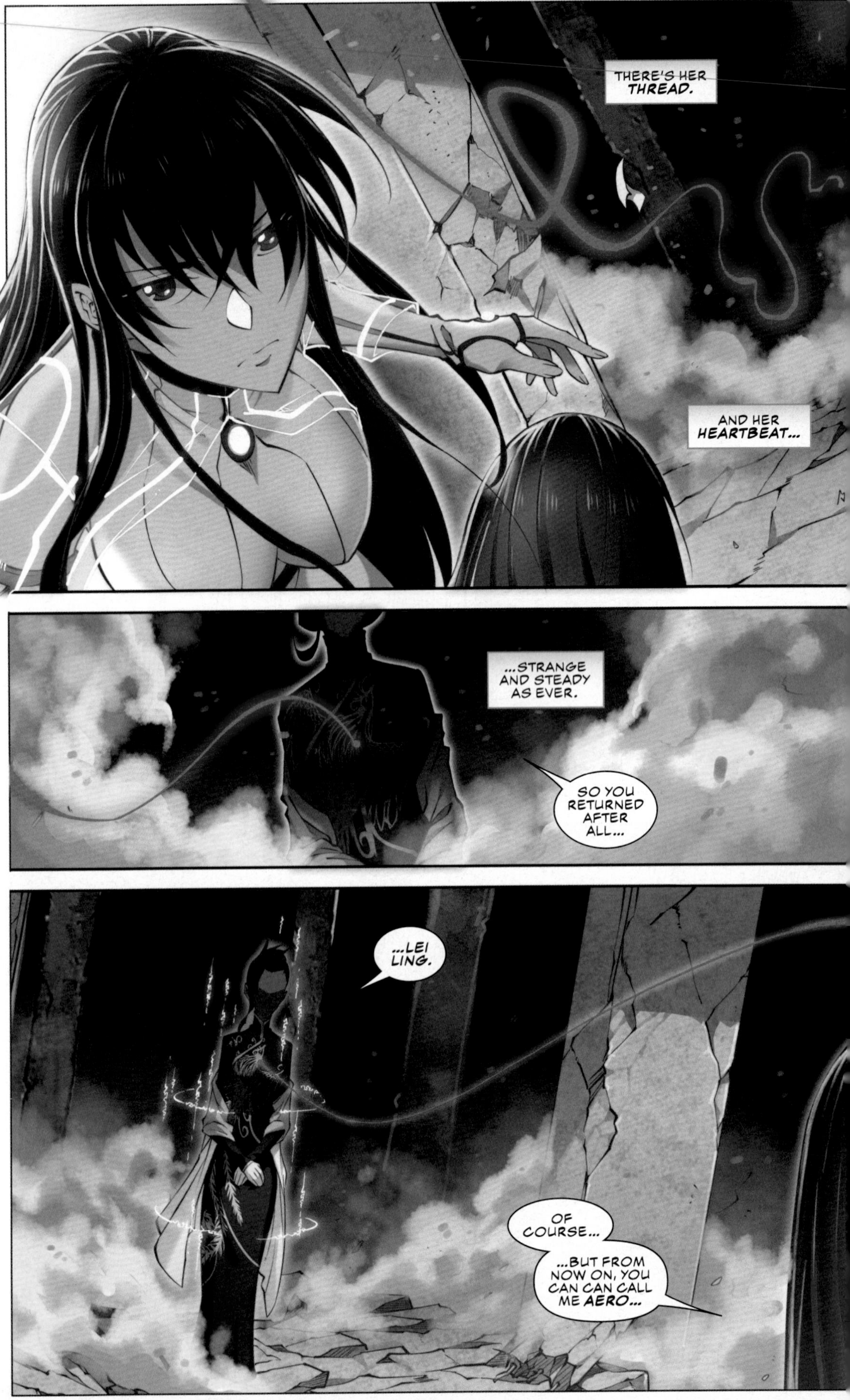
THERE'S HER THREAD.
AND HER HEARTBEAT...
...STRANGE AND STEADY AS EVER.
SO YOU RETURNED AFTER ALL...
...LEI LING.
OF COURSE...
...BUT FROM NOW ON, YOU CAN CAN CALL ME AERO...

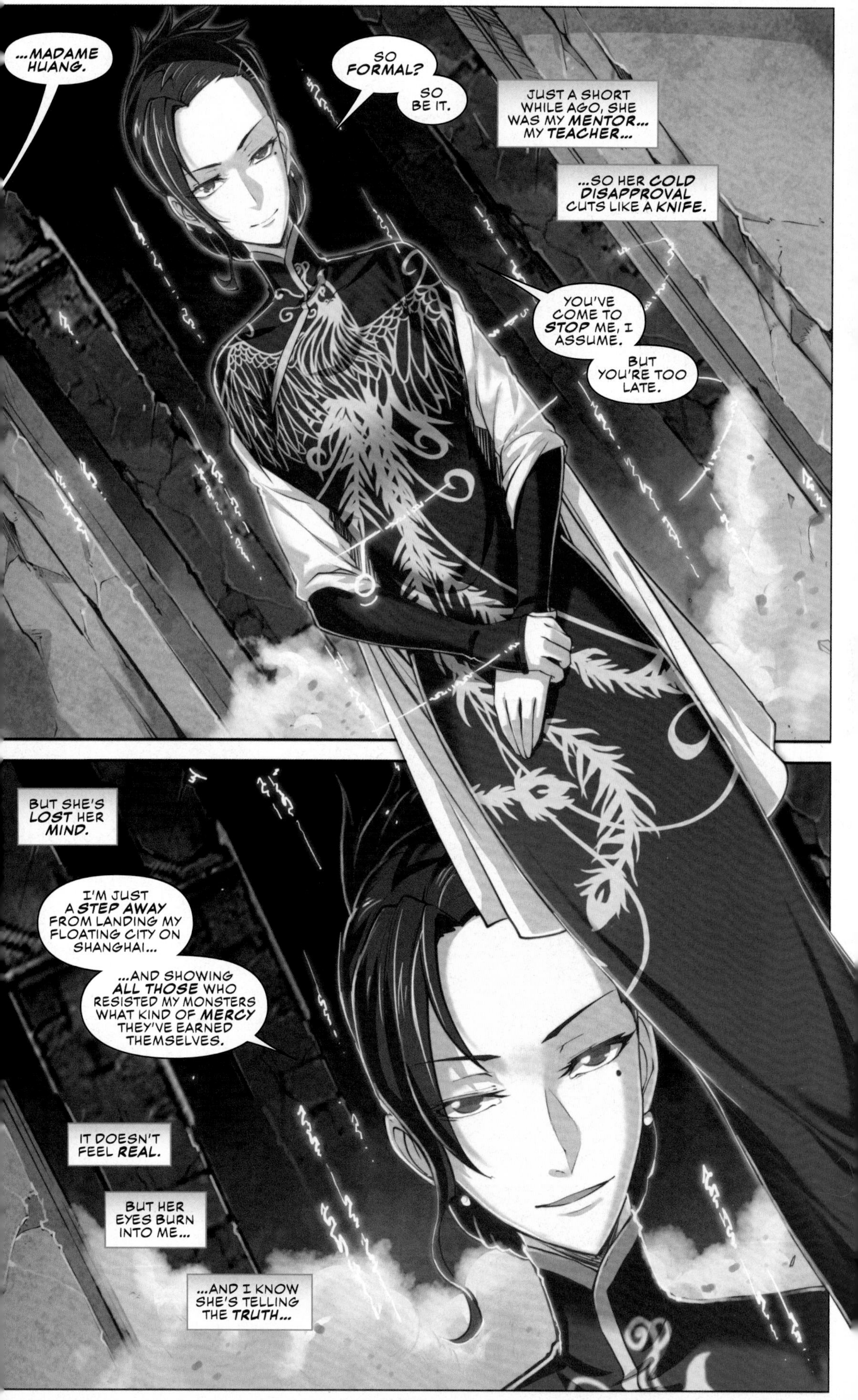
...MADAME HUANG.
SO FORMAL?
SO BE IT.
JUST A SHORT WHILE AGO, SHE WAS MY MENTOR... MY TEACHER...
...SO HER COLD DISAPPROVAL CUTS LIKE A KNIFE.
YOU'VE COME TO STOP ME, I ASSUME.
BUT YOU'RE TOO LATE.
BUT SHE'S LOST HER MIND.
I'M JUST A STEP AWAY FROM LANDING MY FLOATING CITY ON SHANGHAI...
...AND SHOWING ALL THOSE WHO RESISTED MY MONSTERS WHAT KIND OF MERCY THEY'VE EARNED THEMSELVES.
IT DOESN'T FEEL REAL.
BUT HER EYES BURN INTO ME...
...AND I KNOW SHE'S TELLING THE TRUTH...

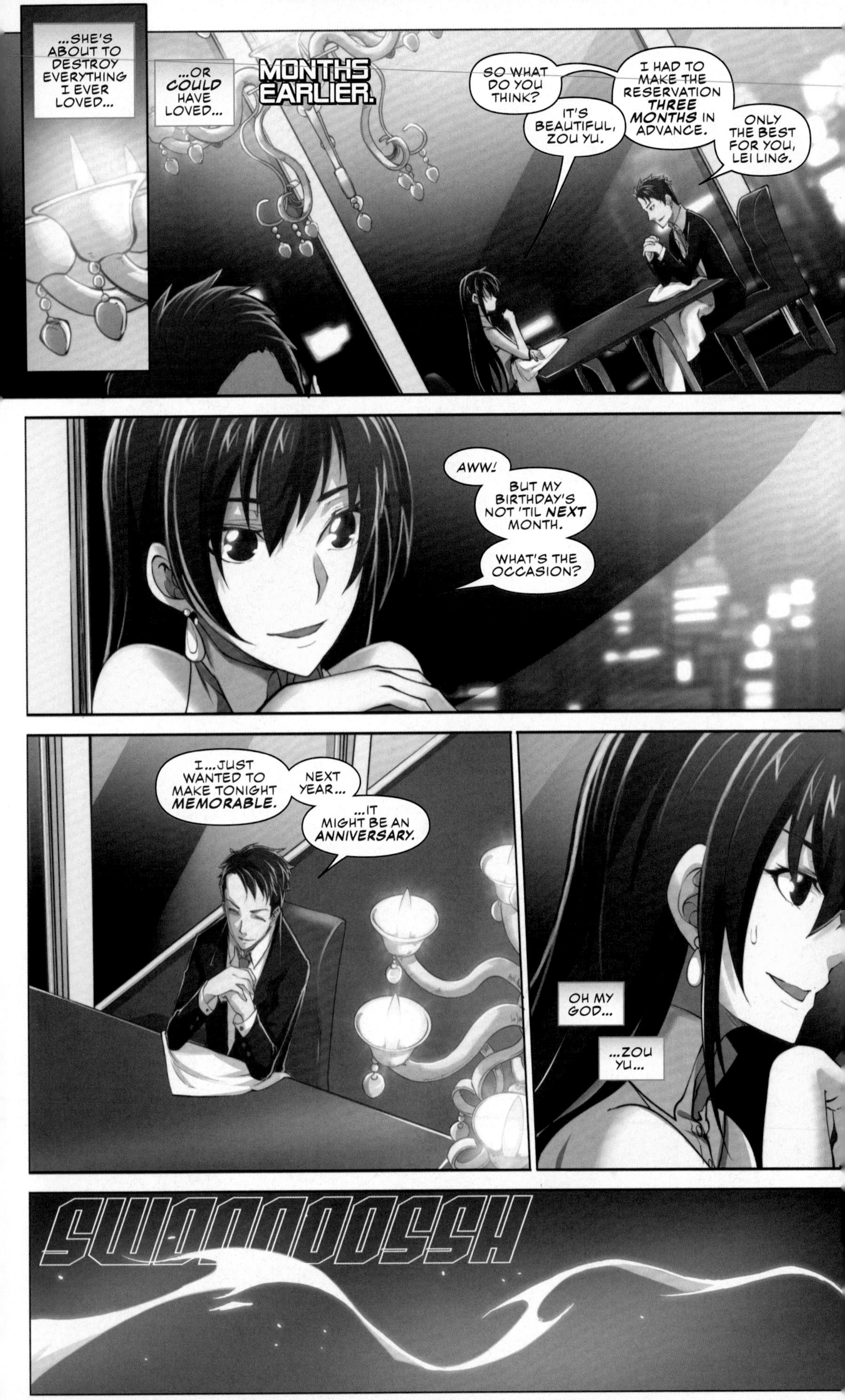
...SHE'S ABOUT TO DESTROY EVERYTHING I EVER LOVED...
...OR COULD HAVE LOVED...
MONTHS EARLIER.
SO WHAT DO YOU THINK?
IT'S BEAUTIFUL, ZOU YU.
I HAD TO MAKE THE RESERVATION THREE MONTHS IN ADVANCE.
ONLY THE BEST FOR YOU, LEI LING.
AWW!
BUT MY BIRTHDAY'S NOT 'TIL NEXT MONTH.
WHAT'S THE OCCASION?
I...JUST WANTED TO MAKE TONIGHT MEMORABLE.
NEXT YEAR...
...IT MIGHT BE AN ANNIVERSARY.
OH MY GOD...
...ZOU YU...
SWOOOOOSH

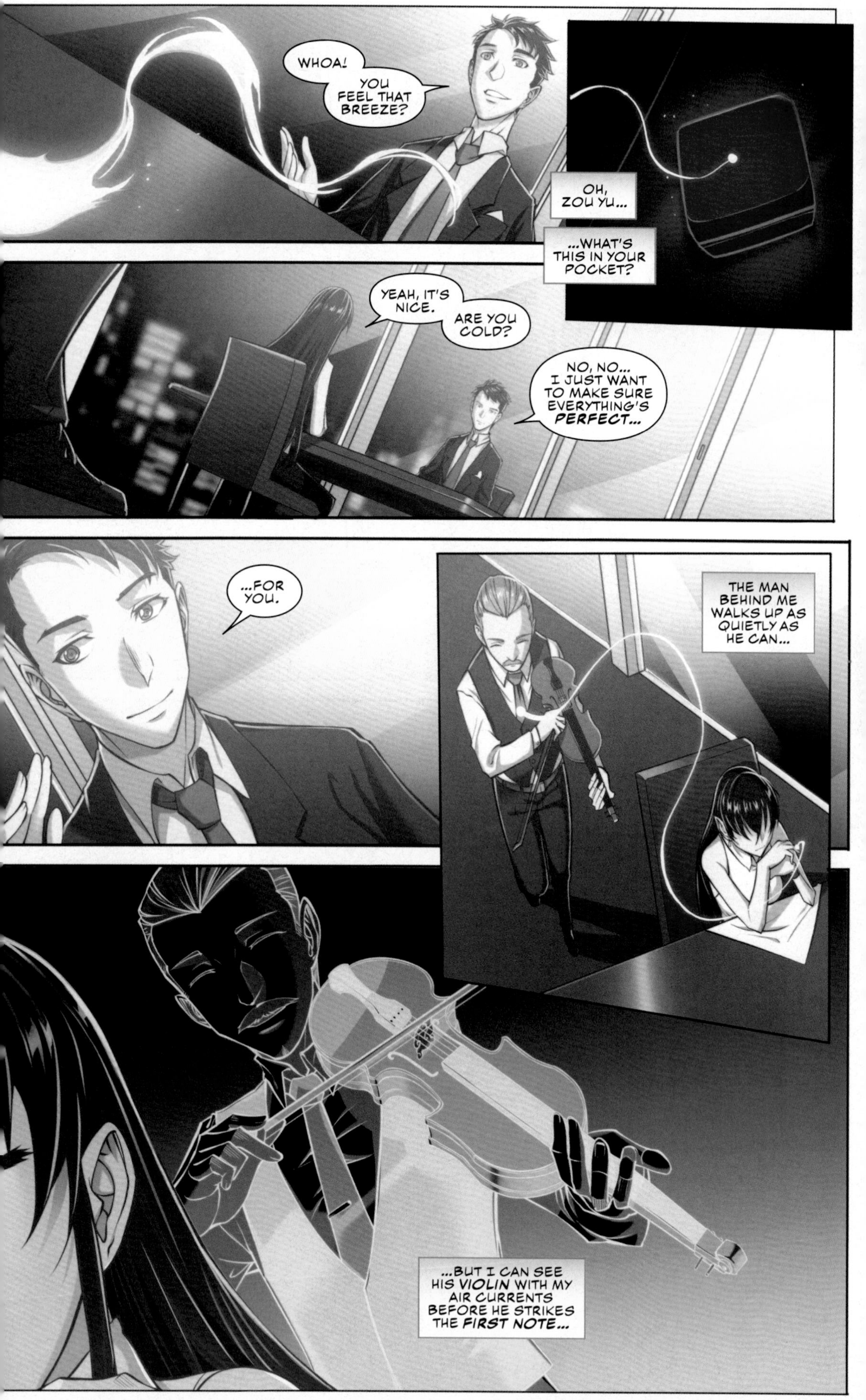
WHOA!
YOU FEEL THAT BREEZE?
OH, ZOU YU...
...WHAT'S THIS IN YOUR POCKET?
YEAH, IT'S NICE.
ARE YOU COLD?
NO, NO... I JUST WANT TO MAKE SURE EVERYTHING'S PERFECT...
...FOR YOU.
THE MAN BEHIND ME WALKS UP AS QUIETLY AS HE CAN...
...BUT I CAN SEE HIS VIOLIN WITH MY AIR CURRENTS BEFORE HE STRIKES THE FIRST NOTE...

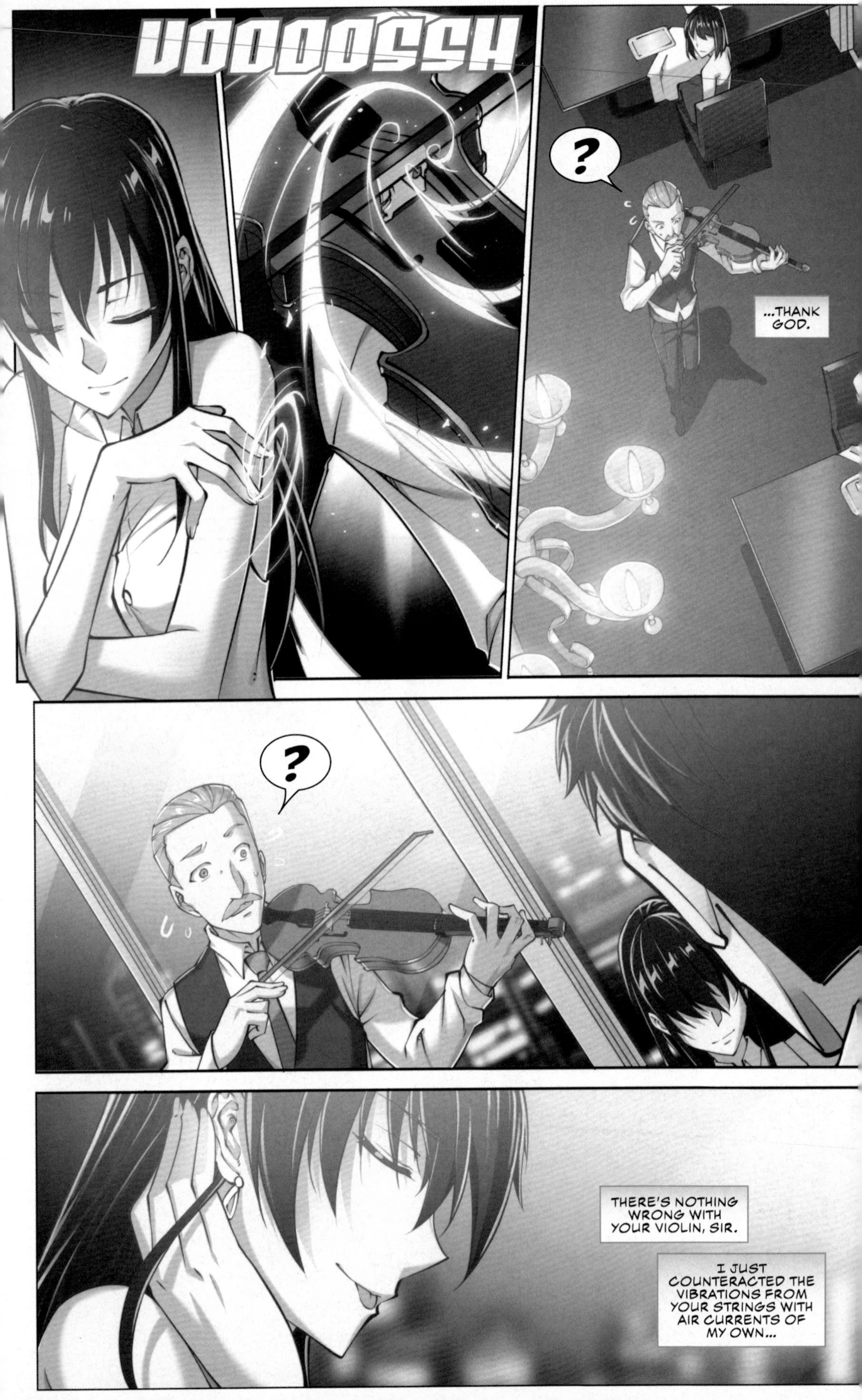
VOOOOSSH
?
...THANK GOD.
?
THERE'S NOTHING WRONG WITH YOUR VIOLIN, SIR.
I JUST COUNTERACTED THE VIBRATIONS FROM YOUR STRINGS WITH AIR CURRENTS OF MY OWN...

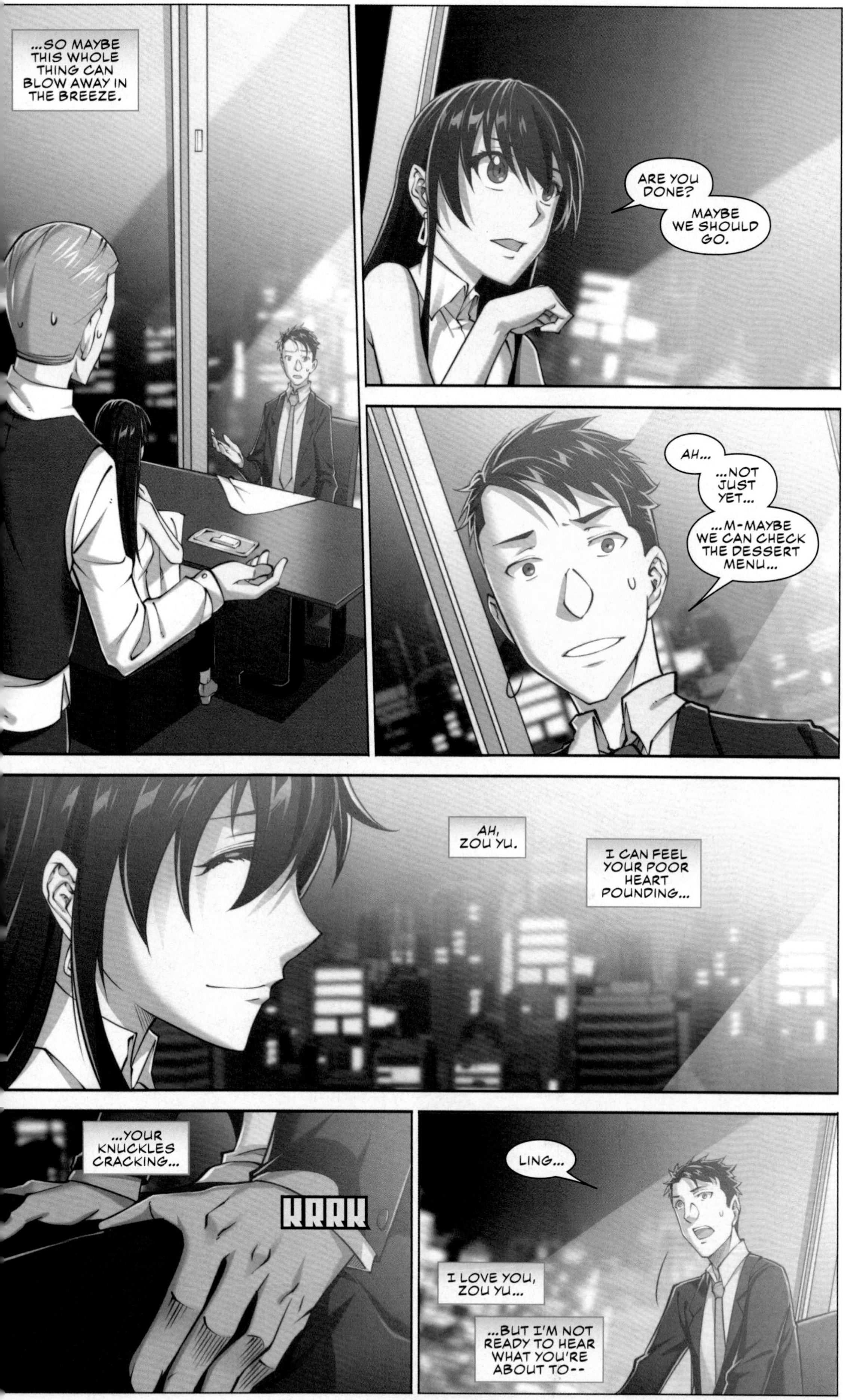
...SO MAYBE THIS WHOLE THING CAN BLOW AWAY IN THE BREEZE.
ARE YOU DONE?
MAYBE WE SHOULD GO.
AH...
...NOT JUST YET...
...M-MAYBE WE CAN CHECK THE DESSERT MENU...
AH, ZOU YU.
I CAN FEEL YOUR POOR HEART POUNDING...
...YOUR KNUCKLES CRACKING...
KRRK
LING...
I LOVE YOU, ZOU YU...
...BUT I'M NOT READY TO HEAR WHAT YOU'RE ABOUT TO--

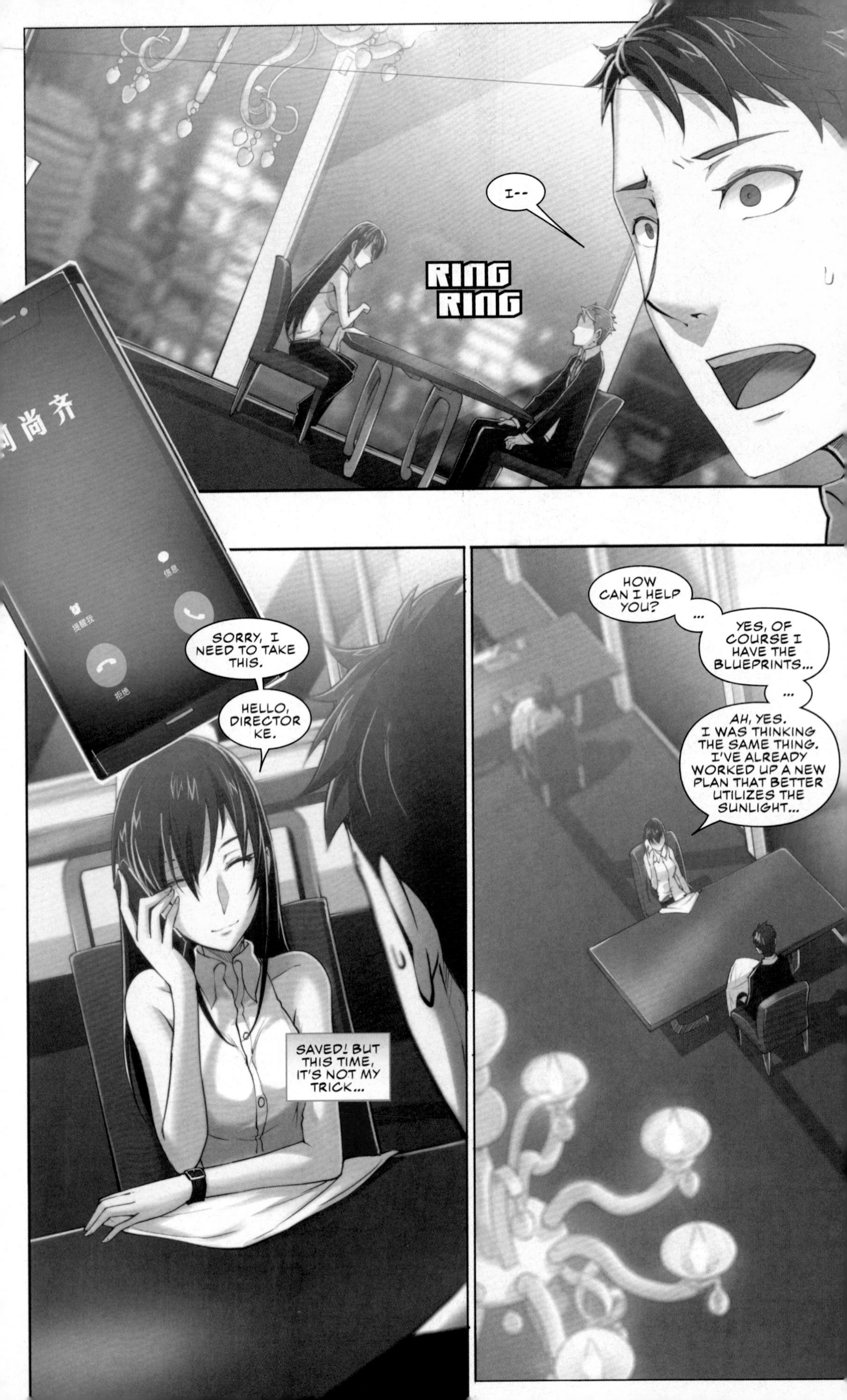
I--
RING RING
信息
提醒我
拒绝
SORRY, I NEED TO TAKE THIS.
HELLO, DIRECTOR KE.
SAVED! BUT THIS TIME, IT'S NOT MY TRICK...
HOW CAN I HELP YOU?
...
YES, OF COURSE I HAVE THE BLUEPRINTS...
...
AH, YES. I WAS THINKING THE SAME THING. I'VE ALREADY WORKED UP A NEW PLAN THAT BETTER UTILIZES THE SUNLIGHT...

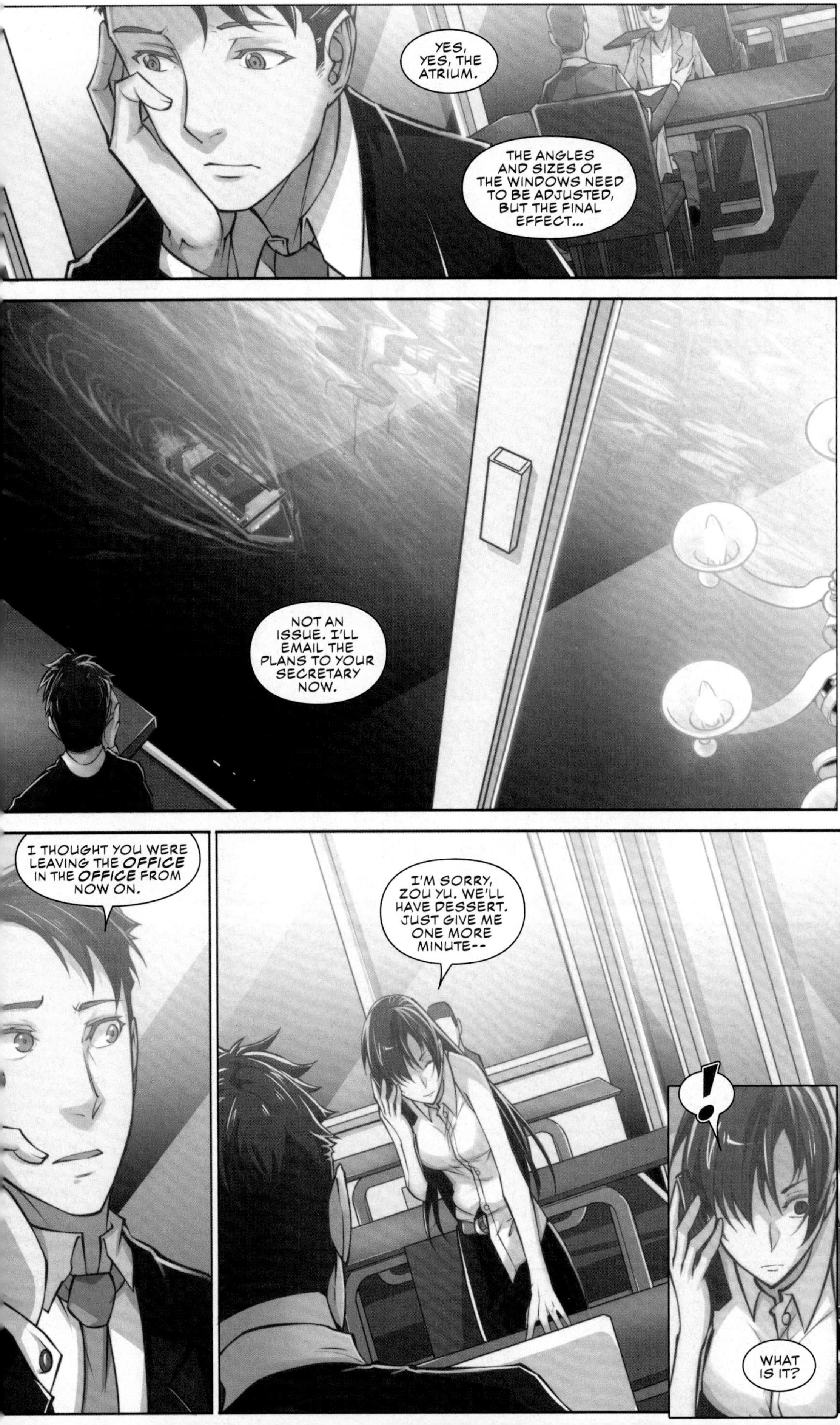
YES, YES, THE ATRIUM.
THE ANGLES AND SIZES OF THE WINDOWS NEED TO BE ADJUSTED, BUT THE FINAL EFFECT...
NOT AN ISSUE. I'LL EMAIL THE PLANS TO YOUR SECRETARY NOW.
I THOUGHT YOU WERE LEAVING THE OFFICE IN THE OFFICE FROM NOW ON.
I'M SORRY, ZOU YU. WE'LL HAVE DESSERT. JUST GIVE ME ONE MORE MINUTE--
!
WHAT IS IT?

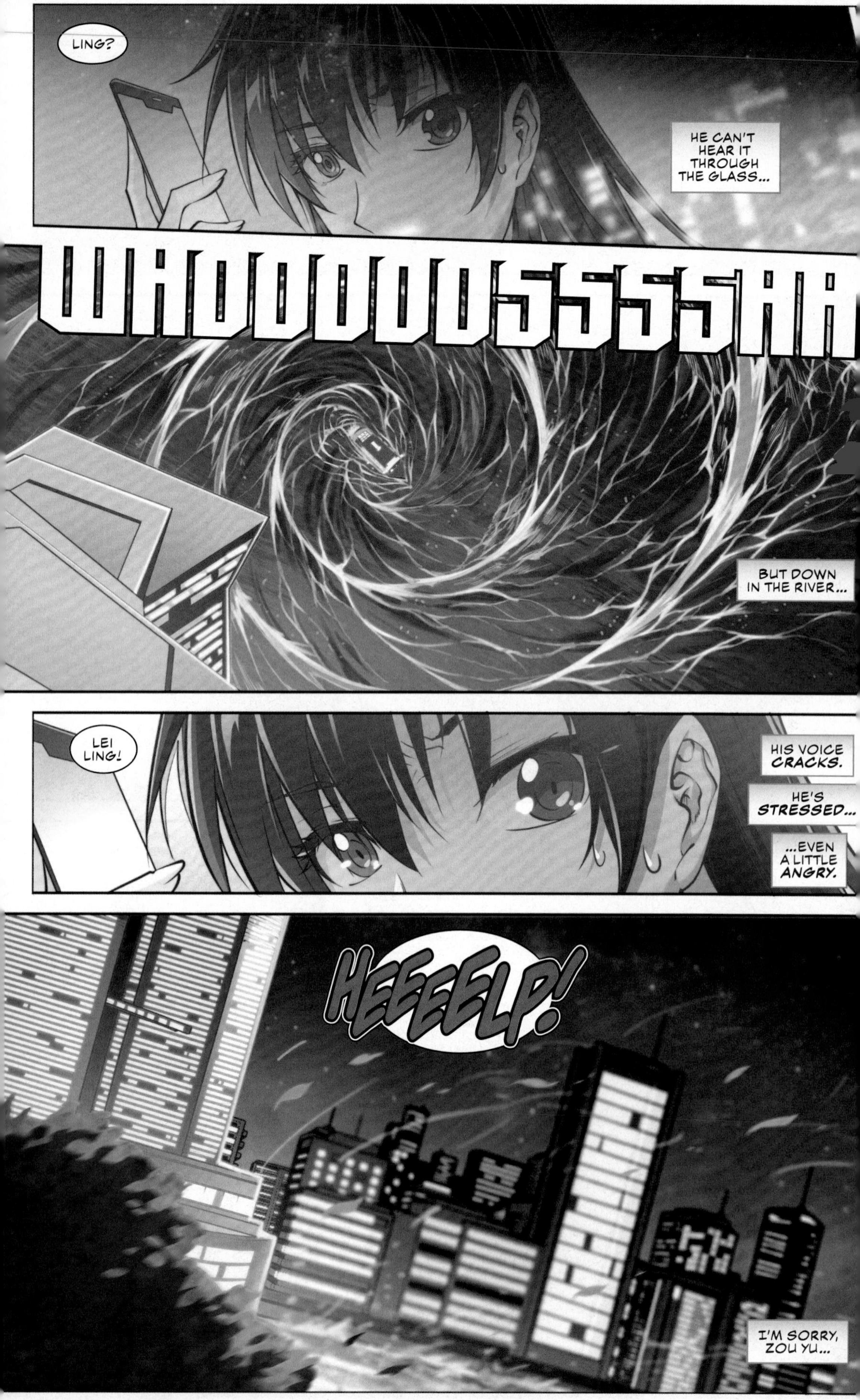
LING?
HE CAN'T HEAR IT THROUGH THE GLASS...
WHOOOOOSSSSSH
BUT DOWN IN THE RIVER...
LEI LING!
HIS VOICE CRACKS.
HE'S STRESSED...
...EVEN A LITTLE ANGRY.
HEEEELP!
I'M SORRY, ZOU YU...

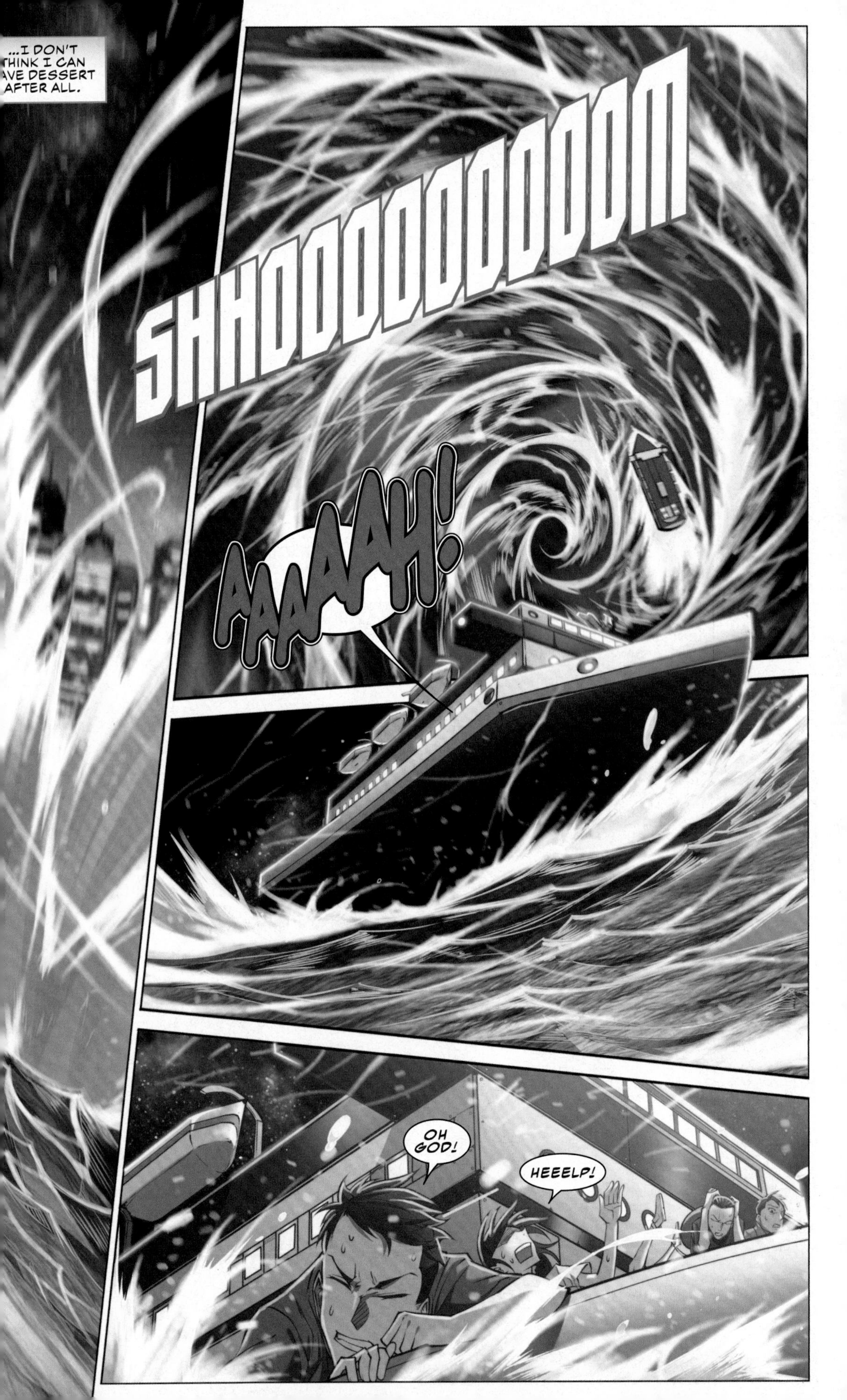
...I DON'T
THINK I CAN
AVE DESSERT
AFTER ALL.
SHHOOOOOOOOOM
AAAAAH!
OH GOD!
HEEELP!

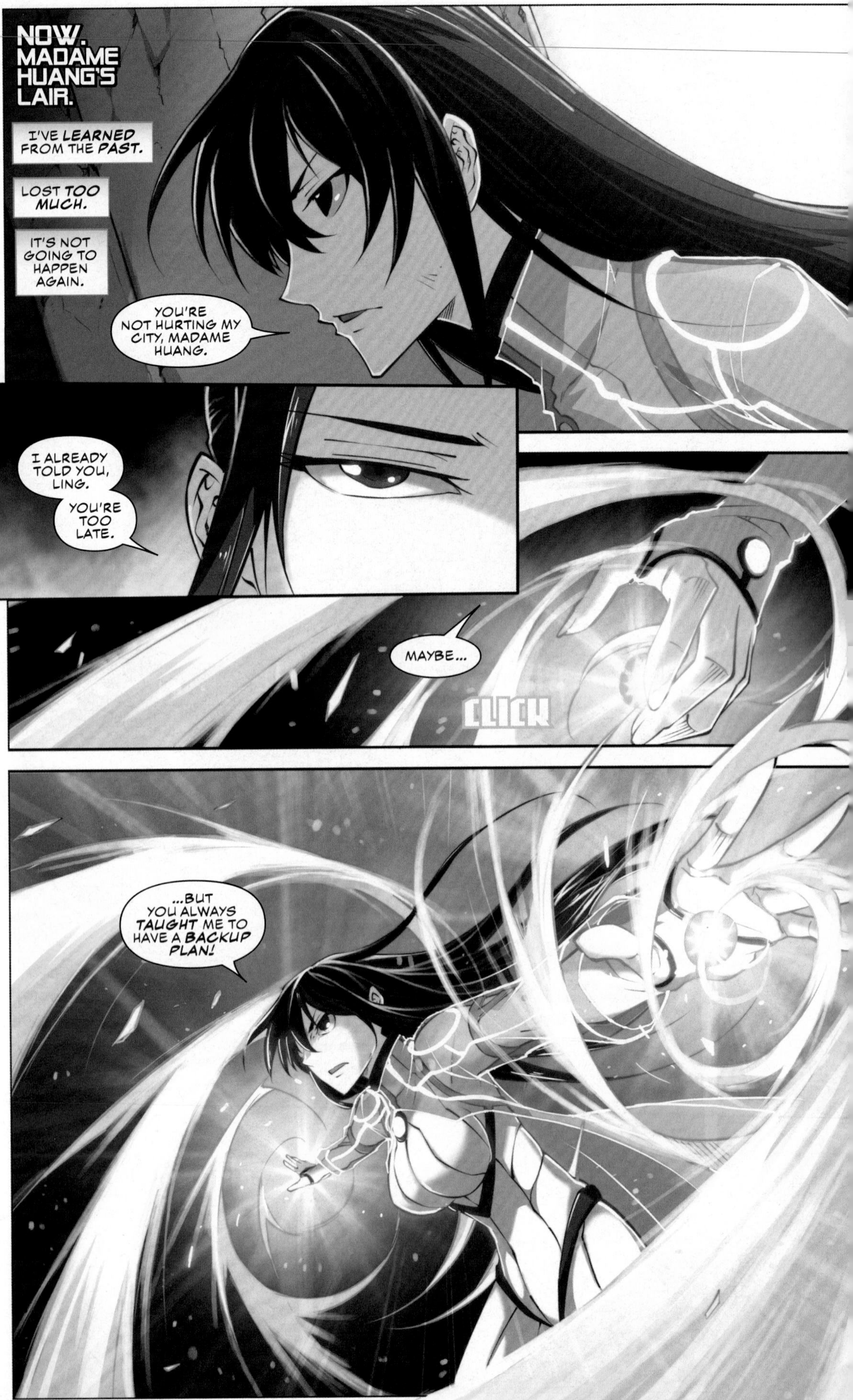
NOW. MADAME HUANG'S LAIR.
I'VE LEARNED FROM THE PAST.
LOST TOO MUCH.
IT'S NOT GOING TO HAPPEN AGAIN.
YOU'RE NOT HURTING MY CITY, MADAME HUANG.
I ALREADY TOLD YOU, LING.
YOU'RE TOO LATE.
MAYBE...
CLICK
...BUT YOU ALWAYS TAUGHT ME TO HAVE A BACKUP PLAN!

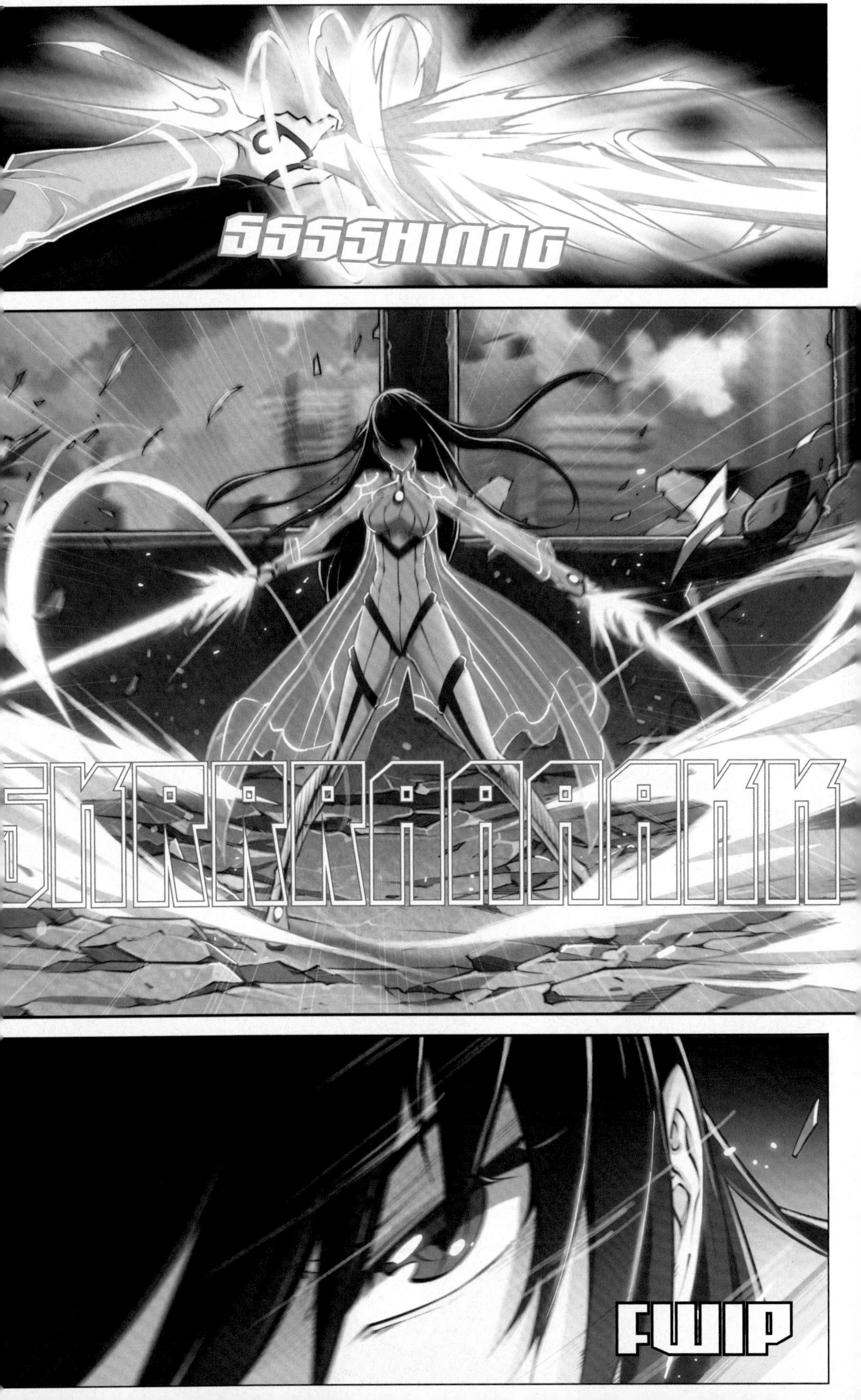
SSSSHINNG
SKRRRAAAAKK
FWIP

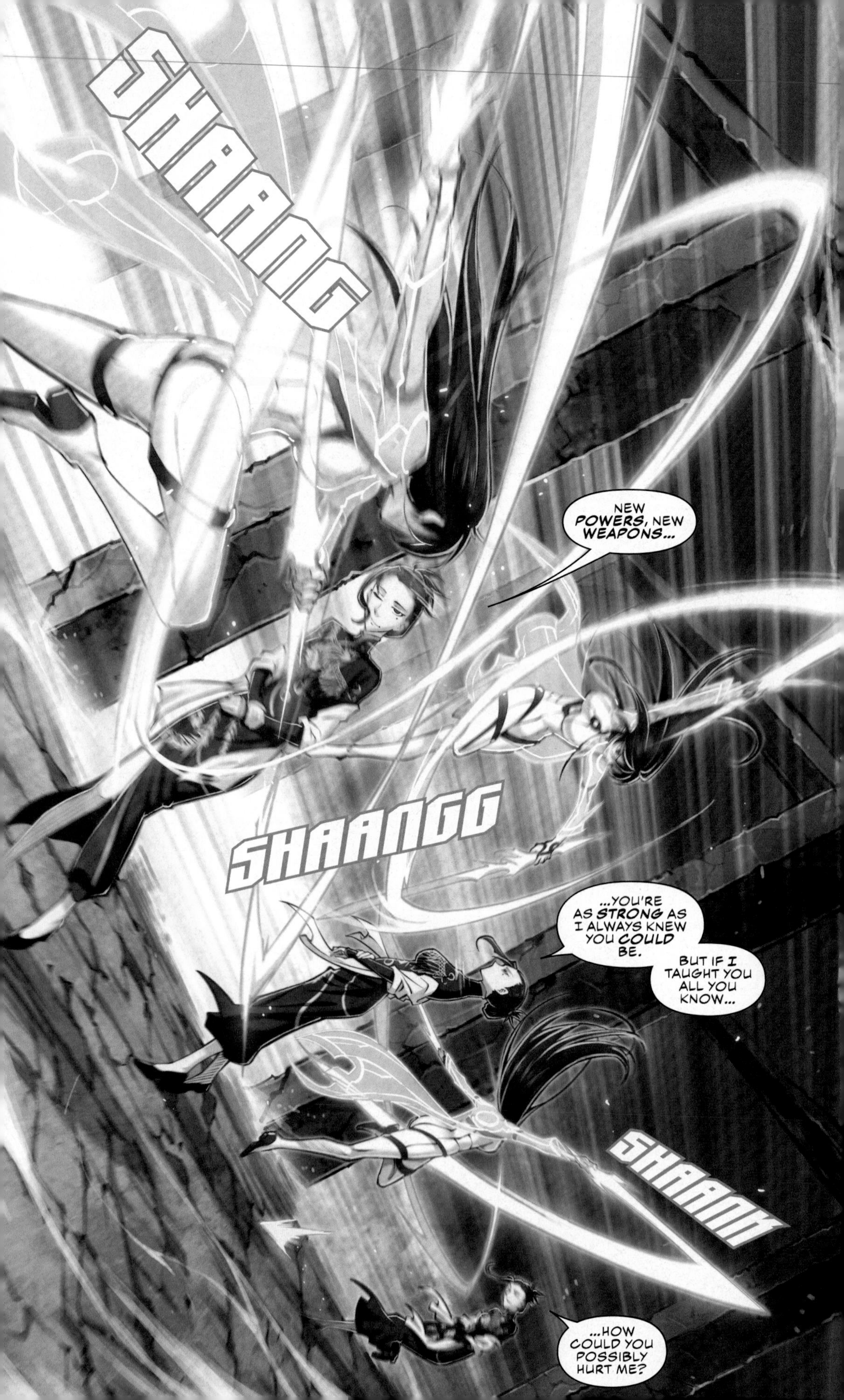
SHAANG
NEW POWERS, NEW WEAPONS...
SHAANGG
...YOU'RE AS STRONG AS I ALWAYS KNEW YOU COULD BE.
BUT IF I TAUGHT YOU ALL YOU KNOW...
SHAANK
...HOW COULD YOU POSSIBLY HURT ME?

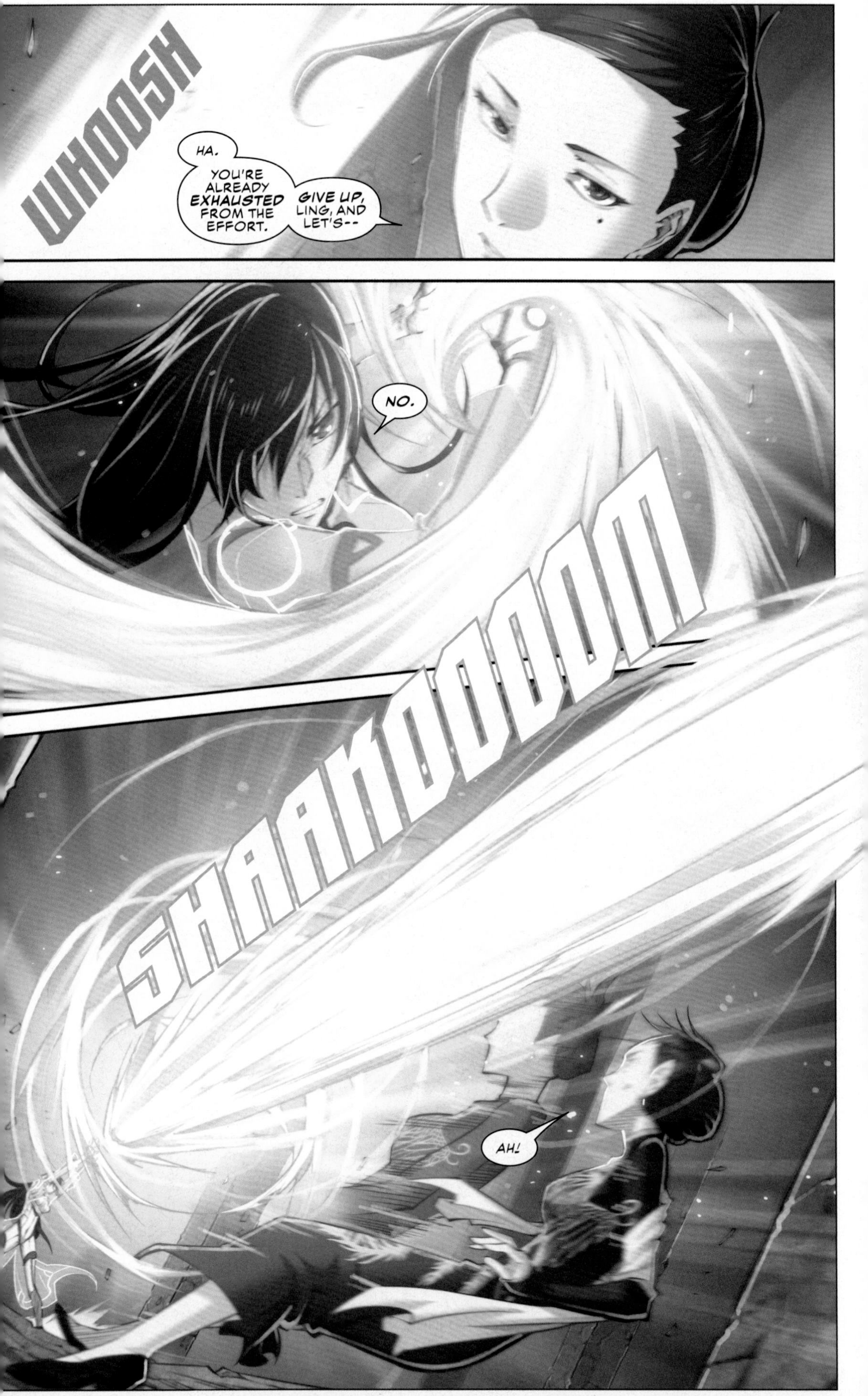
WHOOSH
HA.
YOU'RE ALREADY EXHAUSTED FROM THE EFFORT.
GIVE UP, LING, AND LET'S--
NO.
SHAAKOOOOM
AH!

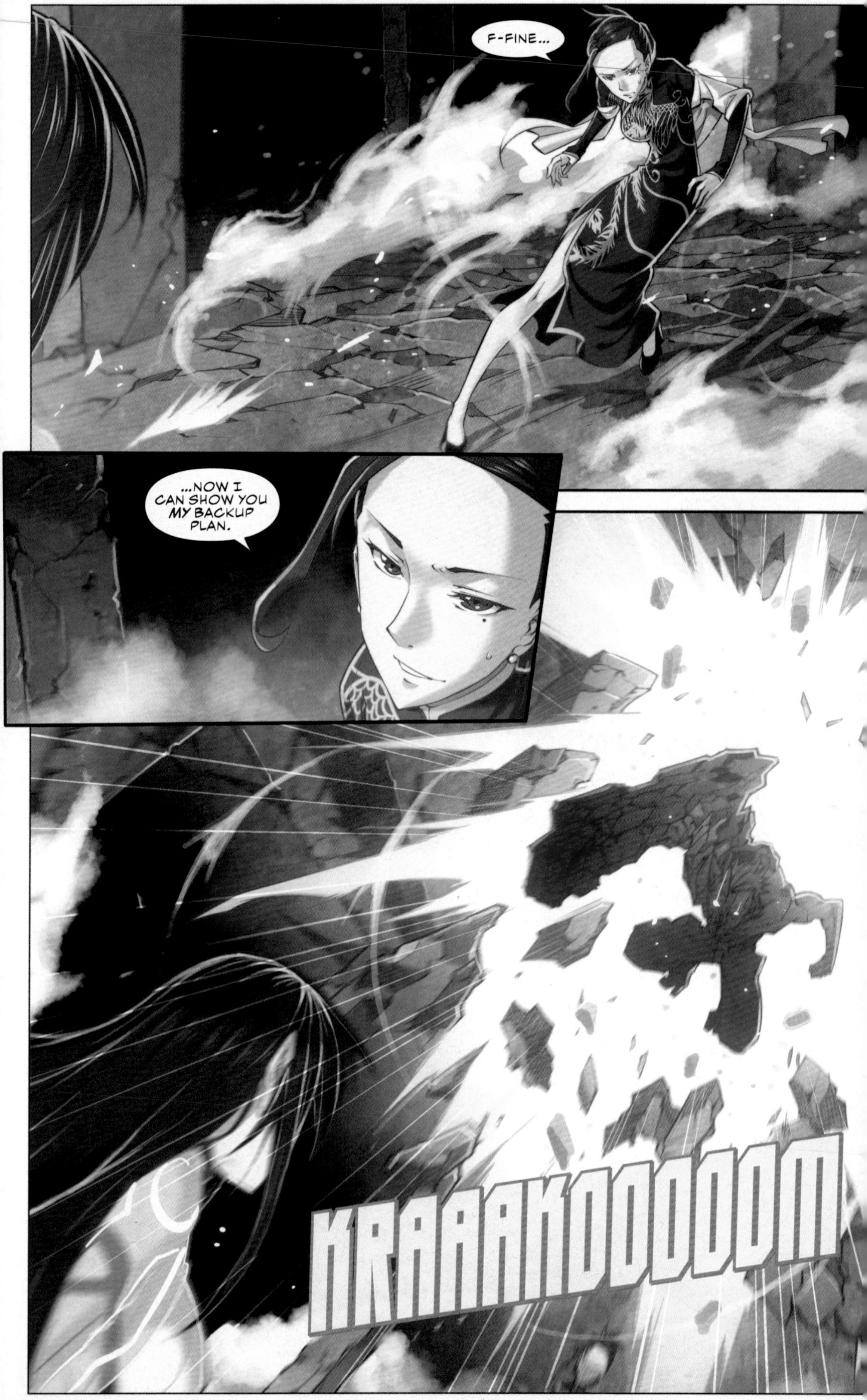
F-FINE...
...NOW I CAN SHOW YOU MY BACKUP PLAN.
KRAAAKOOOOOOM

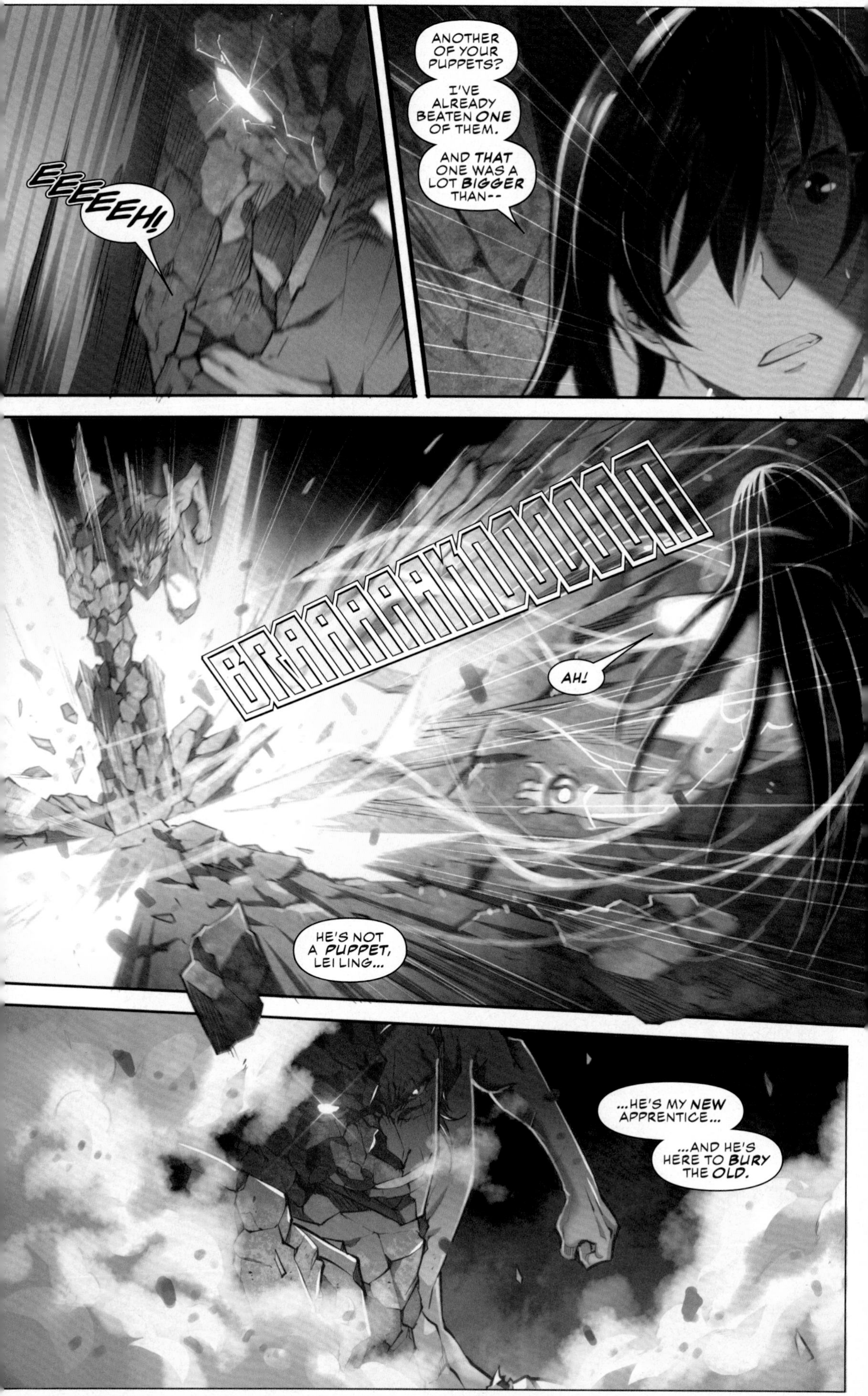
EEEEEEH!
ANOTHER OF YOUR PUPPETS?
I'VE ALREADY BEATEN ONE OF THEM.
AND THAT ONE WAS A LOT BIGGER THAN--
BRAAAAKOOOOM!
AH!
HE'S NOT A PUPPET, LEI LING...
...HE'S MY NEW APPRENTICE...
...AND HE'S HERE TO BURY THE OLD.

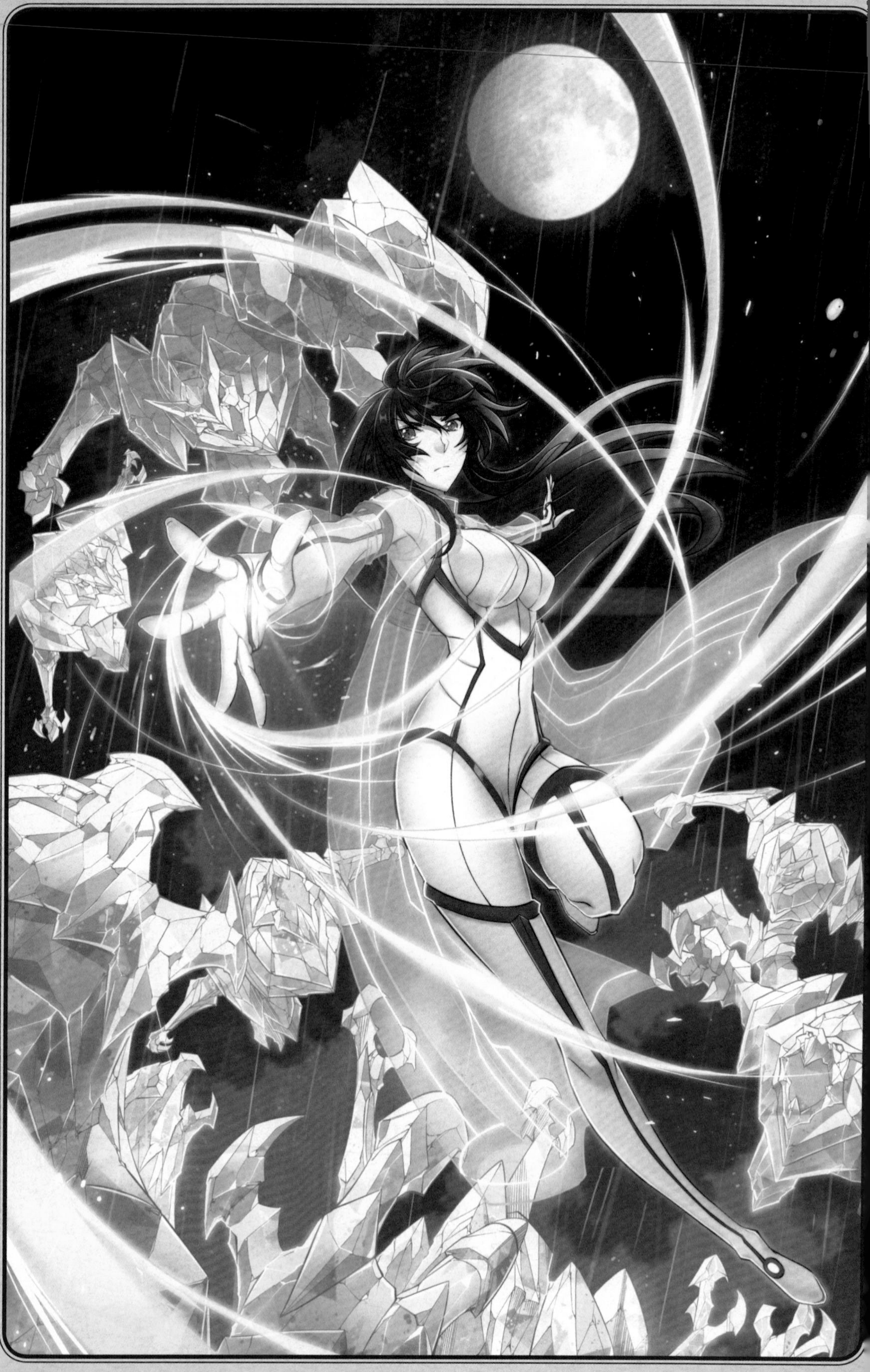

3 Alone Against Stone

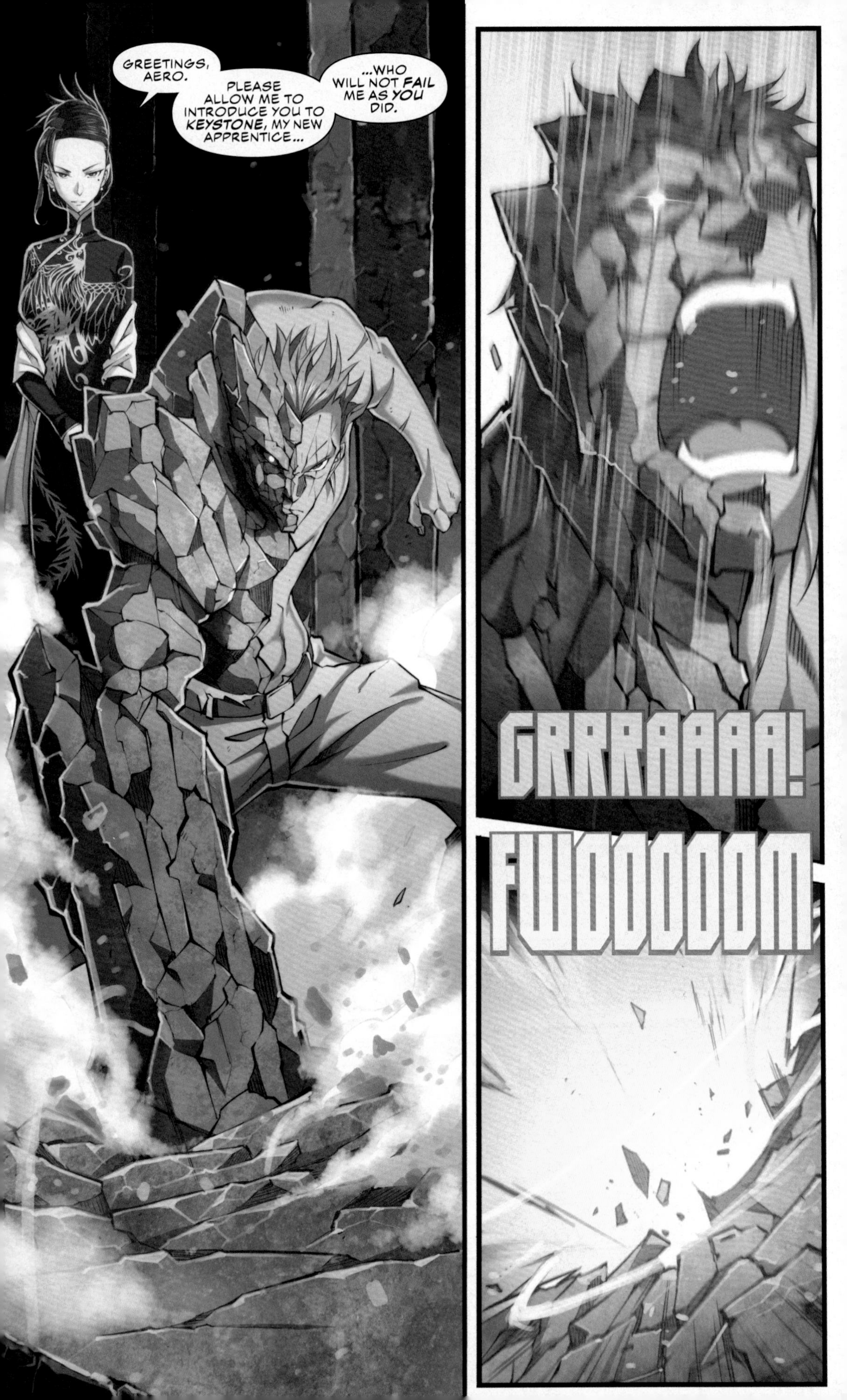
GREETINGS, AERO.
PLEASE ALLOW ME TO INTRODUCE YOU TO KEYSTONE, MY NEW APPRENTICE...
...WHO WILL NOT FAIL ME AS YOU DID.
GRRRAAAAA!
FWOOOOOM

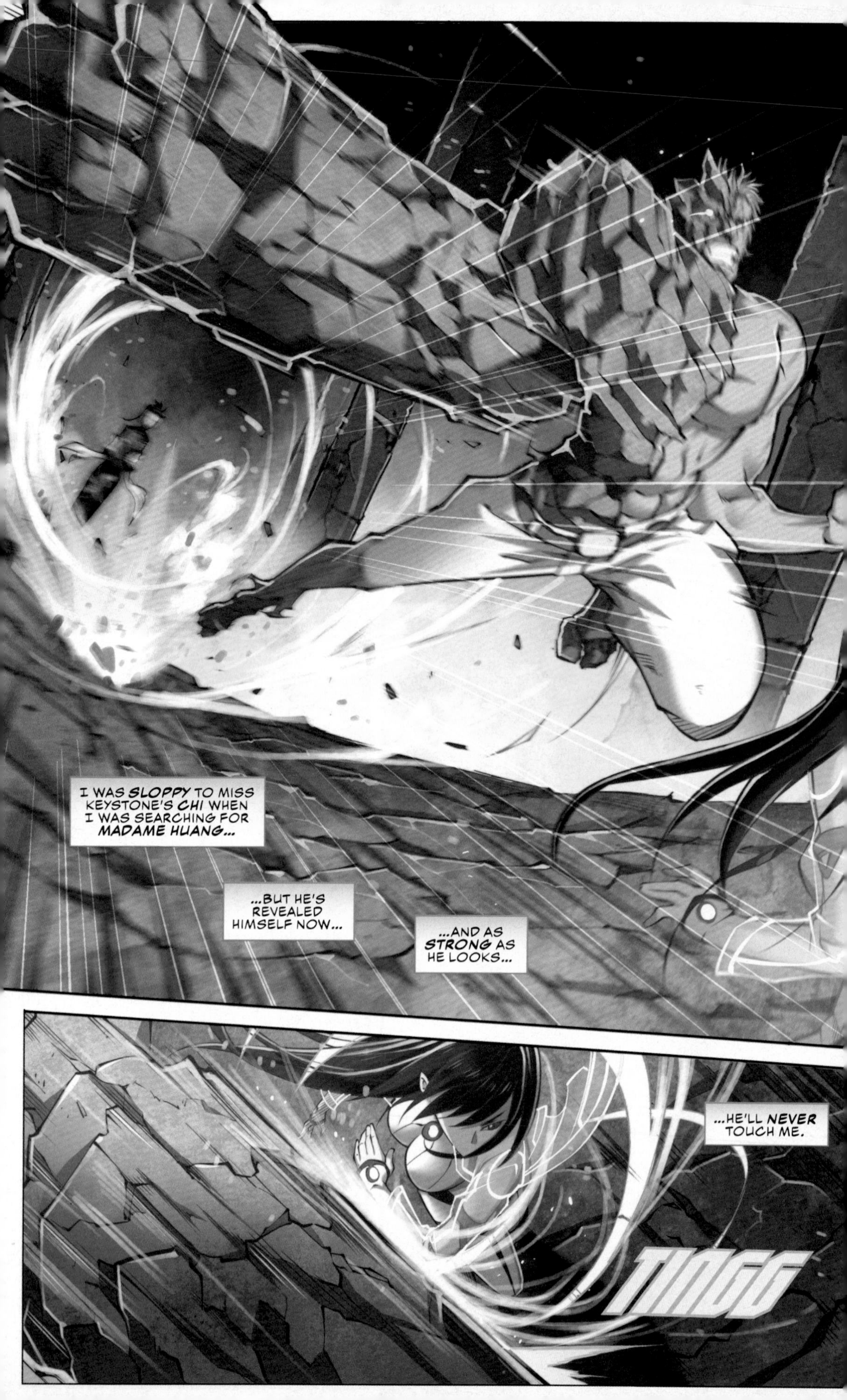
I WAS SLOPPY TO MISS KEYSTONE'S CHI WHEN I WAS SEARCHING FOR MADAME HUANG...
...BUT HE'S REVEALED HIMSELF NOW...
...AND AS STRONG AS HE LOOKS...
...HE'LL NEVER TOUCH ME.
TINGG

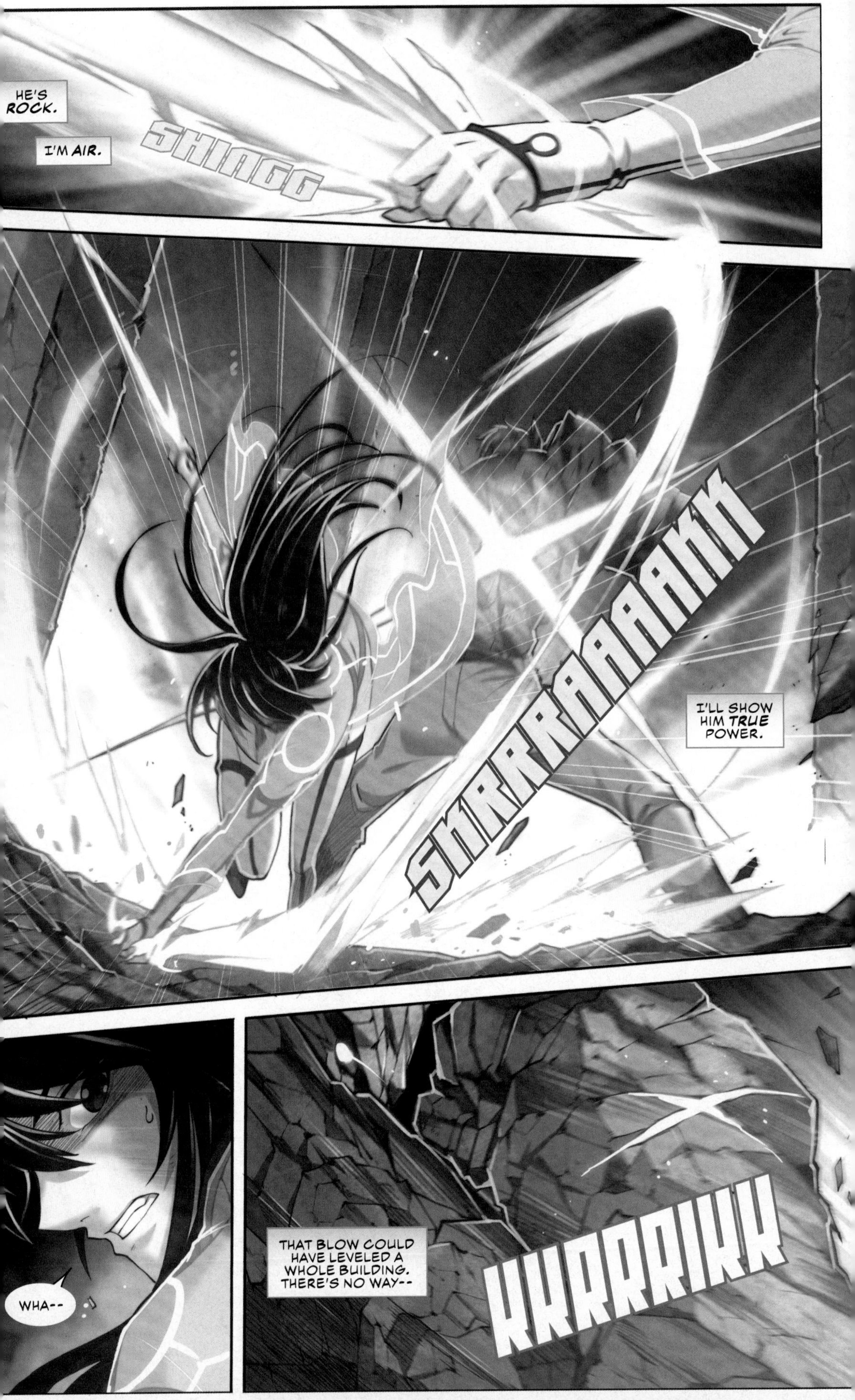
HE'S ROCK.
I'M AIR.
SHINGG
SKRRRAAAAKK
I'LL SHOW HIM TRUE POWER.
WHA--
THAT BLOW COULD HAVE LEVELED A WHOLE BUILDING. THERE'S NO WAY--
KKRRRIKK

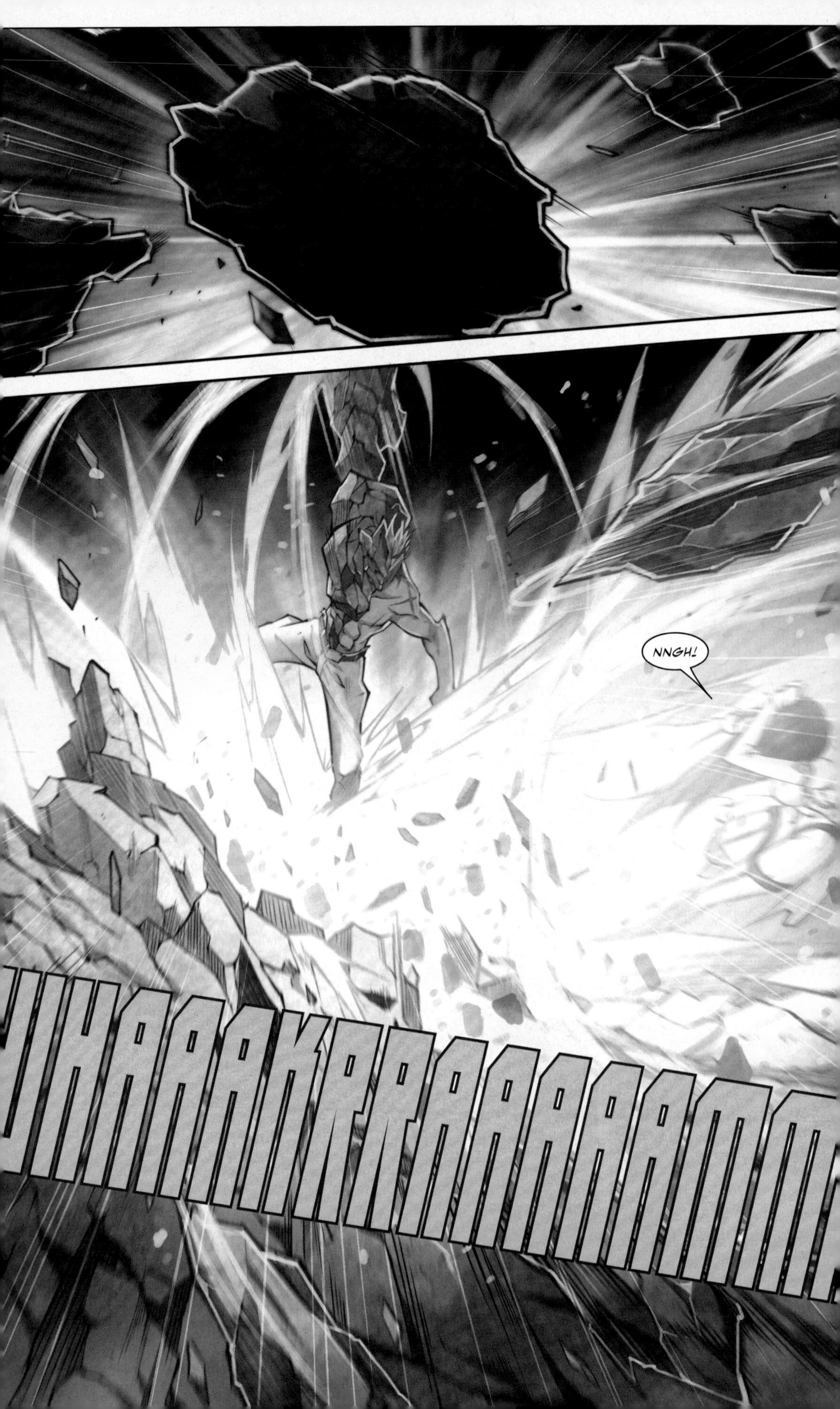
NNGH!
HAAAKRRAAAAAMM

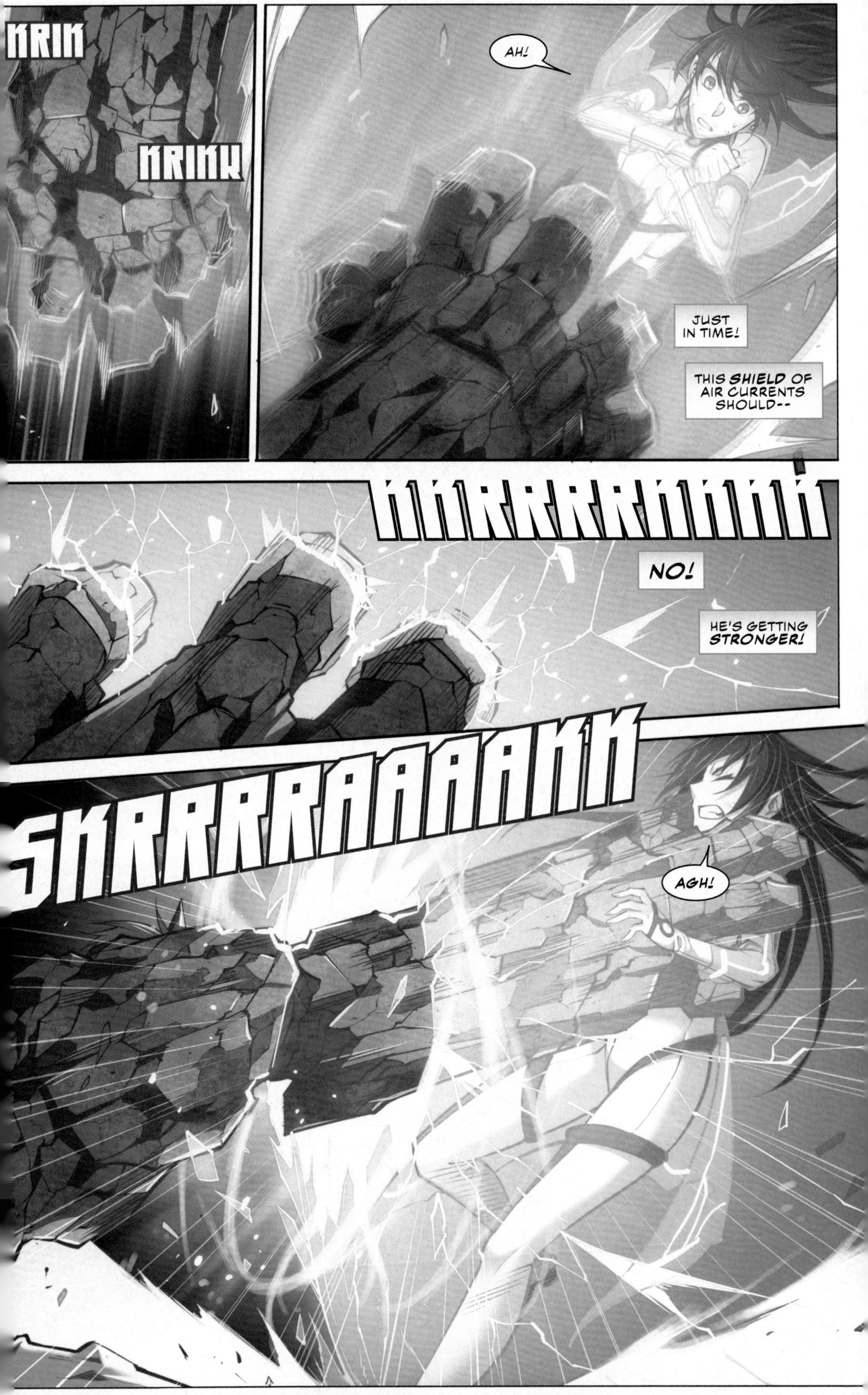
KRIK
KRIKK
AH!
JUST IN TIME!
THIS SHIELD OF AIR CURRENTS SHOULD--
KKRRRRKKKKK
NO!
HE'S GETTING STRONGER!
SKRRRRAAAAAKK
AGH!

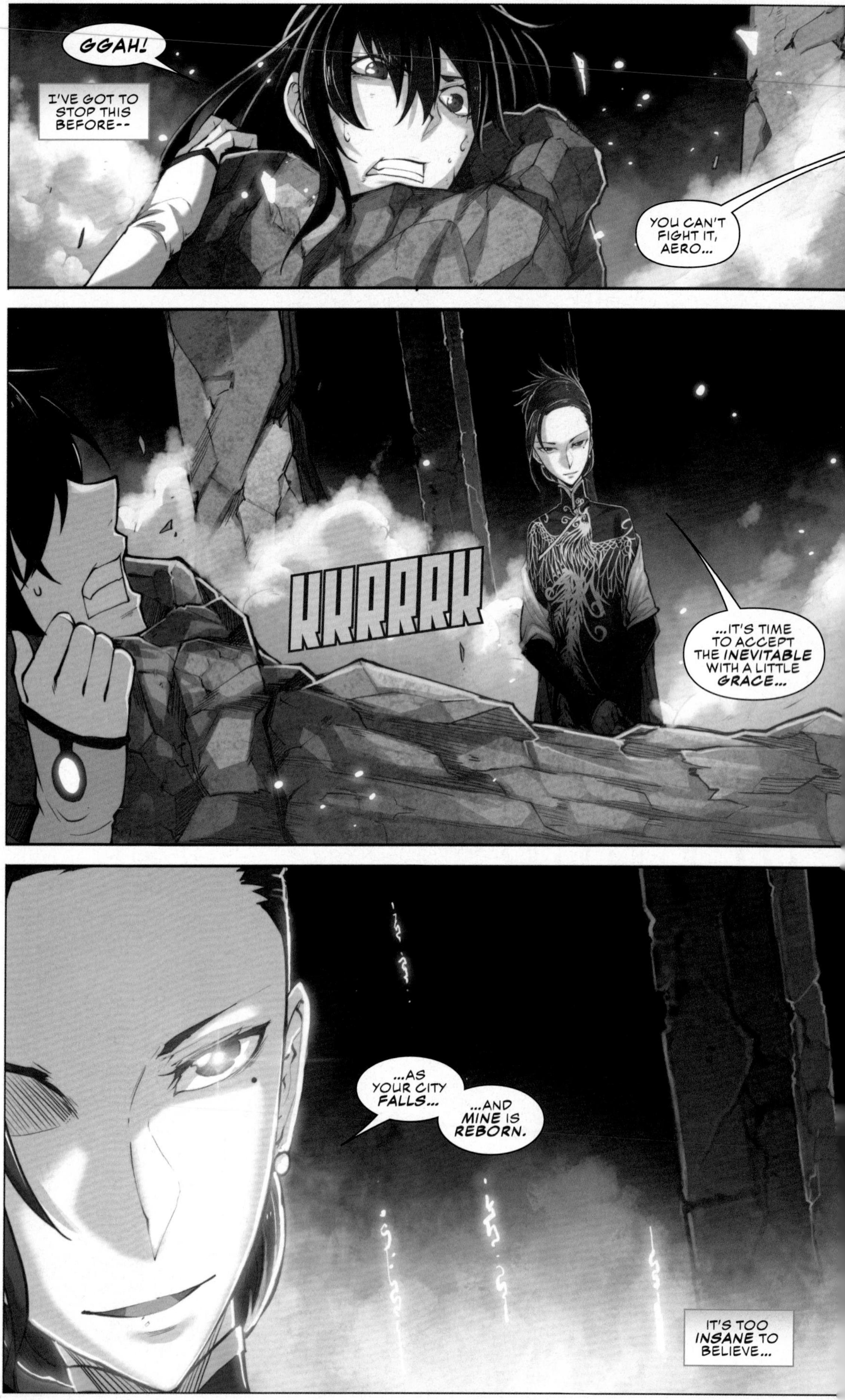
GGAH!
I'VE GOT TO STOP THIS BEFORE--
YOU CAN'T FIGHT IT, AERO...
KKRRRRK
...IT'S TIME TO ACCEPT THE INEVITABLE WITH A LITTLE GRACE...
...AS YOUR CITY FALLS...
...AND MINE IS REBORN.
IT'S TOO INSANE TO BELIEVE...

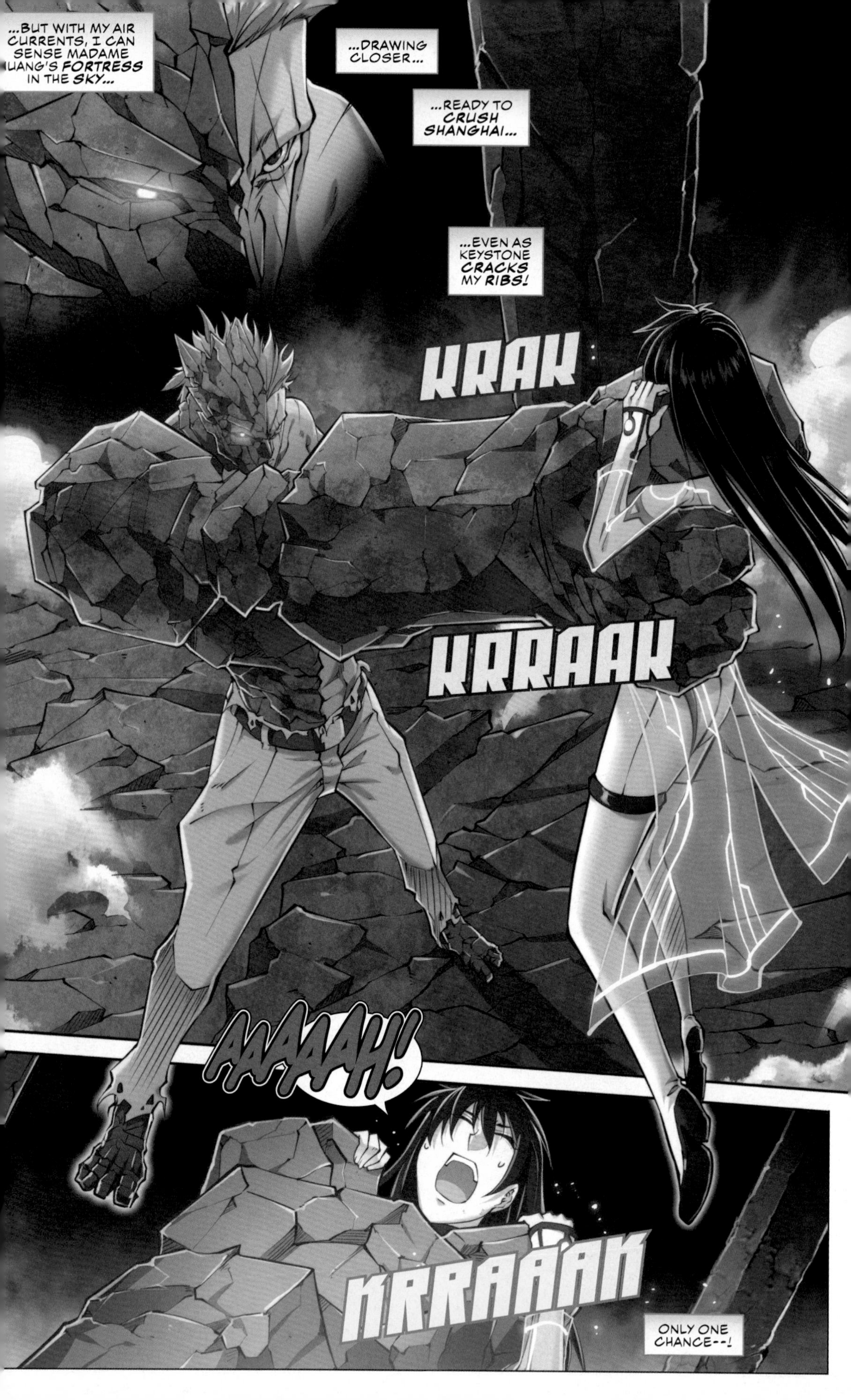

...BUT WITH MY AIR CURRENTS, I CAN SENSE MADAME UANG'S FORTRESS IN THE SKY...
...DRAWING CLOSER...
...READY TO CRUSH SHANGHAI...
...EVEN AS KEYSTONE CRACKS MY RIBS!
KRAK
KRRAAK
AAAAAH!
KRRAAAK
ONLY ONE CHANCE--!

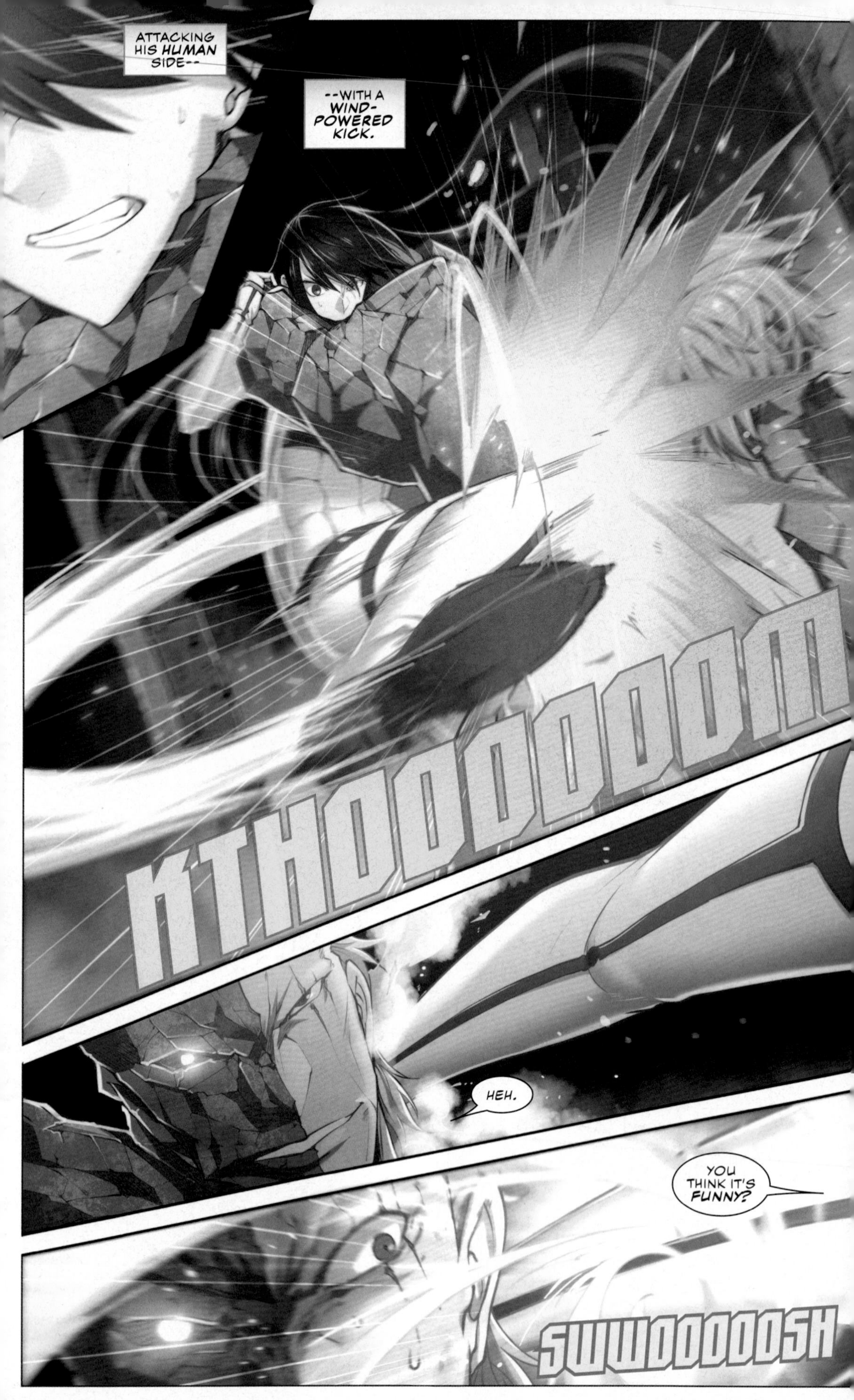
ATTACKING HIS HUMAN SIDE--
--WITH A WIND-POWERED KICK.
KTHOOOOOOM
HEH.
YOU THINK IT'S FUNNY?
SWWOOOOOSH

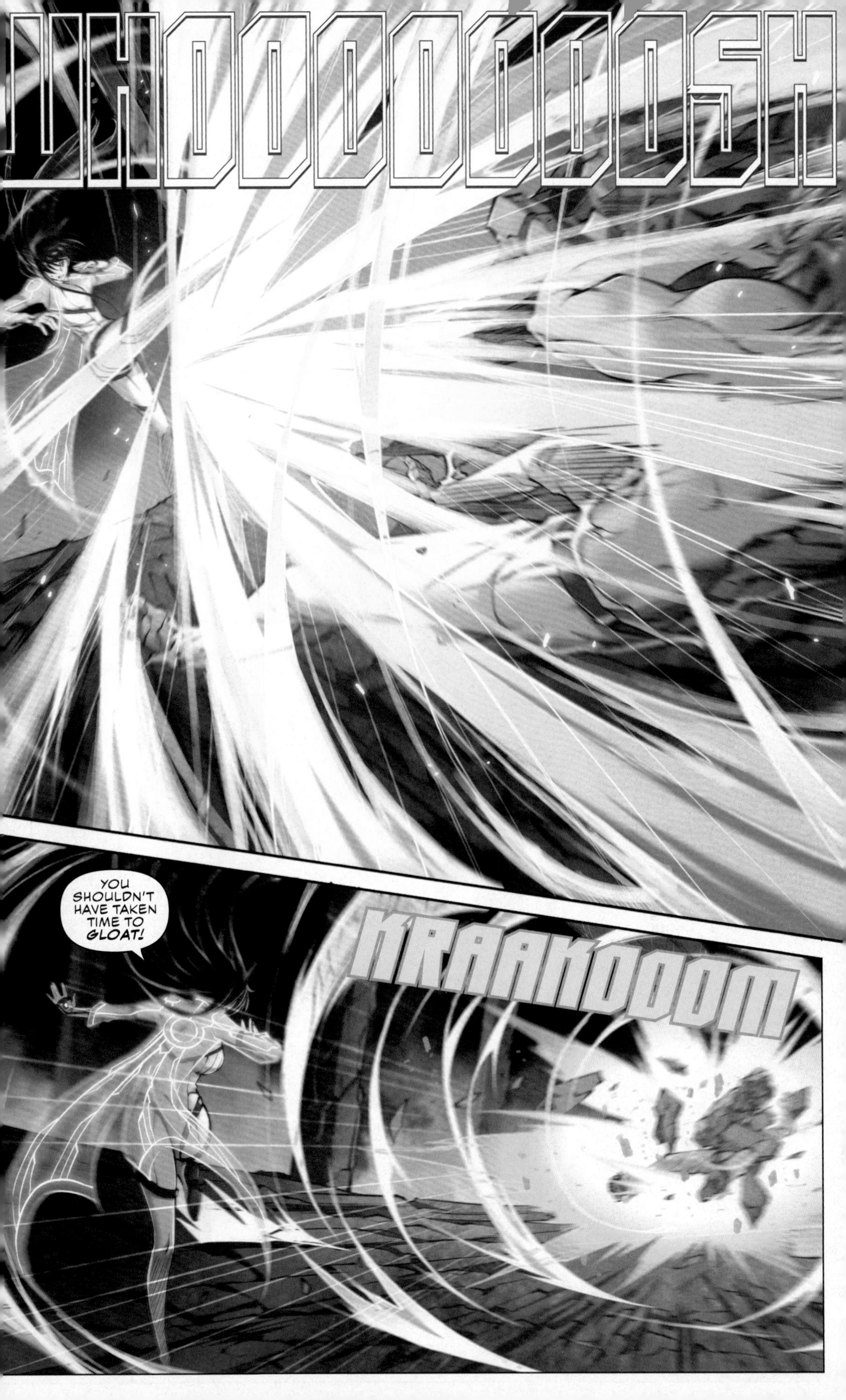
WHOOOOOOOSH
YOU SHOULDN'T HAVE TAKEN TIME TO GLOAT!
KRAAKOOOM

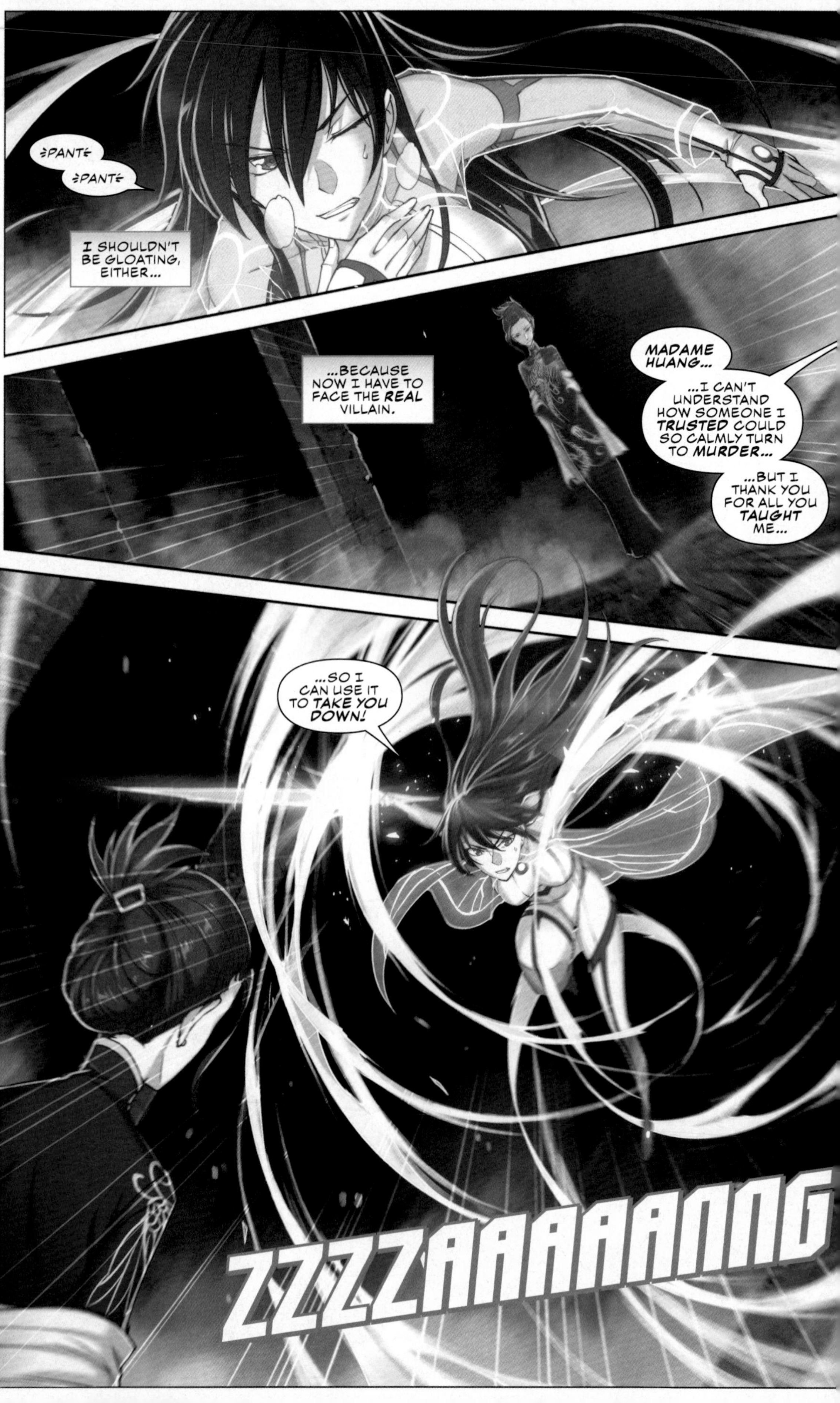

PANT
PANT
I SHOULDN'T BE GLOATING, EITHER...
...BECAUSE NOW I HAVE TO FACE THE REAL VILLAIN.
MADAME HUANG...
...I CAN'T UNDERSTAND HOW SOMEONE I TRUSTED COULD SO CALMLY TURN TO MURDER...
...BUT I THANK YOU FOR ALL YOU TAUGHT ME...
...SO I CAN USE IT TO TAKE YOU DOWN!
ZZZZAAAAAANNG

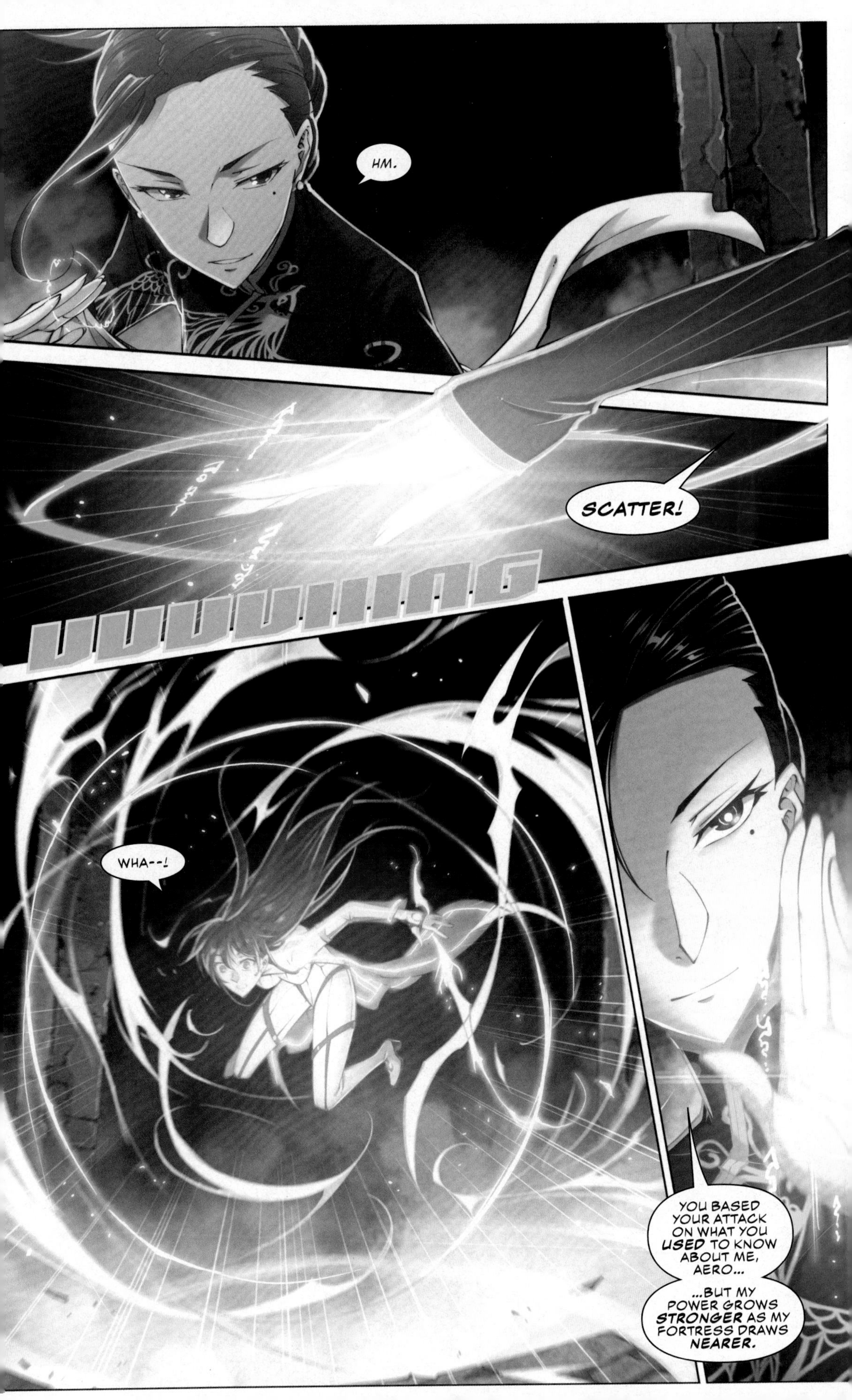

HM.
SCATTER!
VVVVIIING
WHA--!
YOU BASED YOUR ATTACK ON WHAT YOU **USED** TO KNOW ABOUT ME, AERO...
...BUT MY POWER GROWS **STRONGER** AS MY FORTRESS DRAWS **NEARER.**

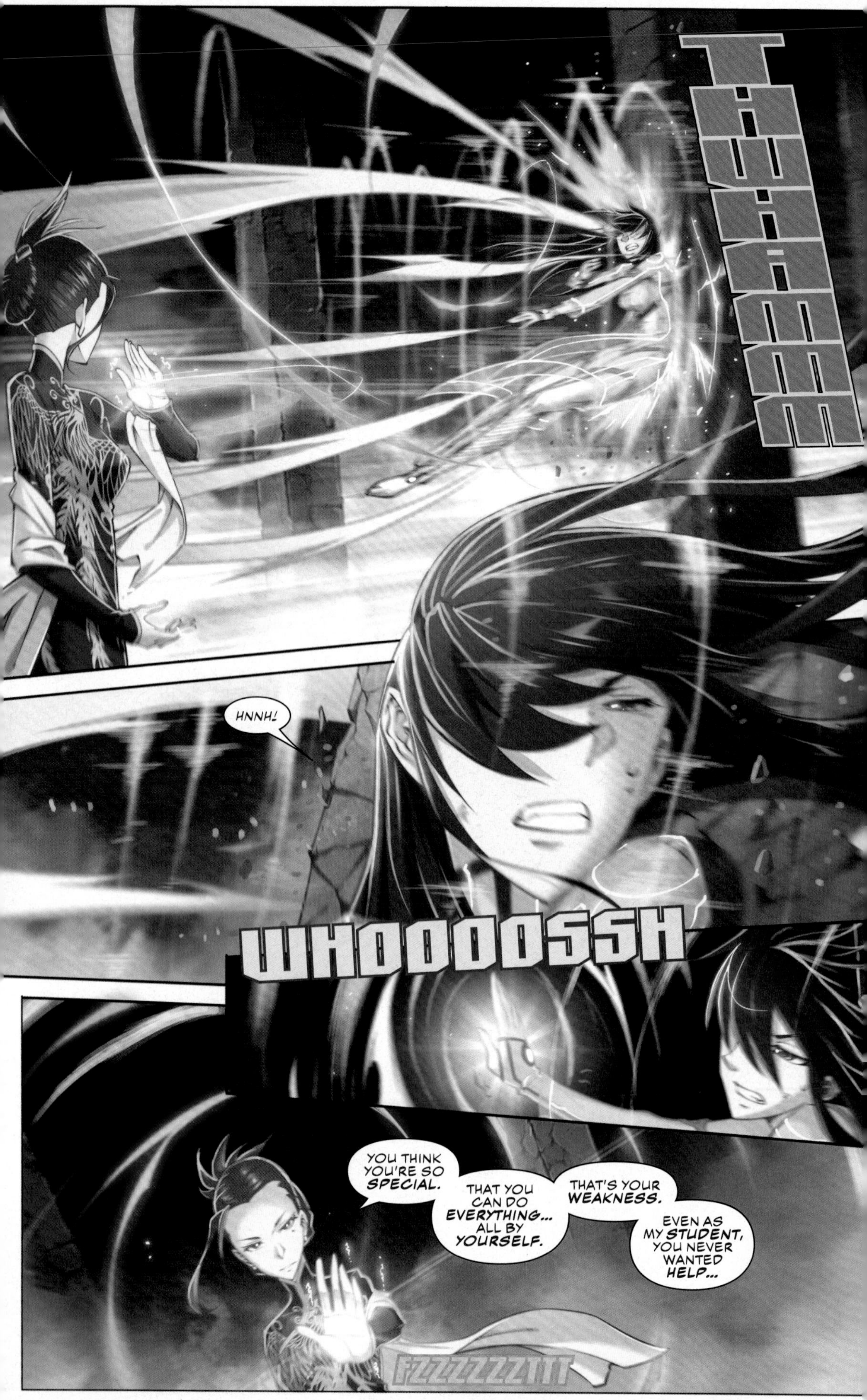
HNNH!
WHOOOOSSH
YOU THINK YOU'RE SO SPECIAL.
THAT YOU CAN DO EVERYTHING... ALL BY YOURSELF.
THAT'S YOUR WEAKNESS.
EVEN AS MY STUDENT, YOU NEVER WANTED HELP...
FZZZZZZTTT

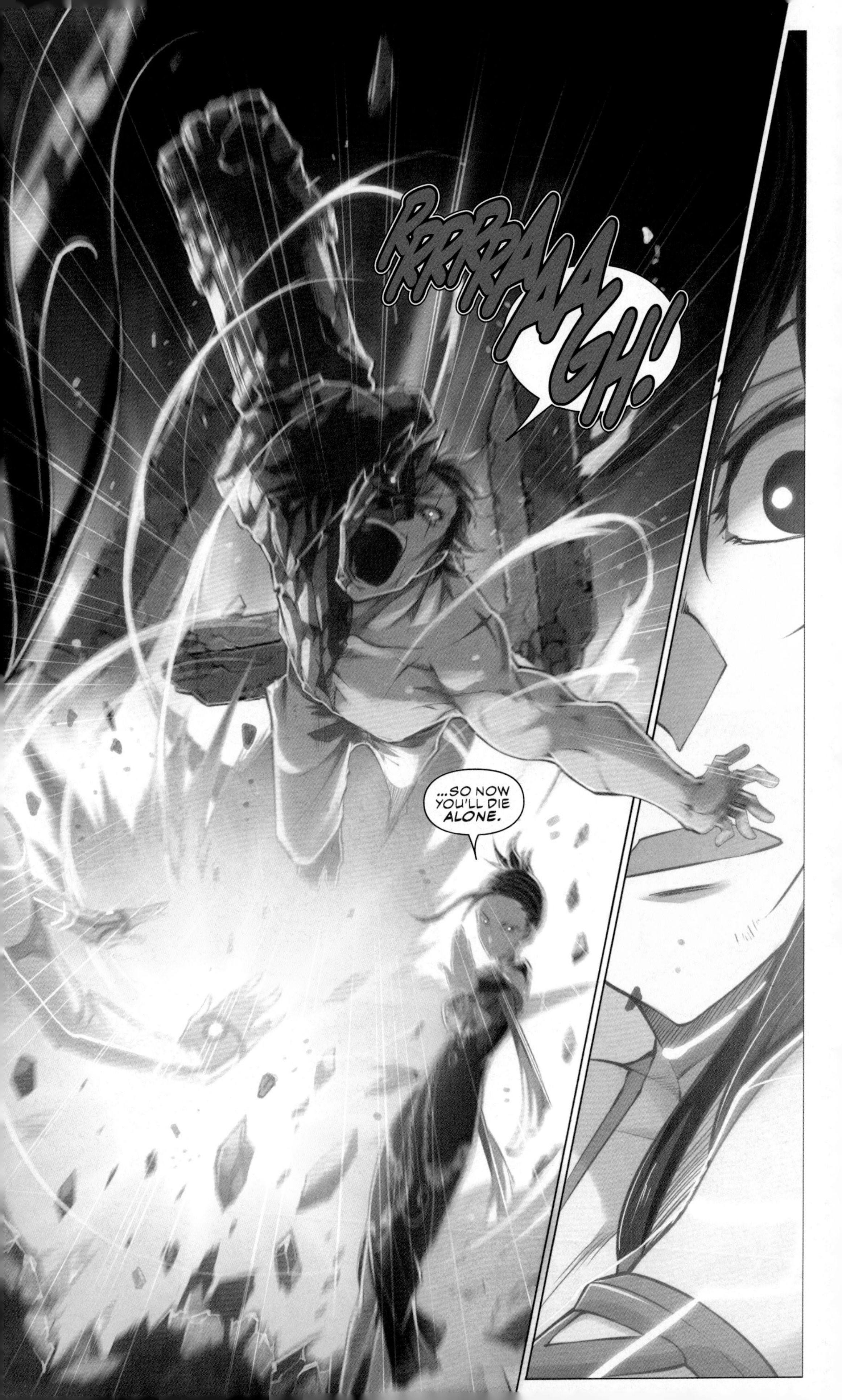
RRRRAAAAGH!
...SO NOW YOU'LL DIE ALONE.

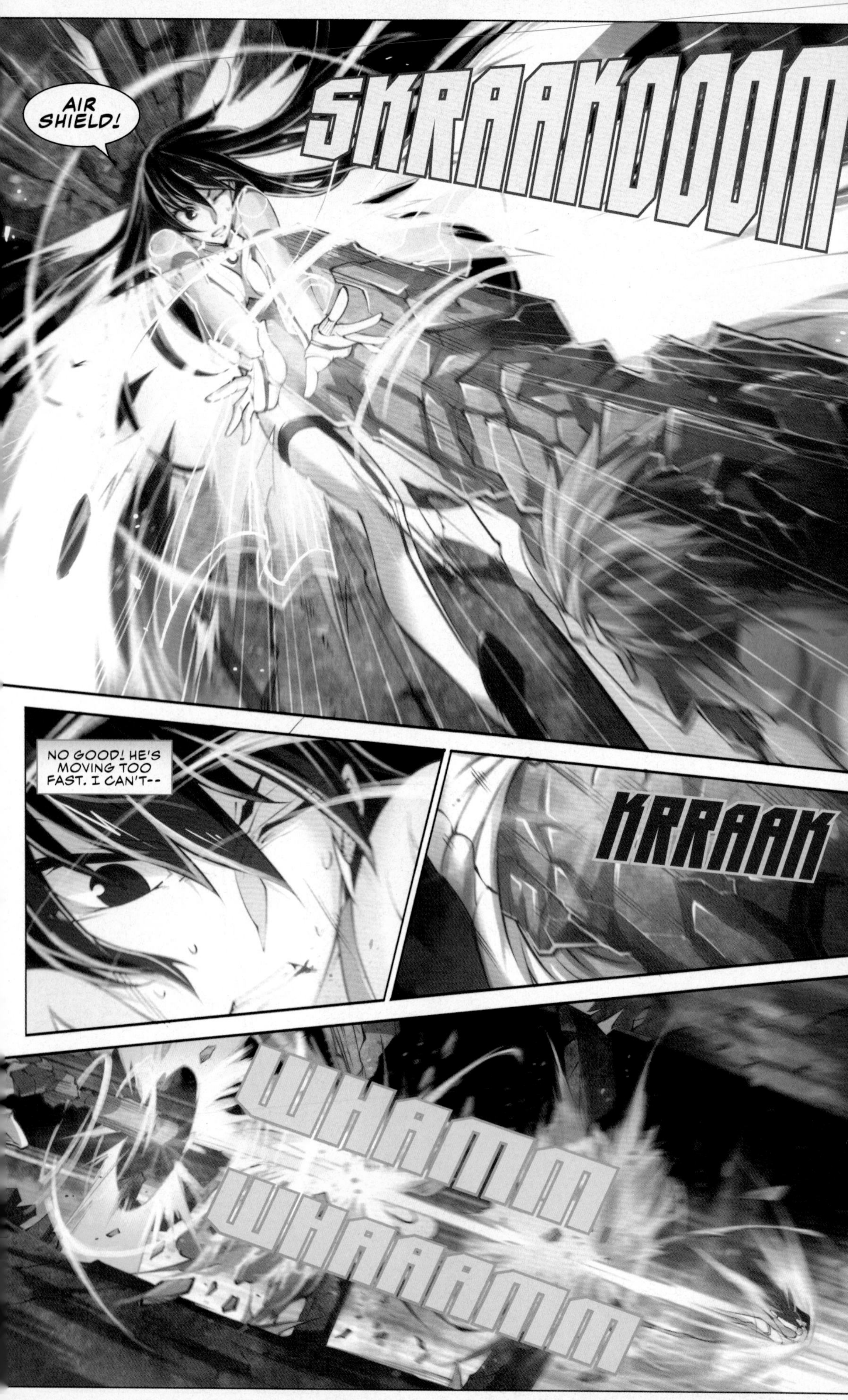
AIR SHIELD!
SKRAAAKOOOM
NO GOOD! HE'S MOVING TOO FAST. I CAN'T--
KRRAAK
WHAMMM
WHAAAMMM

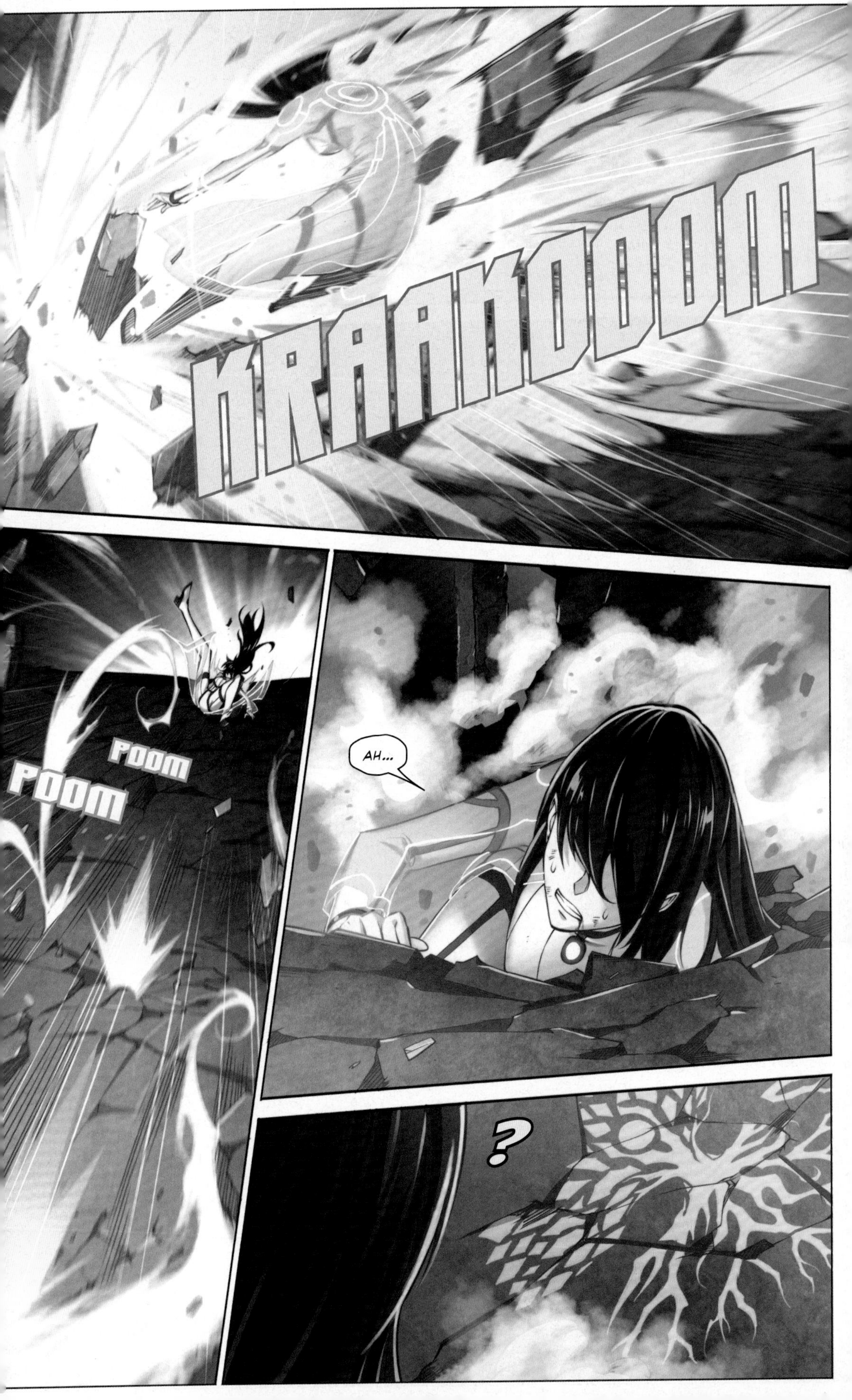
KRAAKOOOM
POOM
POOM
AH...
?

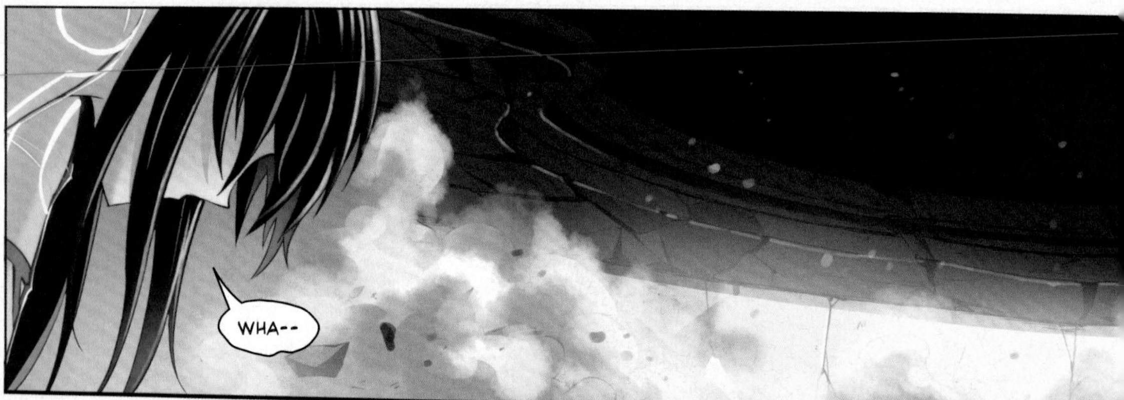
WHA--

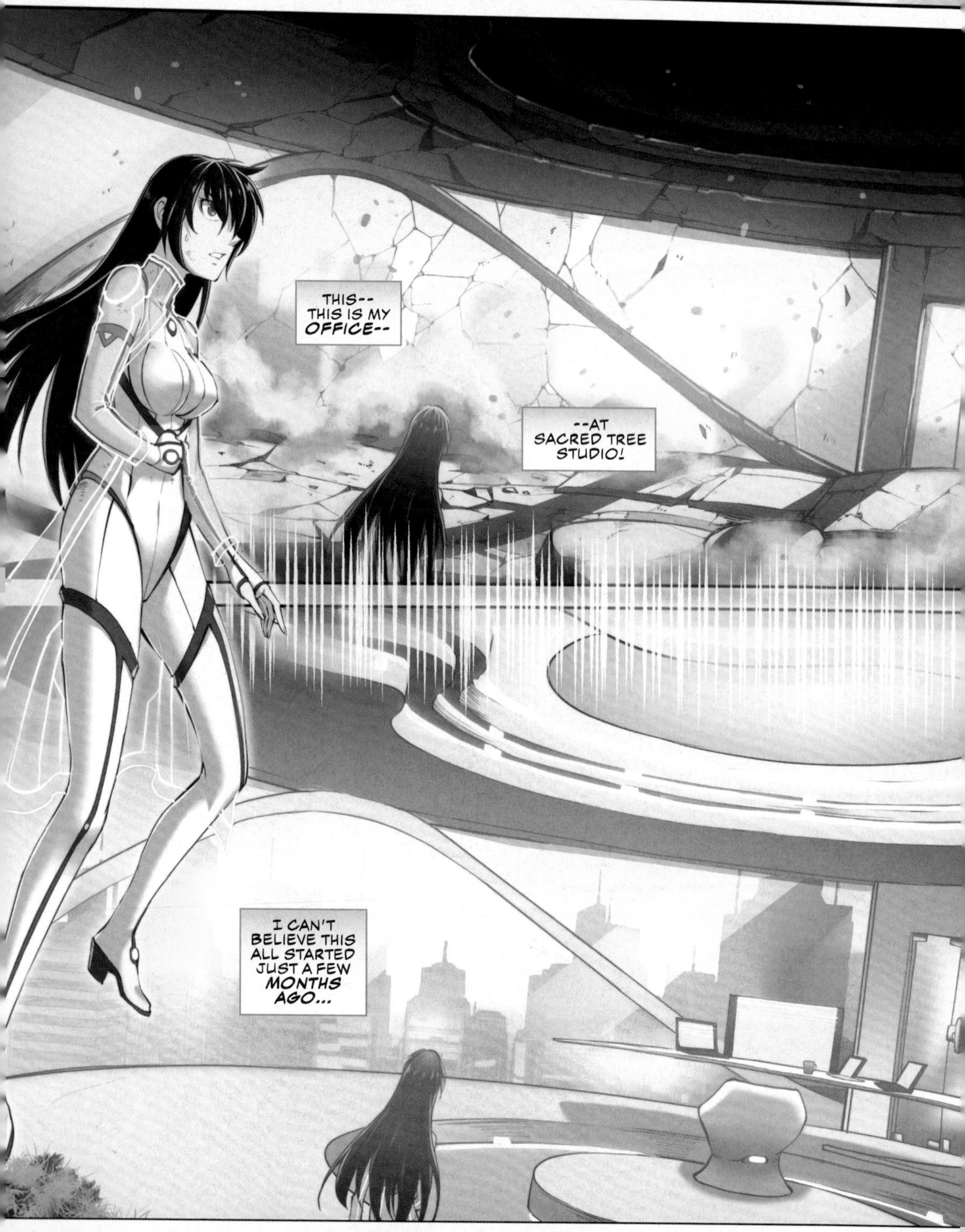
THIS--
THIS IS MY OFFICE--
--AT SACRED TREE STUDIO!
I CAN'T BELIEVE THIS ALL STARTED JUST A FEW MONTHS AGO...

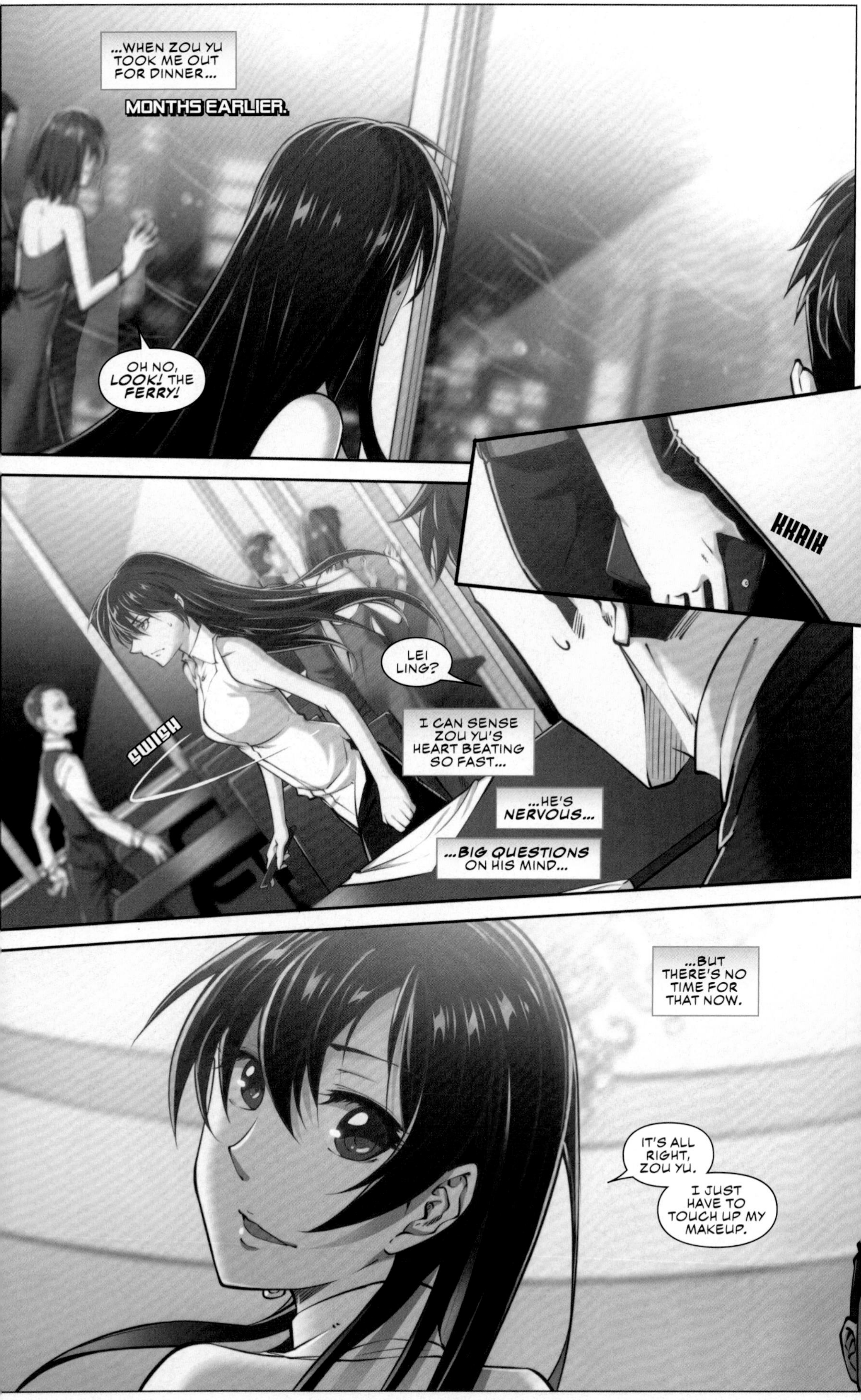
...WHEN ZOU YU TOOK ME OUT FOR DINNER...
MONTHS EARLIER.
OH NO, LOOK! THE FERRY!
KKRIK
LEI LING?
SWISH
I CAN SENSE ZOU YU'S HEART BEATING SO FAST...
...HE'S NERVOUS...
...BIG QUESTIONS ON HIS MIND...
...BUT THERE'S NO TIME FOR THAT NOW.
IT'S ALL RIGHT, ZOU YU.
I JUST HAVE TO TOUCH UP MY MAKEUP.

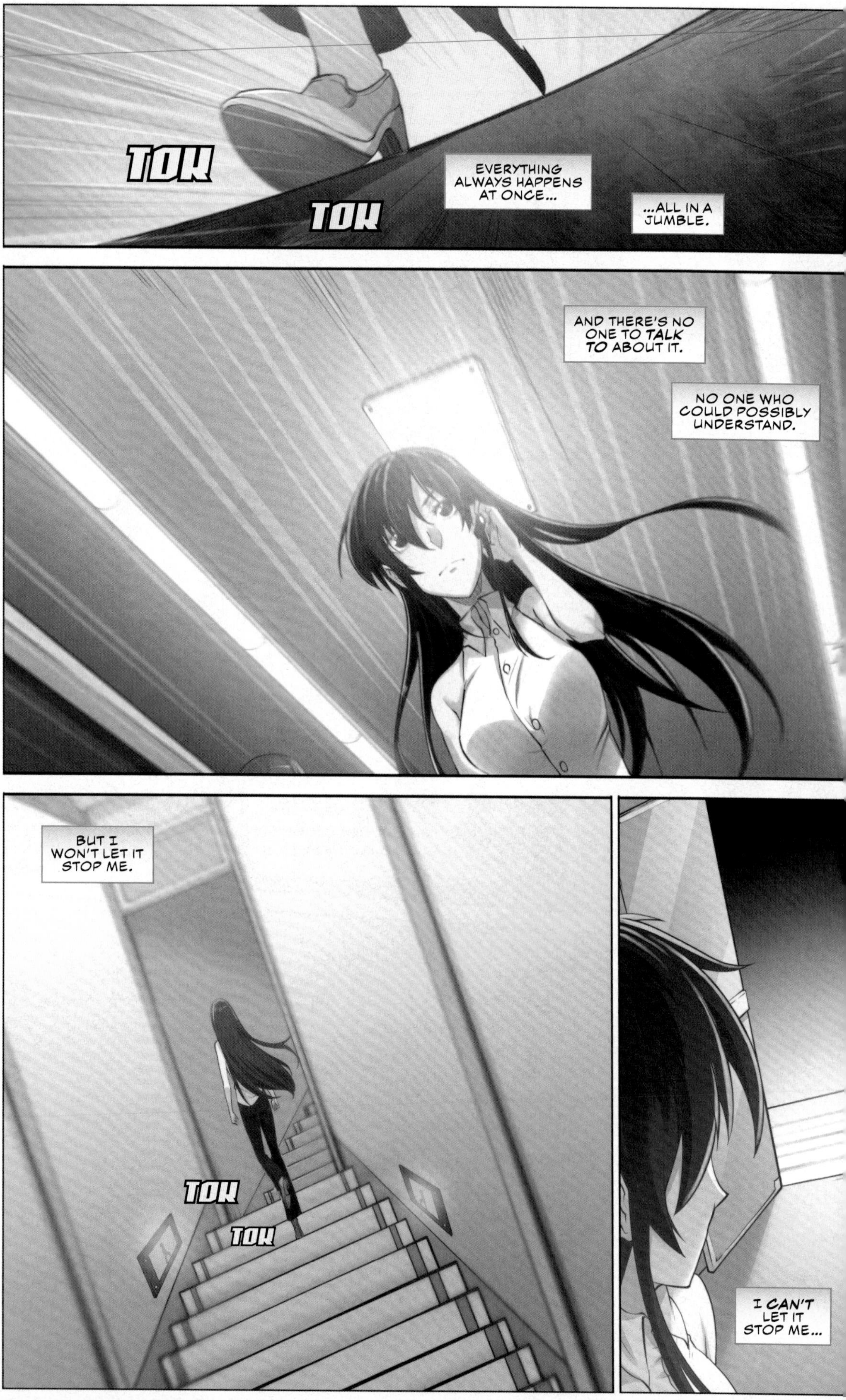
TOK
TOK
EVERYTHING ALWAYS HAPPENS AT ONCE...
...ALL IN A JUMBLE.
AND THERE'S NO ONE TO TALK TO ABOUT IT.
NO ONE WHO COULD POSSIBLY UNDERSTAND.
BUT I WON'T LET IT STOP ME.
TOK
TOK
I CAN'T LET IT STOP ME...

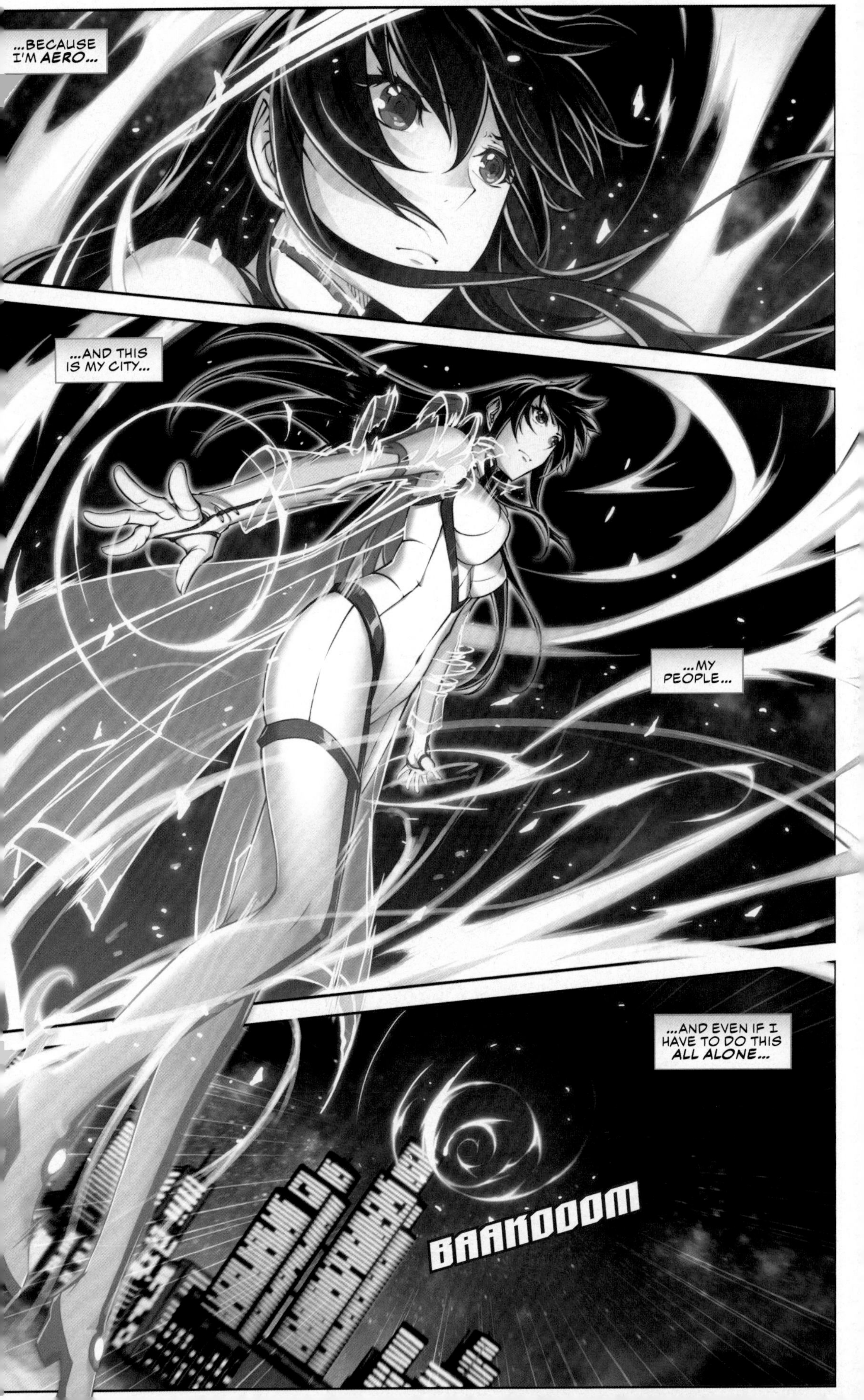
...BECAUSE I'M AERO...
...AND THIS IS MY CITY...
...MY PEOPLE...
...AND EVEN IF I HAVE TO DO THIS ALL ALONE...
BAAKOOOM

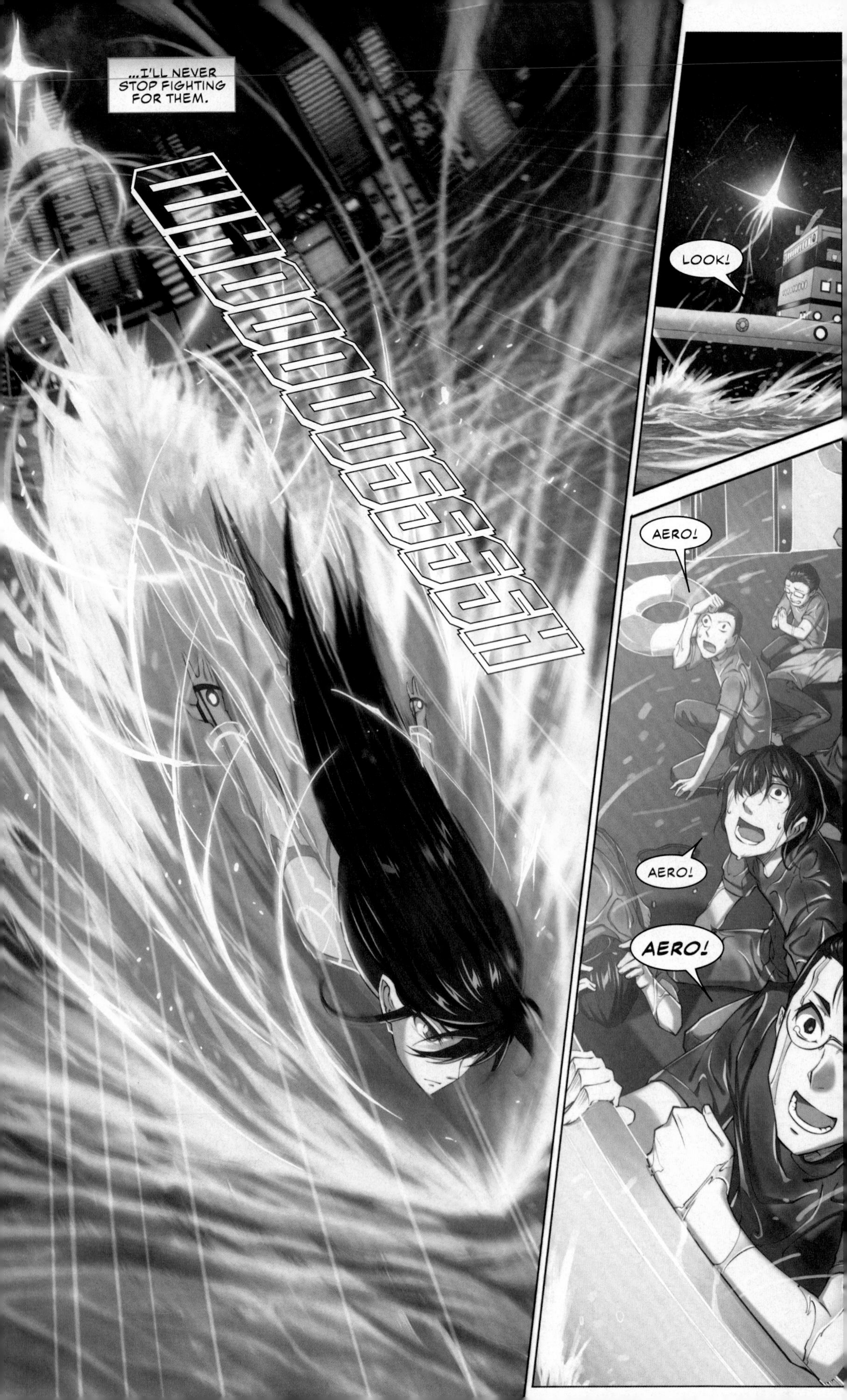
...I'LL NEVER STOP FIGHTING FOR THEM.
WHOOOOOSSSSH!!
LOOK!
AERO!
AERO!
AERO!

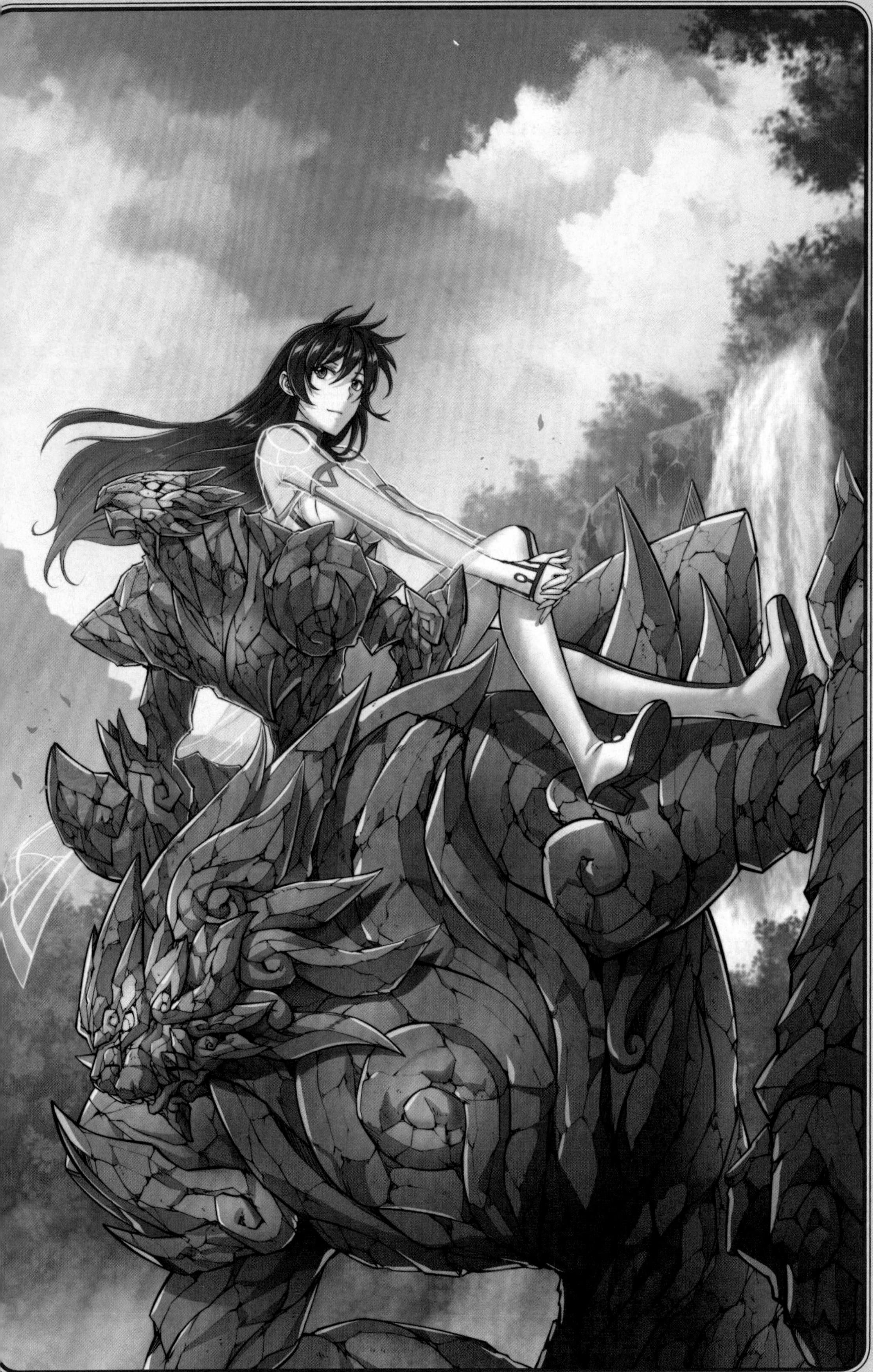

4 **The Tower**

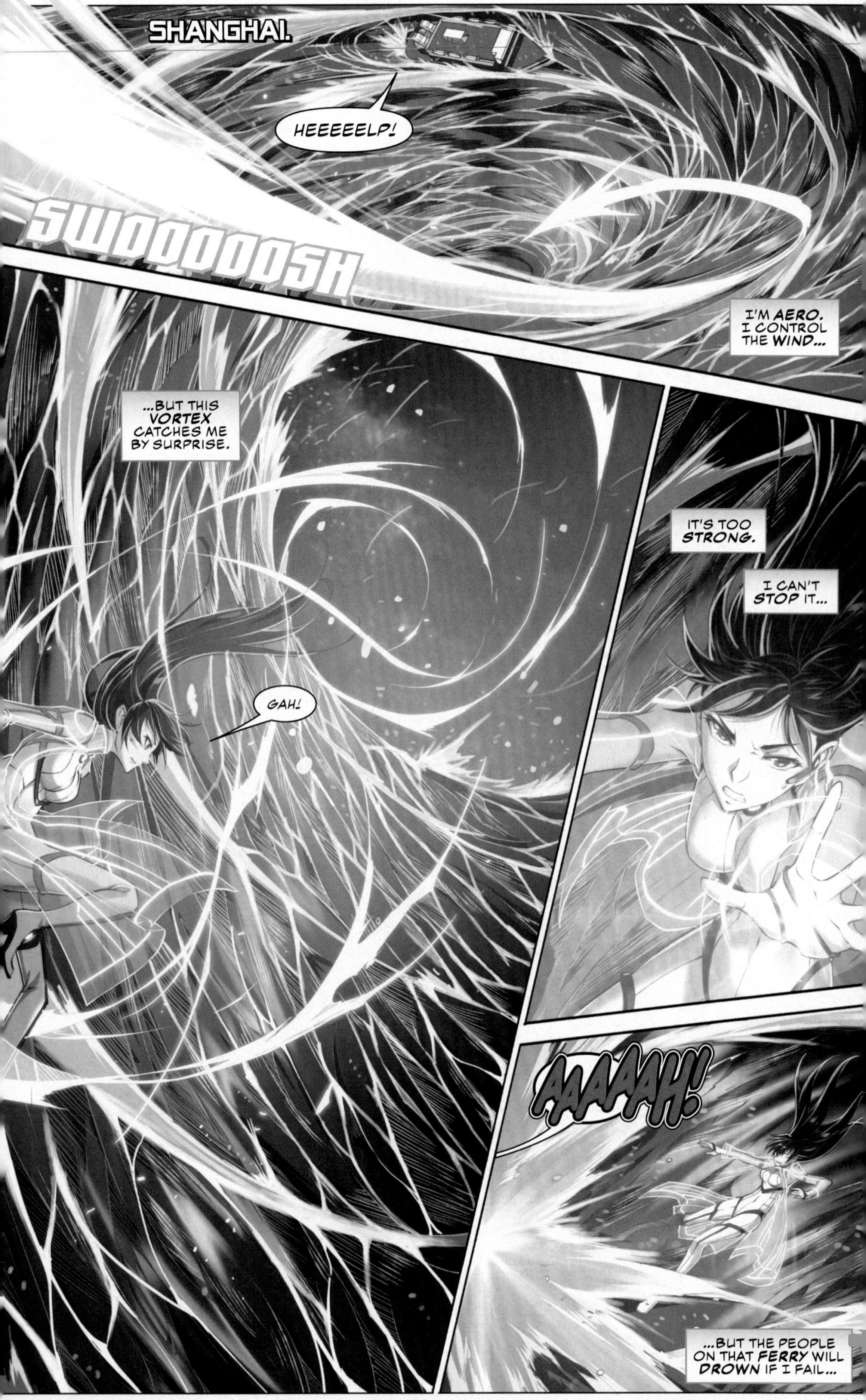

SHANGHAI.
HEEEEELP!
SWOOOOOOSH
I'M AERO. I CONTROL THE WIND...
...BUT THIS VORTEX CATCHES ME BY SURPRISE.
GAH!
IT'S TOO STRONG.
I CAN'T STOP IT...
AAAAAH!
...BUT THE PEOPLE ON THAT FERRY WILL DROWN IF I FAIL...

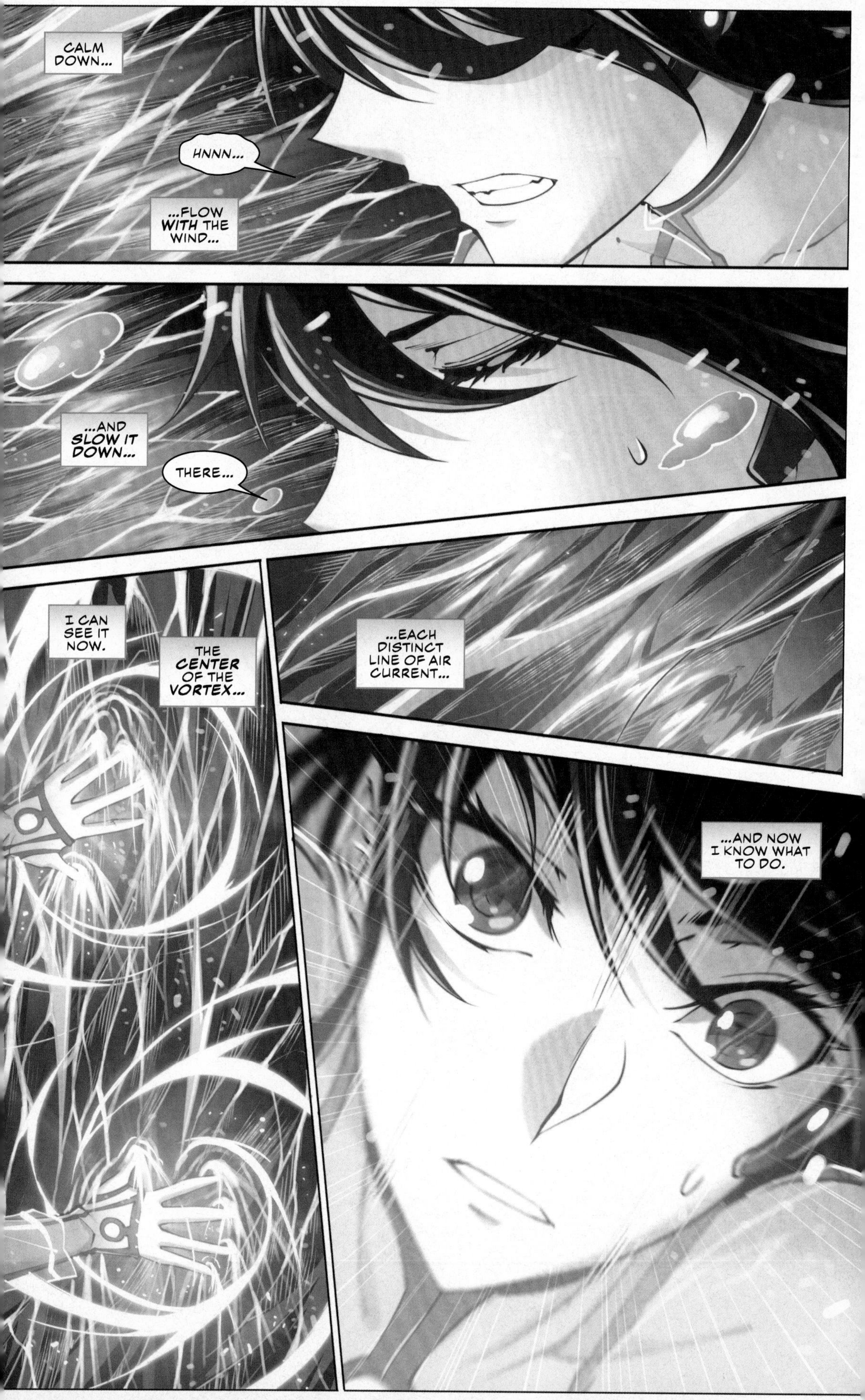
CALM DOWN...
HNNN...
...FLOW WITH THE WIND...
...AND SLOW IT DOWN...
THERE...
I CAN SEE IT NOW.
THE CENTER OF THE VORTEX...
...EACH DISTINCT LINE OF AIR CURRENT...
...AND NOW I KNOW WHAT TO DO.

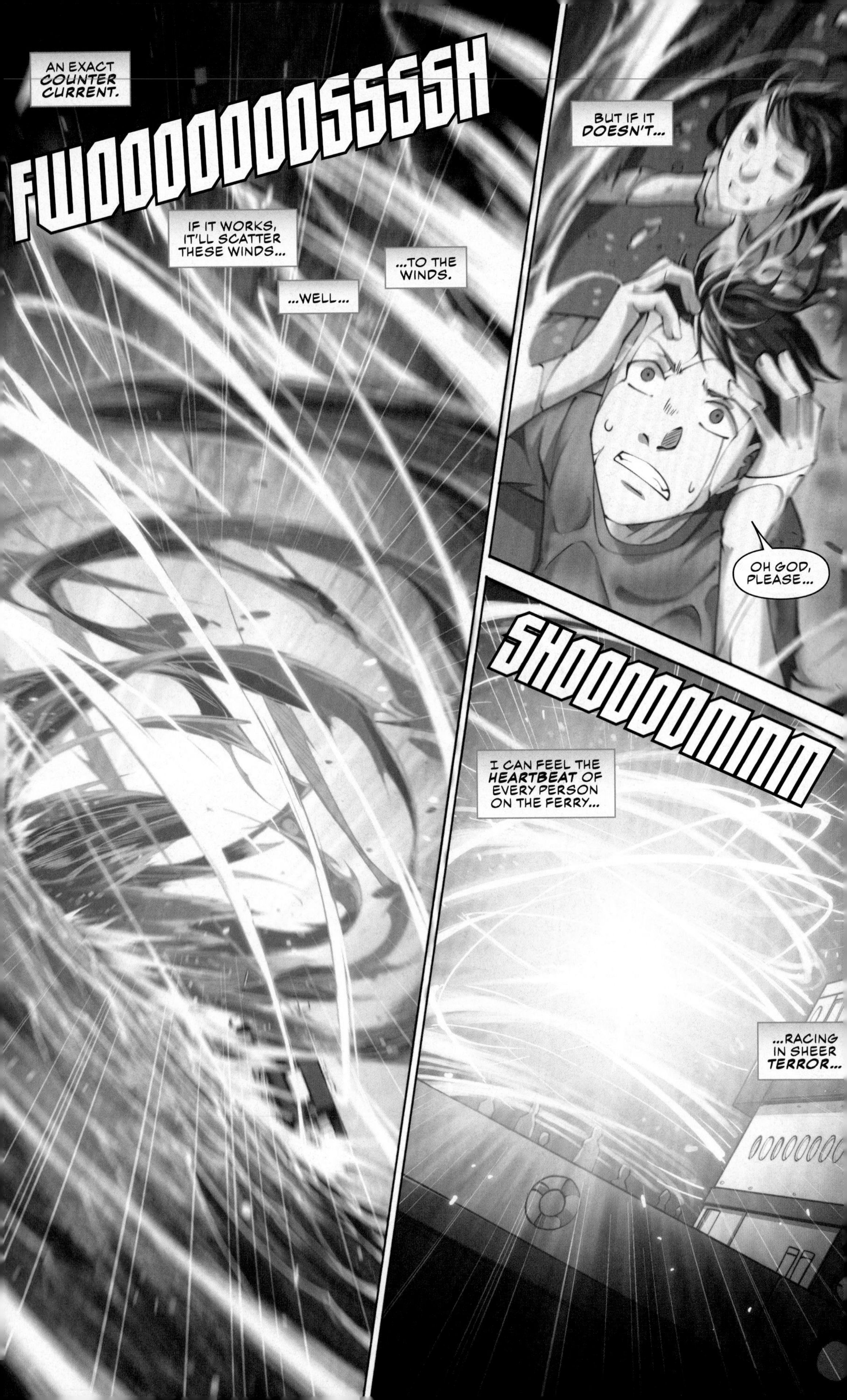
AN EXACT COUNTER CURRENT.
FWOOOOOOOSSSSH
IF IT WORKS, IT'LL SCATTER THESE WINDS...
...WELL...
...TO THE WINDS.
BUT IF IT DOESN'T...
OH GOD, PLEASE...
SHOOOOOMMM
I CAN FEEL THE HEARTBEAT OF EVERY PERSON ON THE FERRY...
...RACING IN SHEER TERROR...

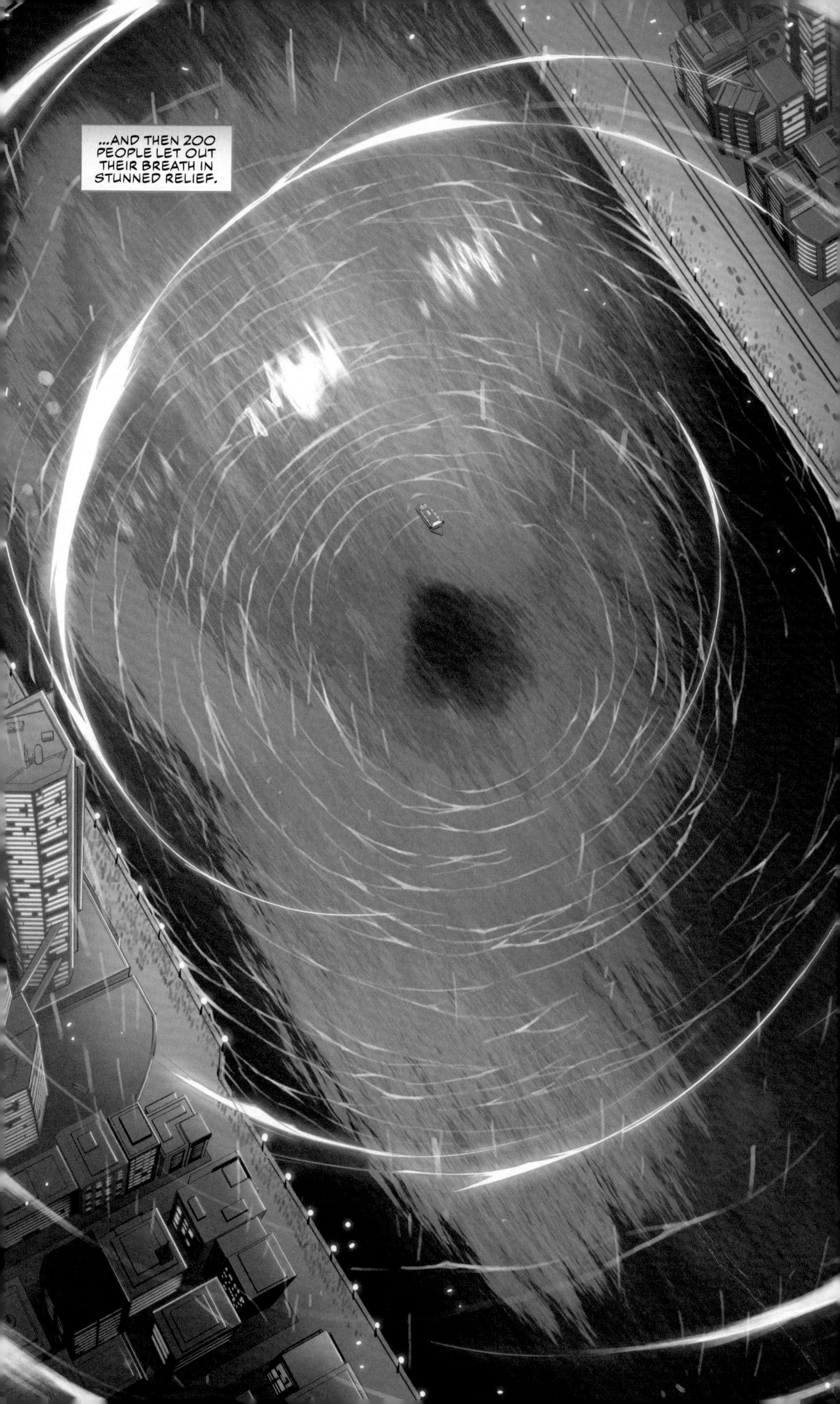
...AND THEN 200 PEOPLE LET OUT THEIR BREATH IN STUNNED RELIEF.

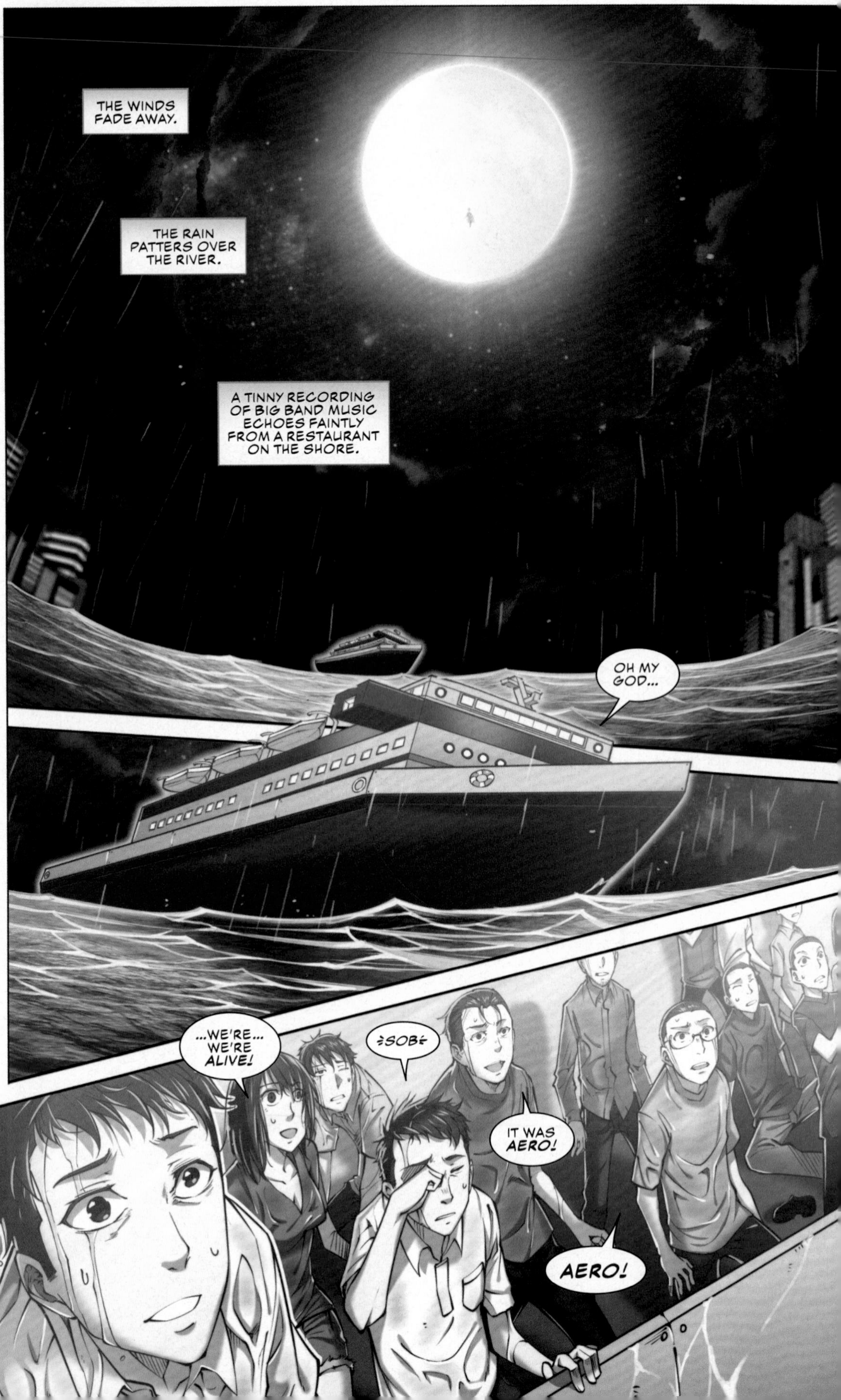

THE WINDS FADE AWAY.
THE RAIN PATTERS OVER THE RIVER.
A TINNY RECORDING OF BIG BAND MUSIC ECHOES FAINTLY FROM A RESTAURANT ON THE SHORE.
OH MY GOD...
...WE'RE... WE'RE ALIVE!
SOB
IT WAS AERO!
AERO!

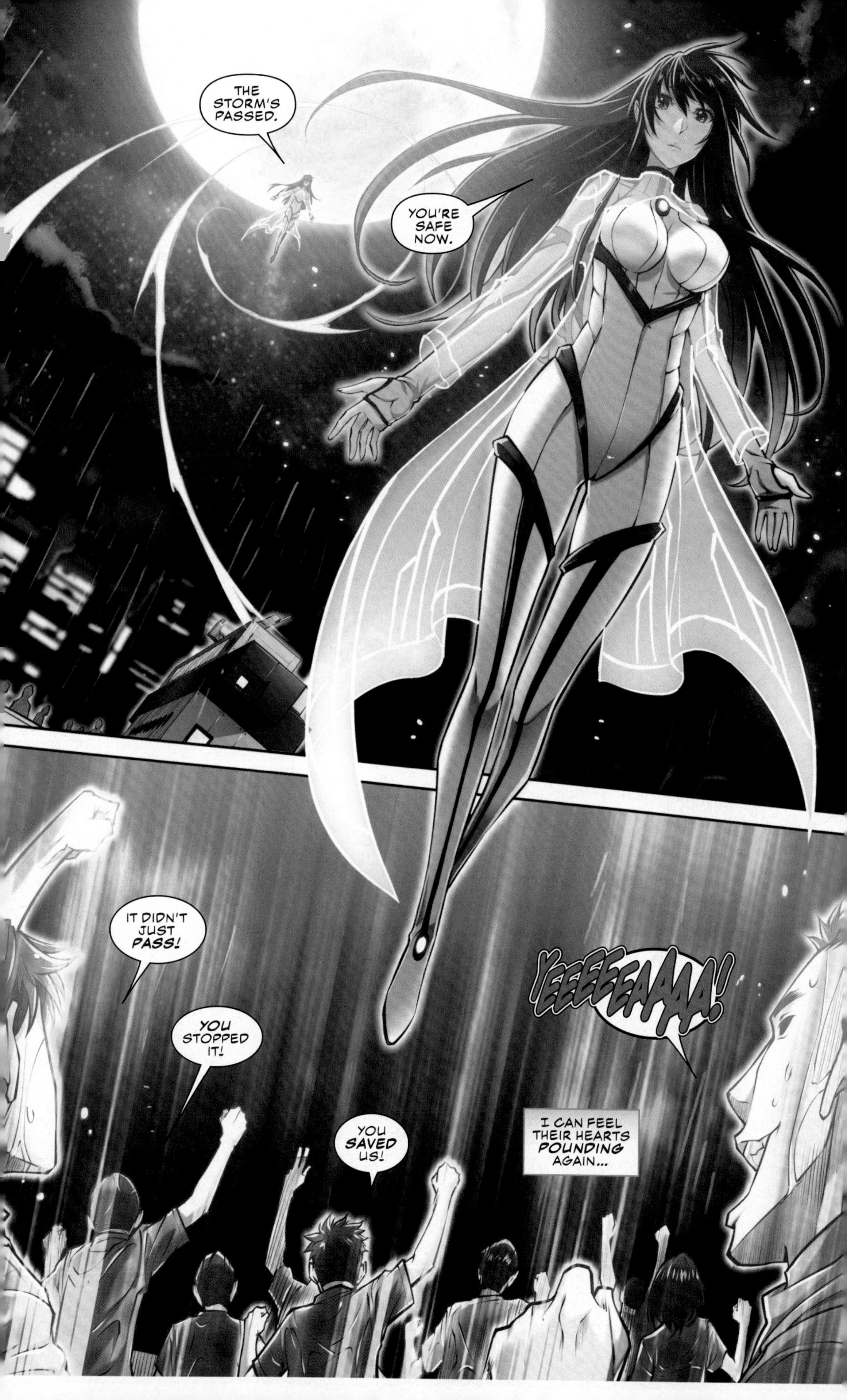
THE STORM'S PASSED.
YOU'RE SAFE NOW.
IT DIDN'T JUST PASS!
YOU STOPPED IT!
YOU SAVED US!
YEEEEEAAAA!
I CAN FEEL THEIR HEARTS POUNDING AGAIN...

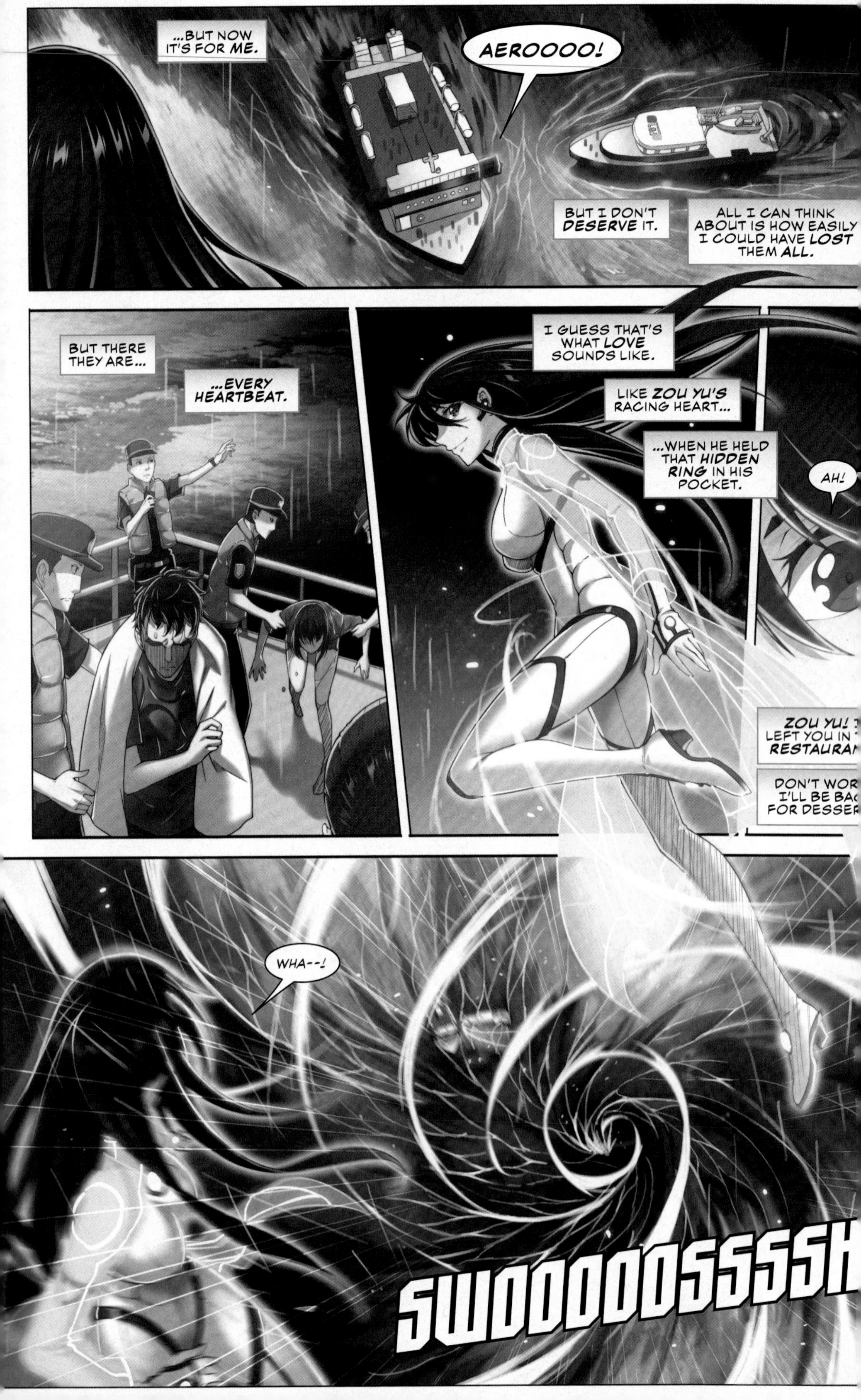
...BUT NOW IT'S FOR ME.
AEROOOO!
BUT I DON'T DESERVE IT.
ALL I CAN THINK ABOUT IS HOW EASILY I COULD HAVE LOST THEM ALL.
BUT THERE THEY ARE...
...EVERY HEARTBEAT.
I GUESS THAT'S WHAT LOVE SOUNDS LIKE.
LIKE ZOU YU'S RACING HEART...
...WHEN HE HELD THAT HIDDEN RING IN HIS POCKET.
AH!
ZOU YU!
LEFT YOU IN
DON'T WOR
I'LL BE BA
FOR DESSE
WHA--!
SWOOOOOOSSSSSH

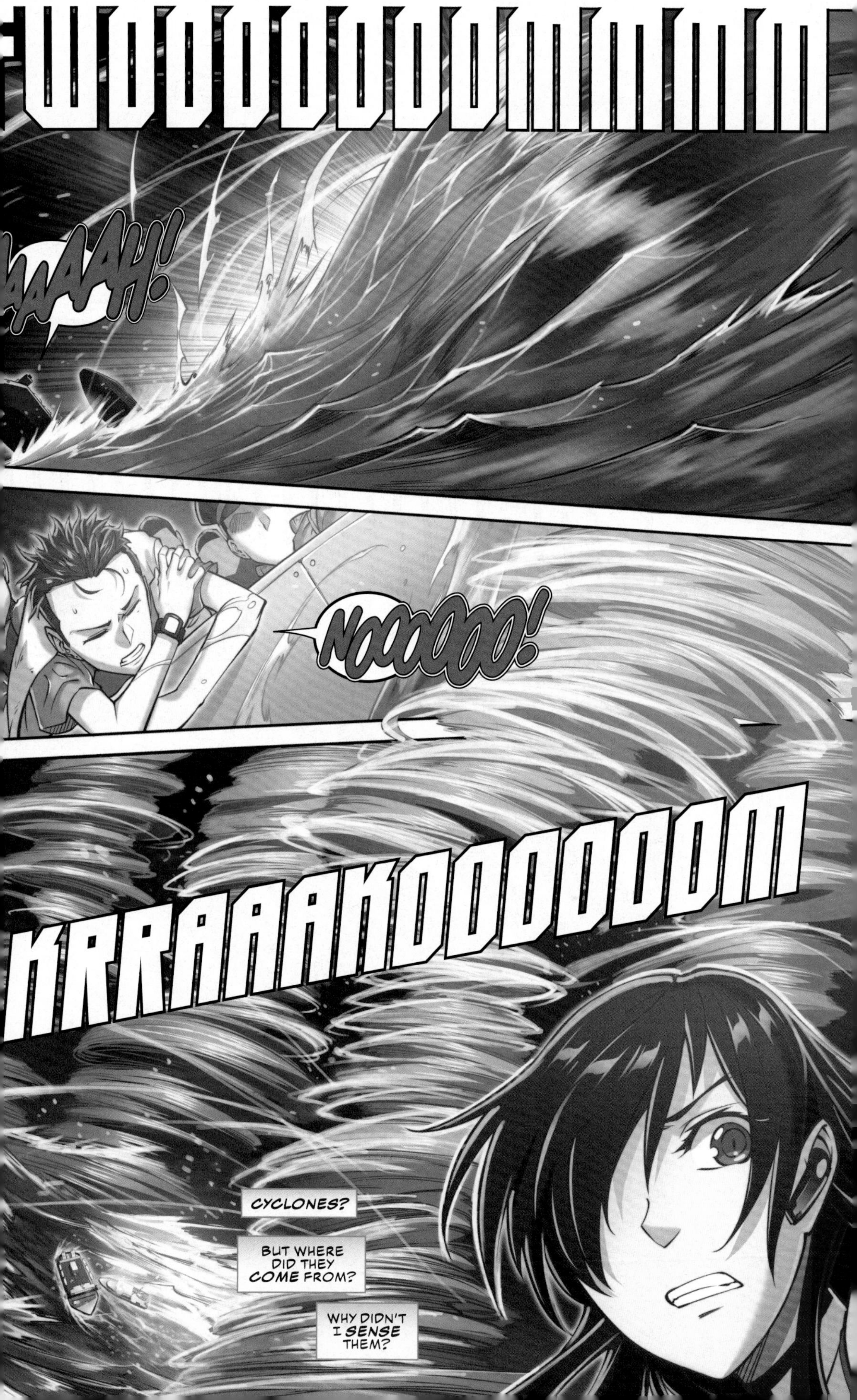
WOOOOOOOMMMM
AAAAH!
NOOOOOO!
KRRAAAKOOOOOOM
CYCLONES?
BUT WHERE DID THEY COME FROM?
WHY DIDN'T I SENSE THEM?

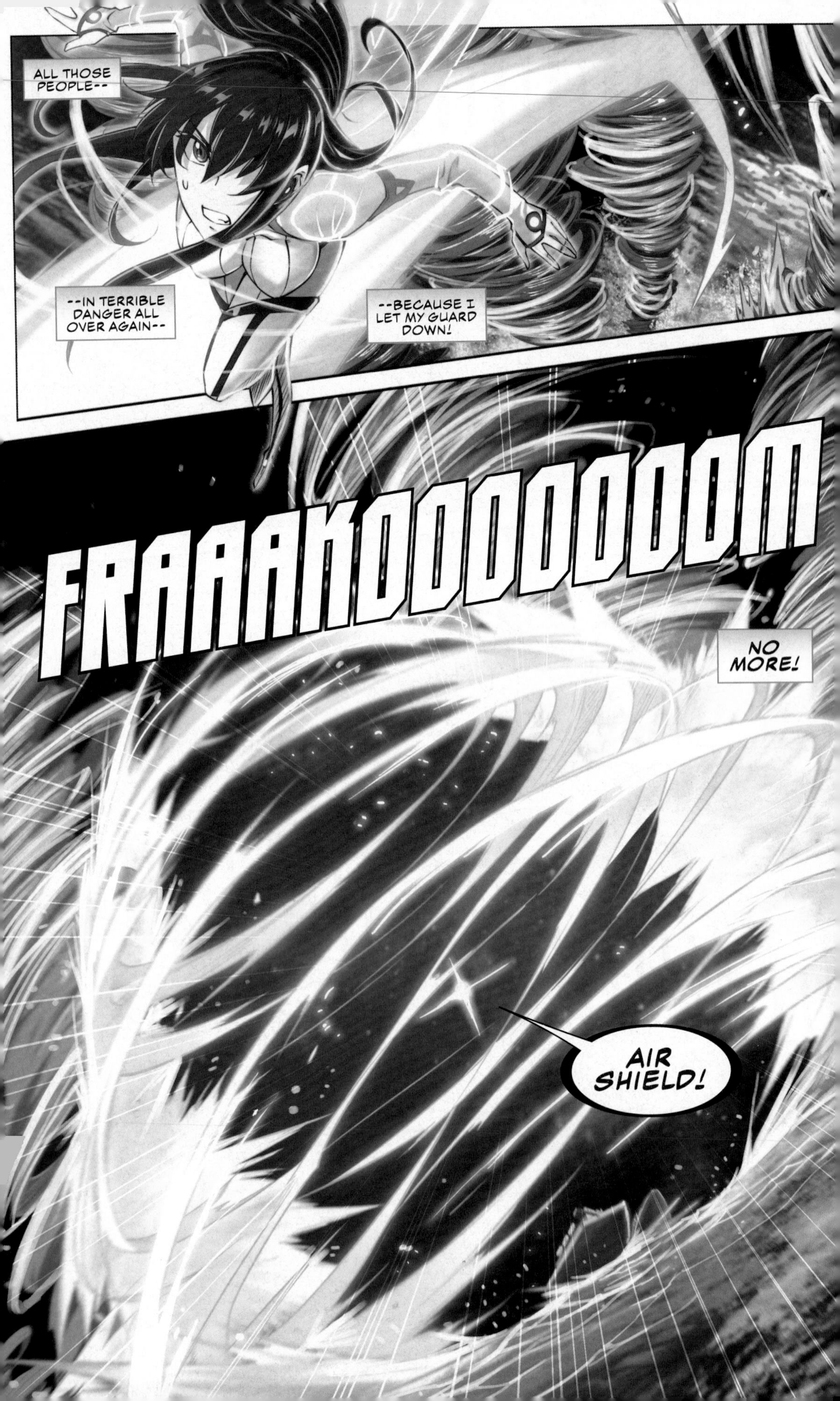
ALL THOSE PEOPLE--
--IN TERRIBLE DANGER ALL OVER AGAIN--
--BECAUSE I LET MY GUARD DOWN!
FRAAAKOOOOOOOOM
NO MORE!
AIR SHIELD!

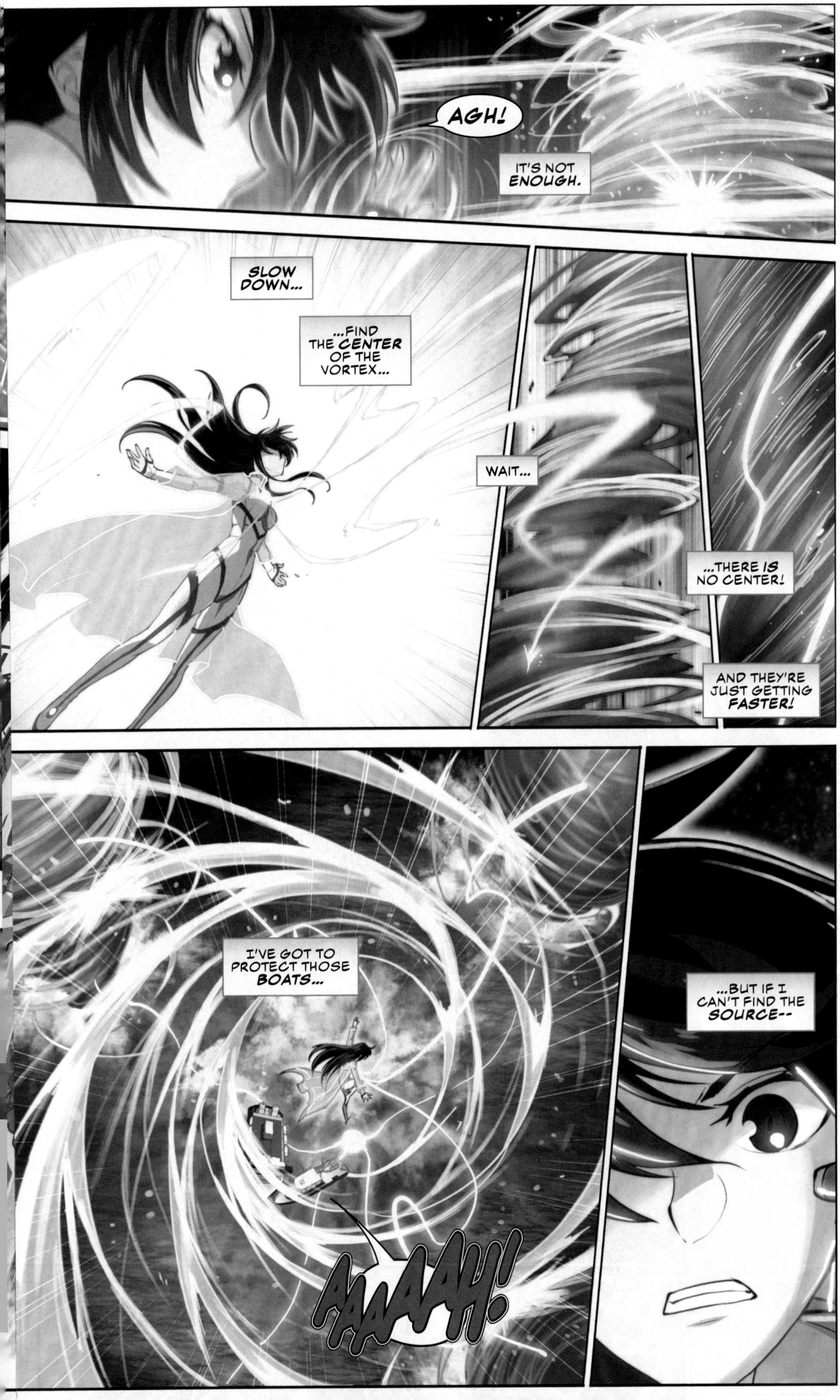
AGH!
IT'S NOT ENOUGH.
SLOW DOWN...
...FIND THE CENTER OF THE VORTEX...
WAIT...
...THERE IS NO CENTER!
AND THEY'RE JUST GETTING FASTER!
I'VE GOT TO PROTECT THOSE BOATS...
AAAAAH!
...BUT IF I CAN'T FIND THE SOURCE--

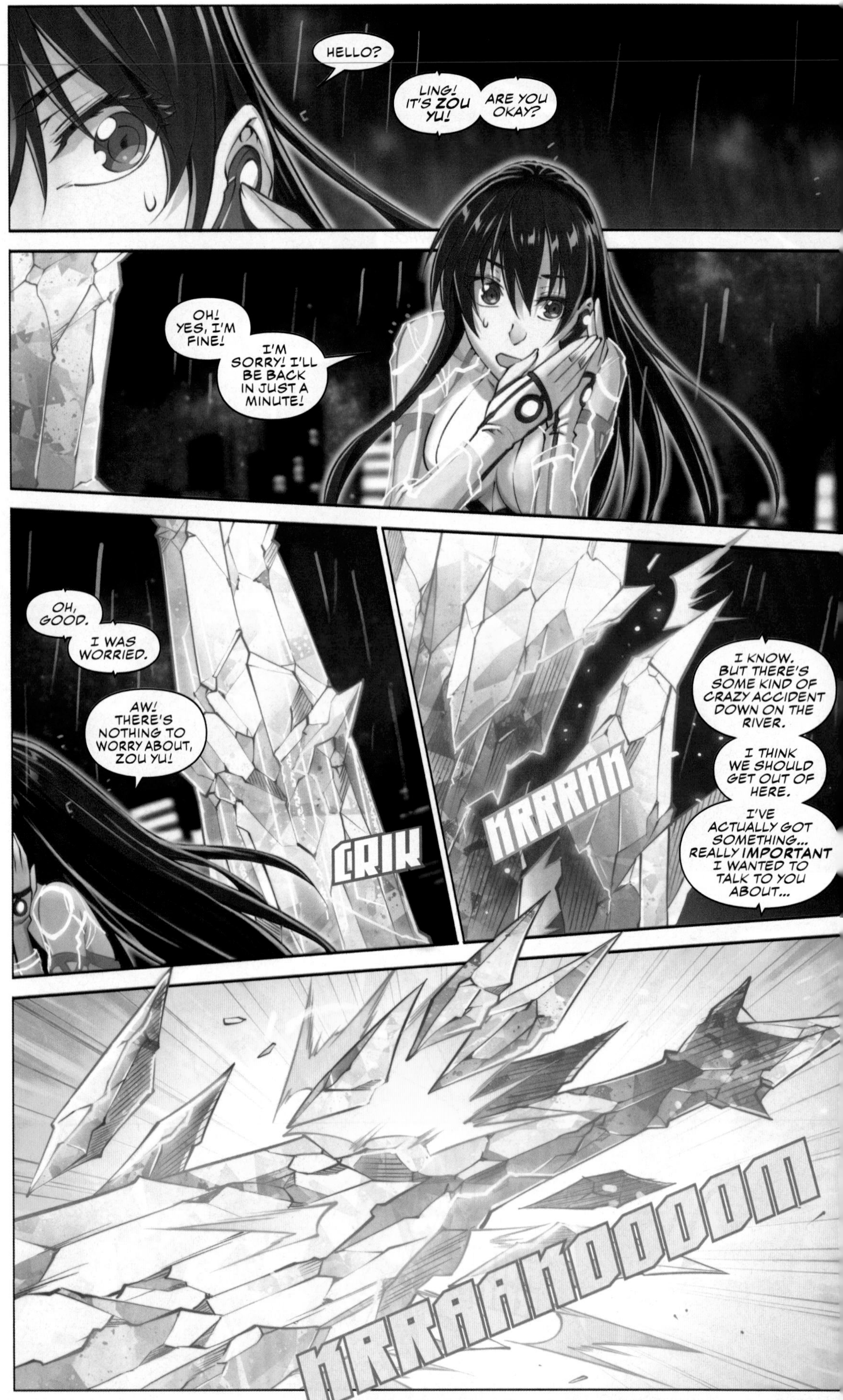
HELLO?
LING! IT'S ZOU YU!
ARE YOU OKAY?
OH! YES, I'M FINE!
I'M SORRY! I'LL BE BACK IN JUST A MINUTE!
OH, GOOD.
I WAS WORRIED.
AW! THERE'S NOTHING TO WORRY ABOUT, ZOU YU!
CRIK
KRRRKK
I KNOW. BUT THERE'S SOME KIND OF CRAZY ACCIDENT DOWN ON THE RIVER.
I THINK WE SHOULD GET OUT OF HERE.
I'VE ACTUALLY GOT SOMETHING... REALLY IMPORTANT I WANTED TO TALK TO YOU ABOUT...
KRRAAKOOOOOM

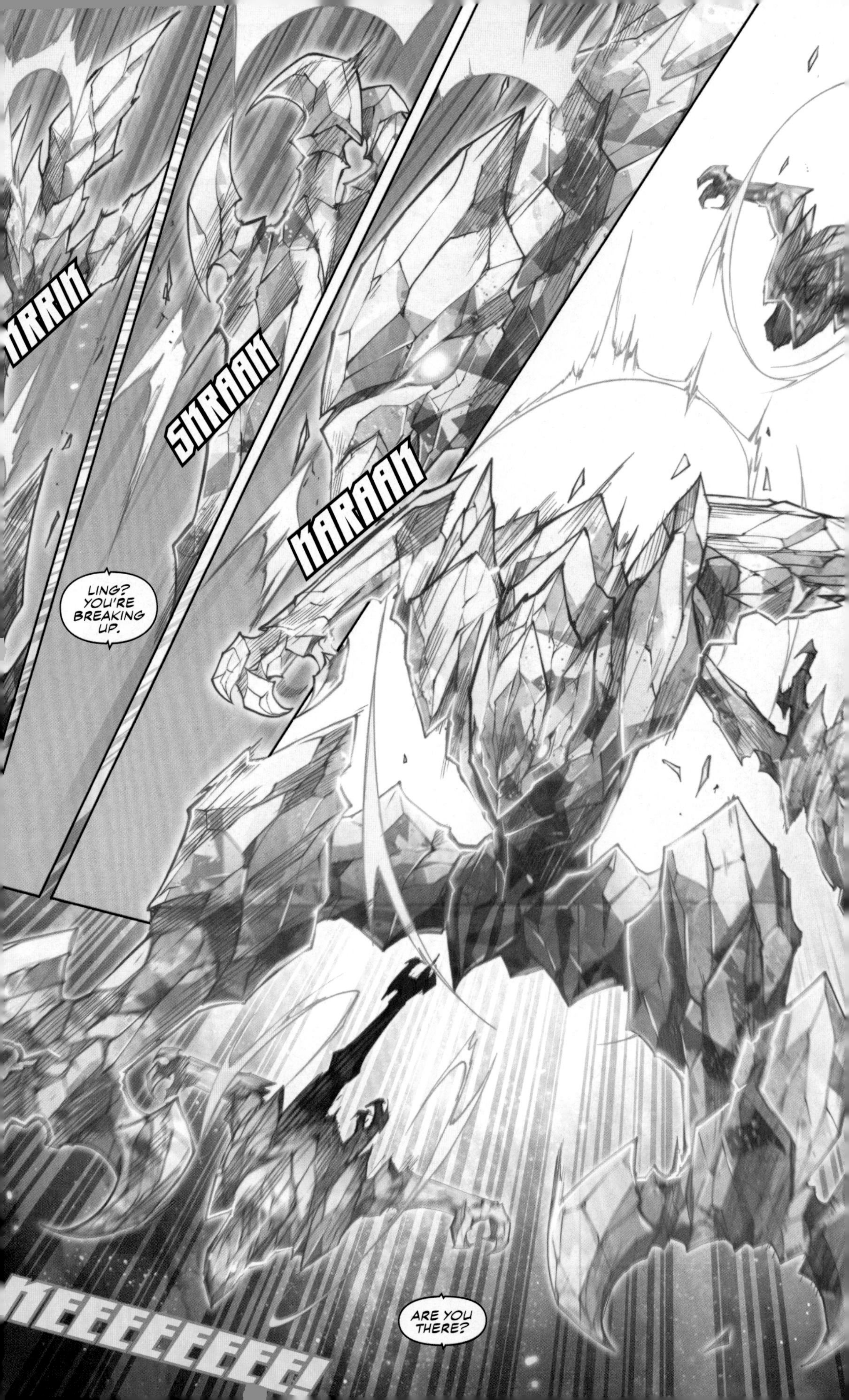
KRRIK
SKRAAK
KARAAK
LING? YOU'RE BREAKING UP.
KEEEEEEEE!
ARE YOU THERE?

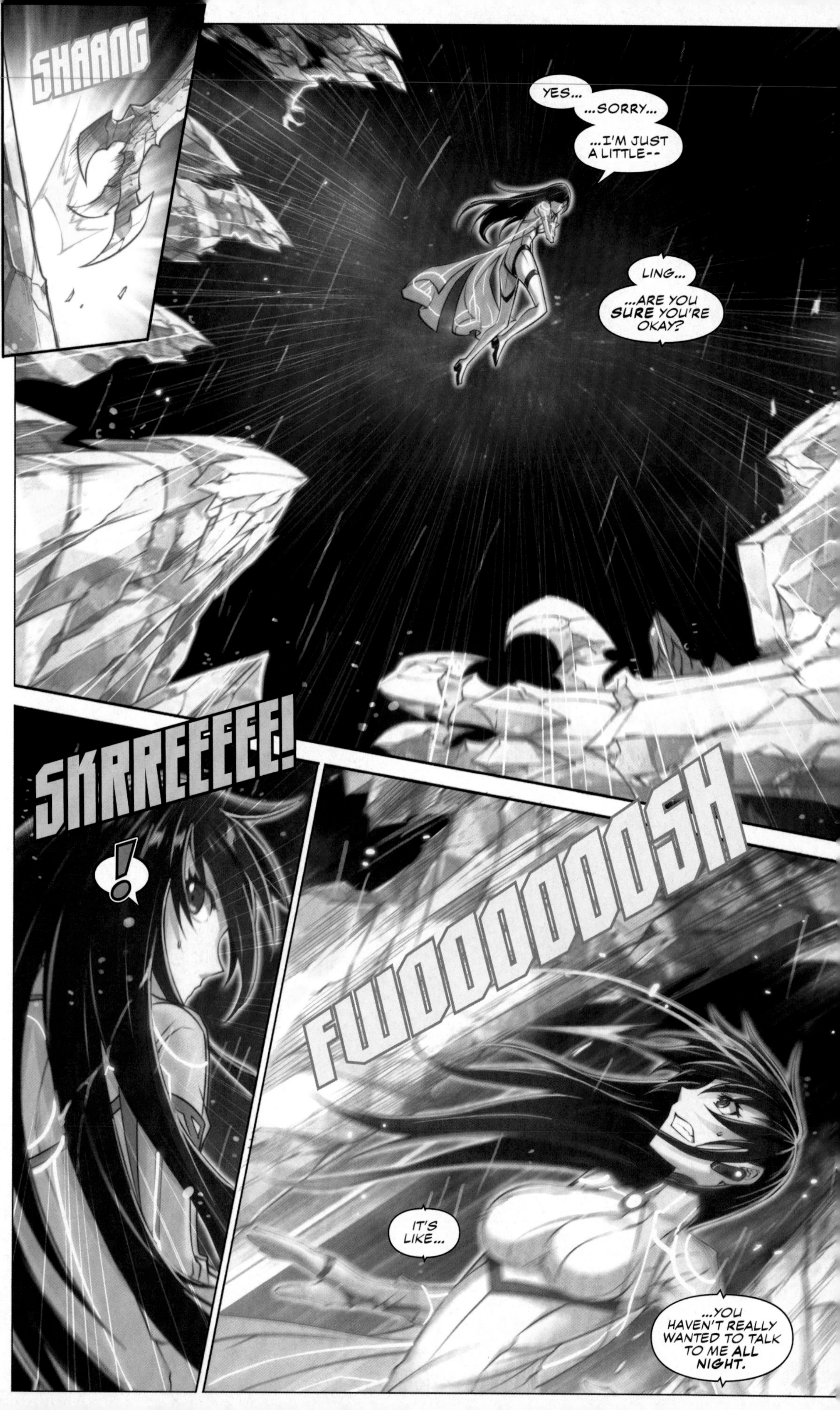
SHAANG
YES...
...SORRY...
...I'M JUST A LITTLE--
LING...
...ARE YOU SURE YOU'RE OKAY?
SKRREEEEE!
!
FWOOOOOOOSH
IT'S LIKE...
...YOU HAVEN'T REALLY WANTED TO TALK TO ME ALL NIGHT.

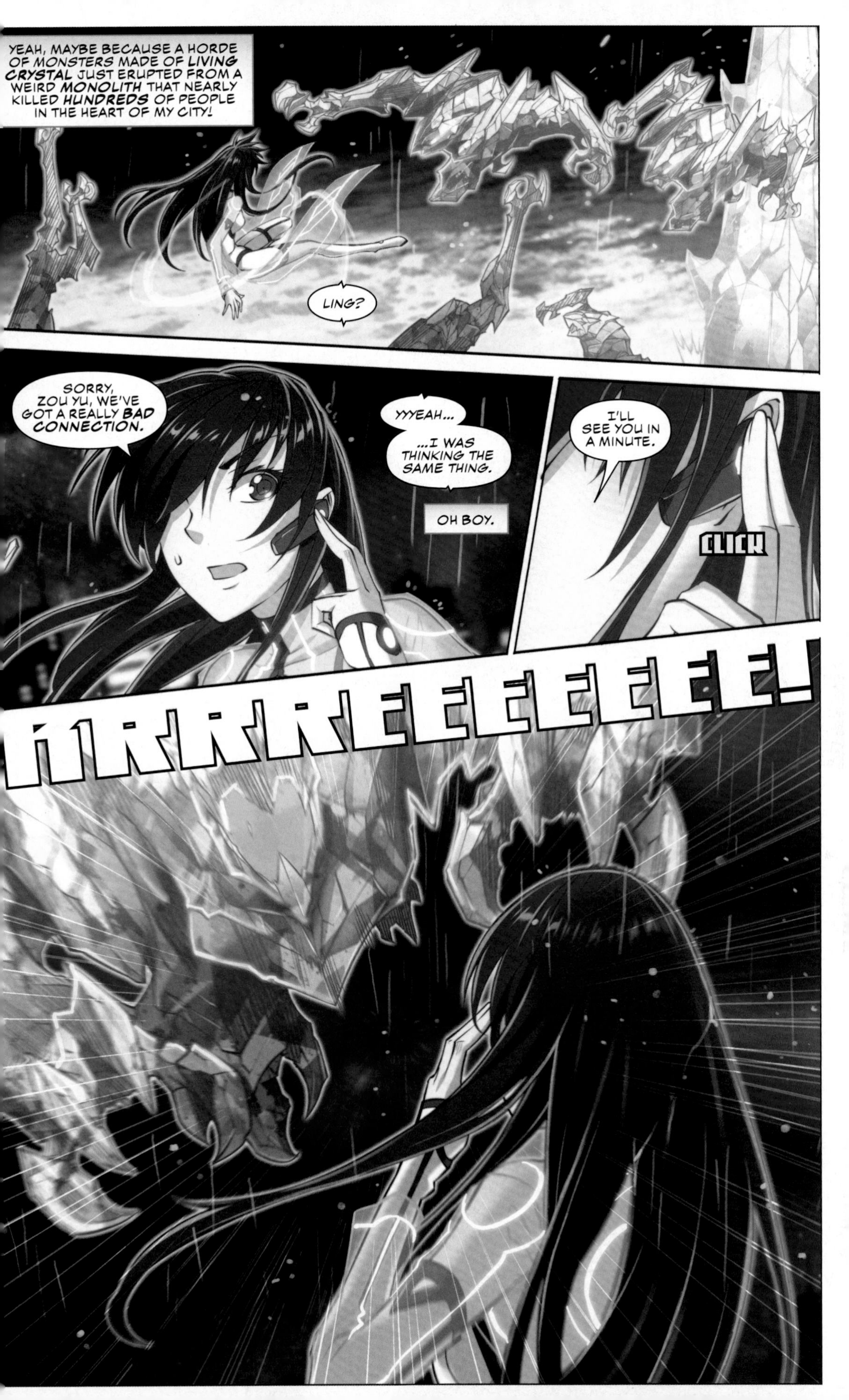

YEAH, MAYBE BECAUSE A HORDE OF MONSTERS MADE OF LIVING CRYSTAL JUST ERUPTED FROM A WEIRD MONOLITH THAT NEARLY KILLED HUNDREDS OF PEOPLE IN THE HEART OF MY CITY!
LING?
SORRY, ZOU YU, WE'VE GOT A REALLY BAD CONNECTION.
YYYEAH...
...I WAS THINKING THE SAME THING.
OH BOY.
I'LL SEE YOU IN A MINUTE.
CLICK
ARRRREEEEEEEEE!

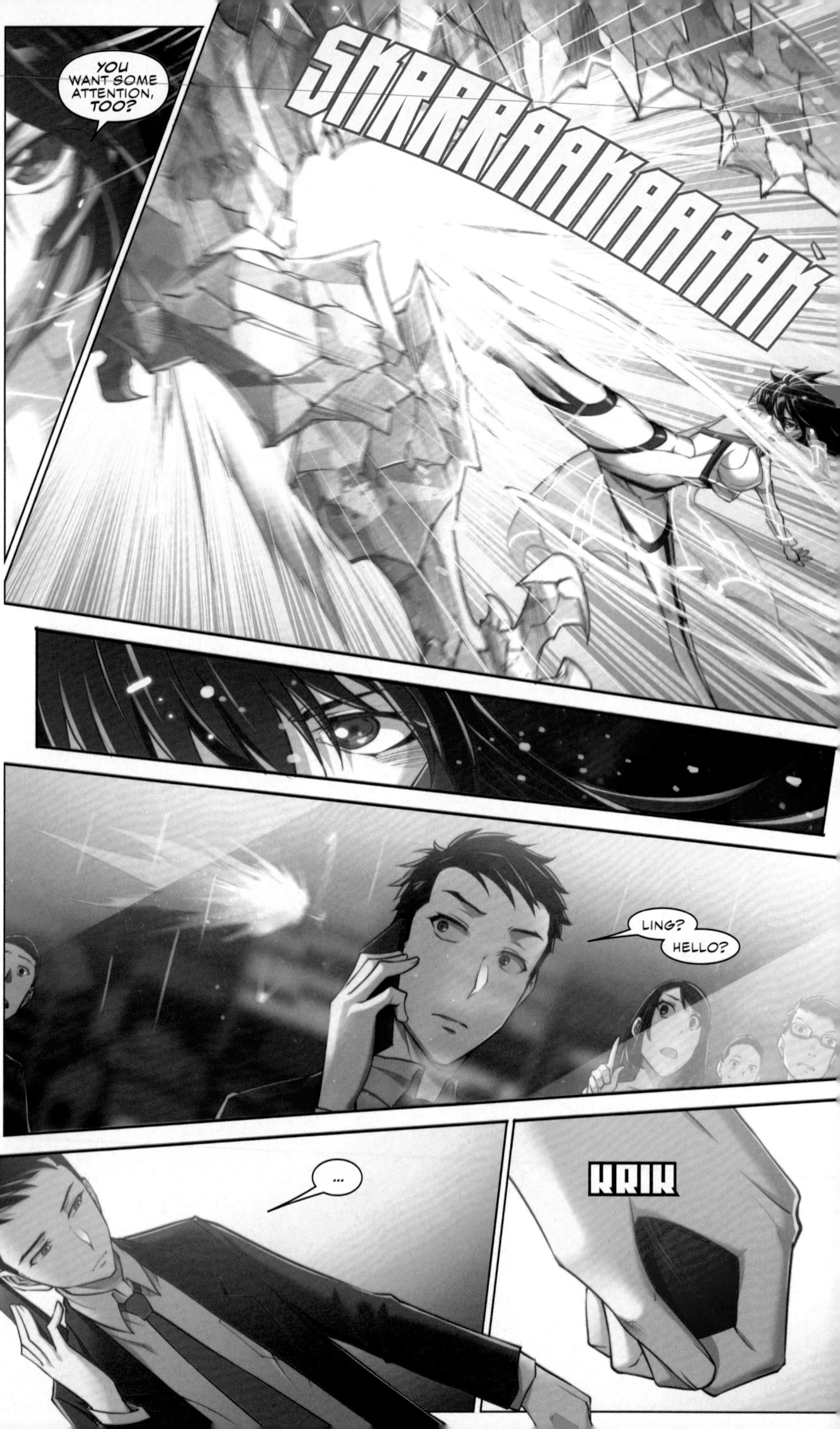
YOU WANT SOME ATTENTION, TOO?
SKRRRAAKAAAAK
LING? HELLO?
...
KRIK

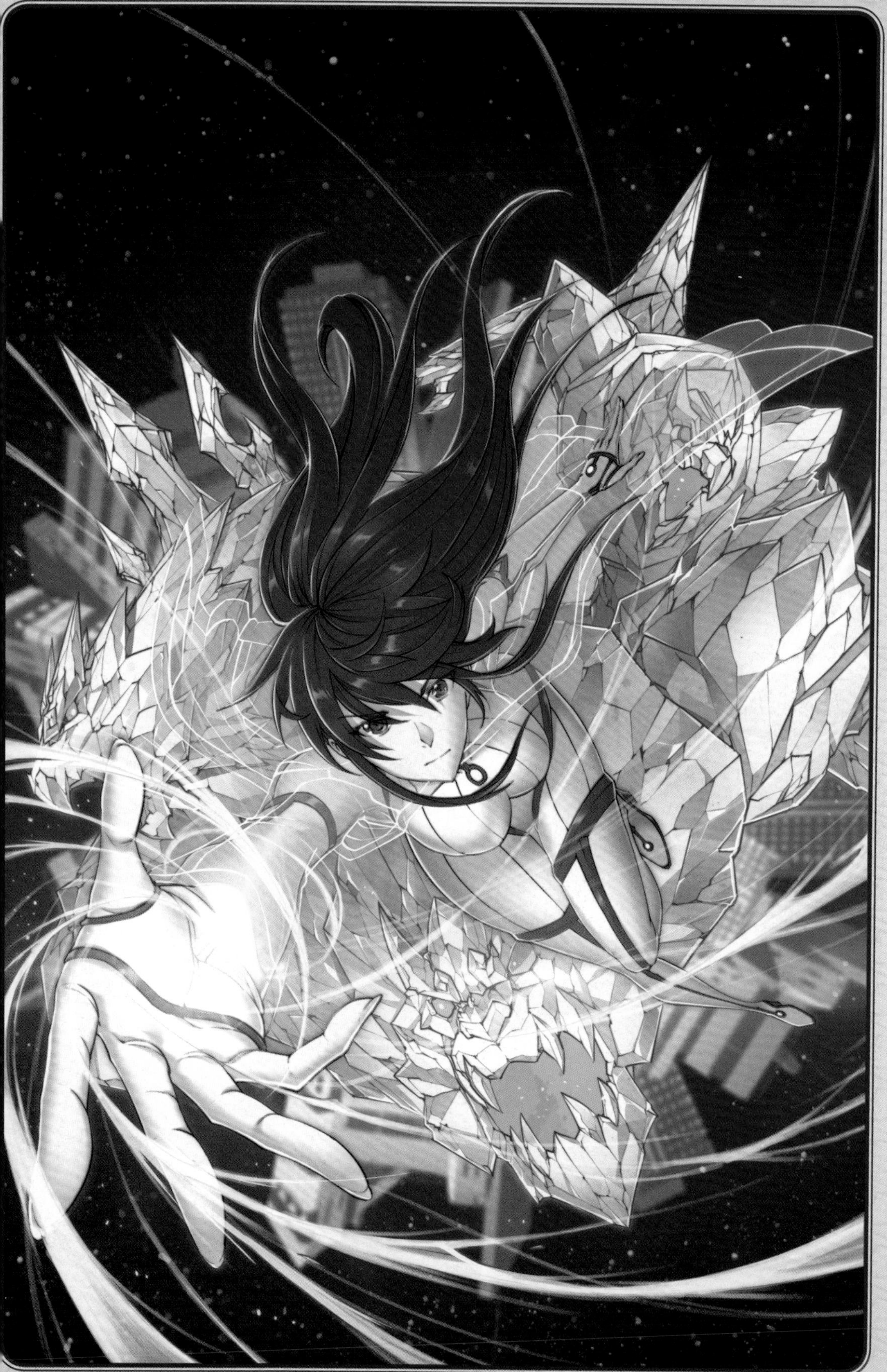

5 Secrets of the Crystal Heart

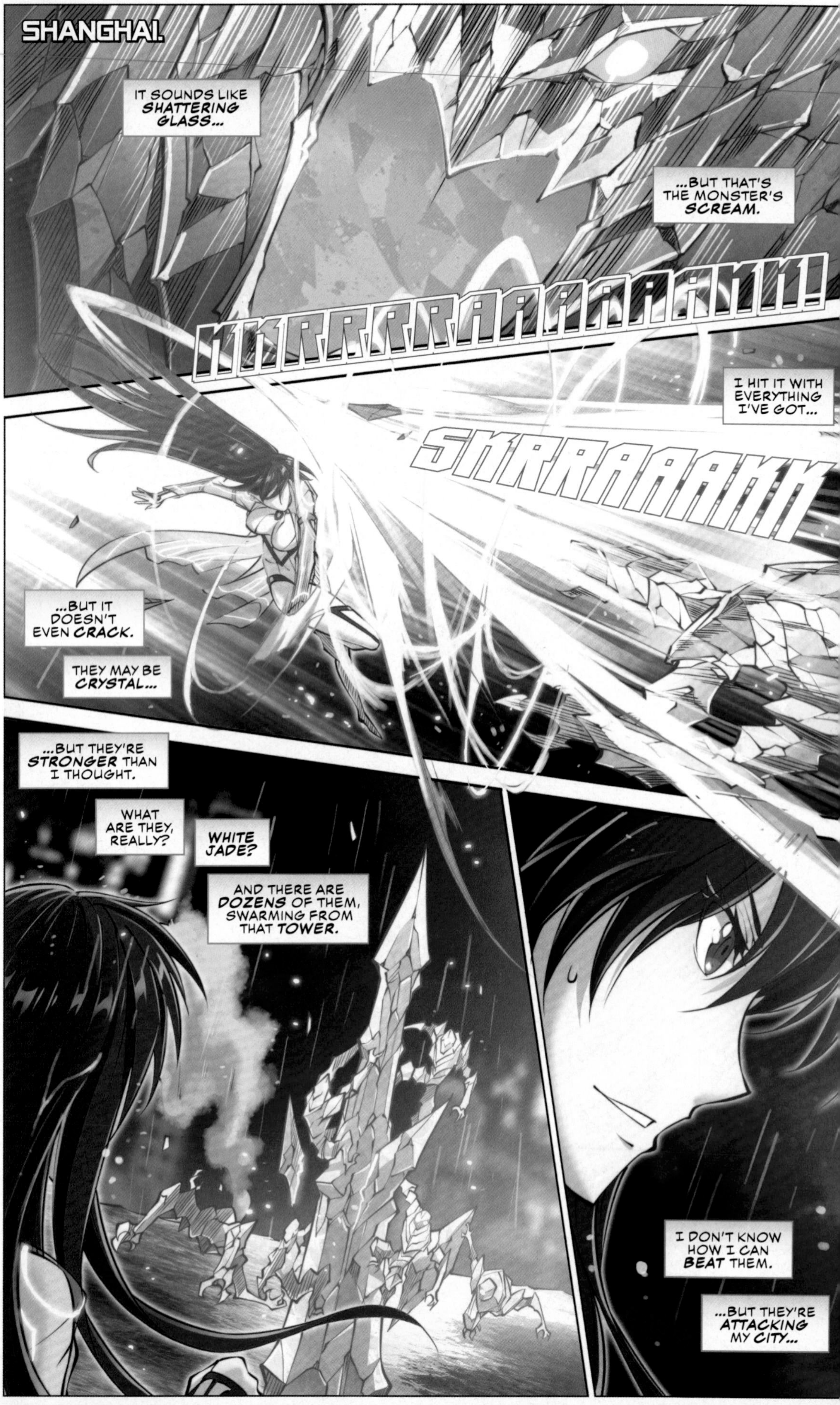
SHANGHAI.
IT SOUNDS LIKE SHATTERING GLASS...
...BUT THAT'S THE MONSTER'S SCREAM.
KKRRRRAAAAAAAKK!
I HIT IT WITH EVERYTHING I'VE GOT...
SKRRAAAAKK
...BUT IT DOESN'T EVEN CRACK.
THEY MAY BE CRYSTAL...
...BUT THEY'RE STRONGER THAN I THOUGHT.
WHAT ARE THEY, REALLY?
WHITE JADE?
AND THERE ARE DOZENS OF THEM, SWARMING FROM THAT TOWER.
I DON'T KNOW HOW I CAN BEAT THEM.
...BUT THEY'RE ATTACKING MY CITY...

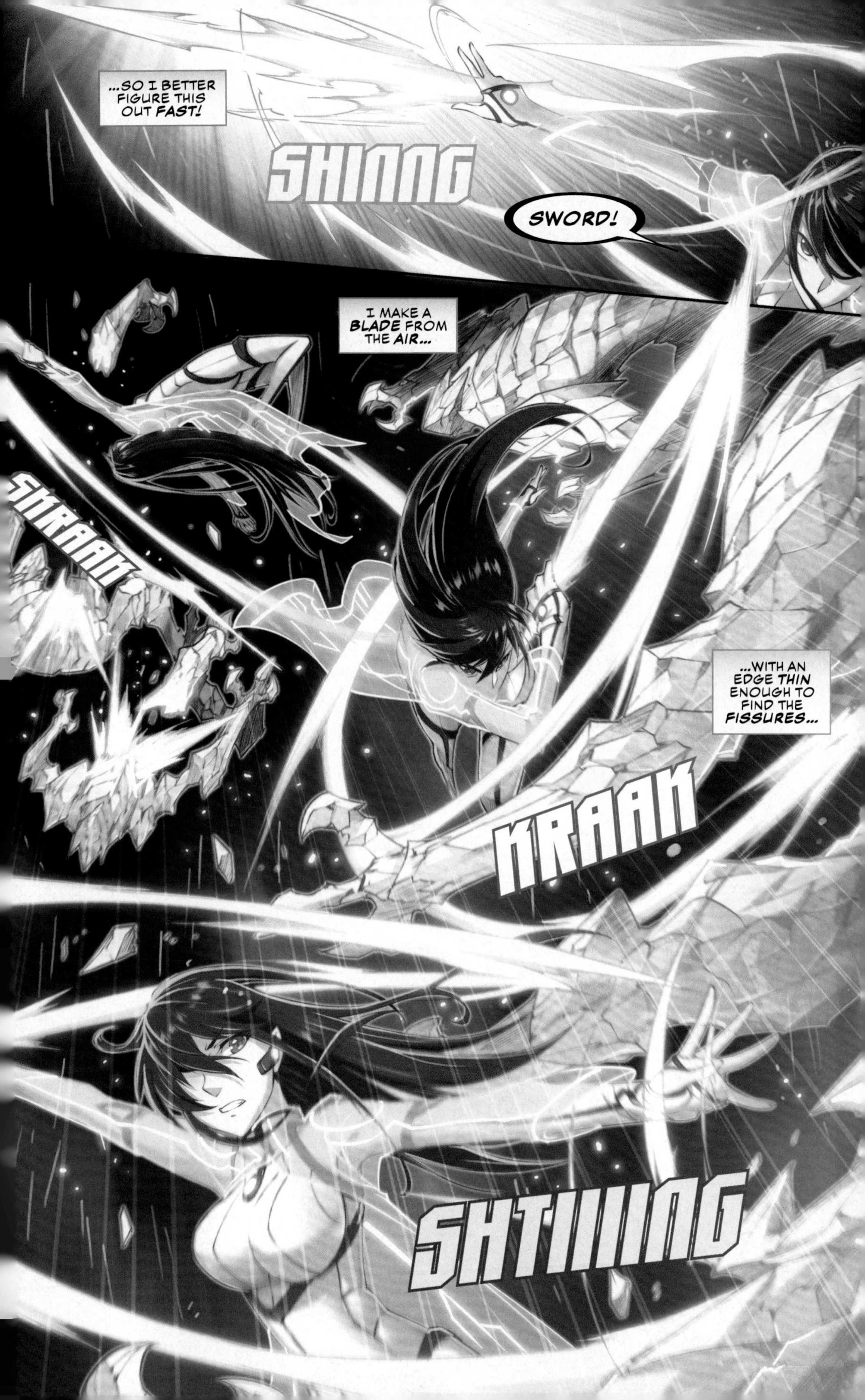
...SO I BETTER FIGURE THIS OUT FAST!
SHINNG
SWORD!
I MAKE A BLADE FROM THE AIR...
SKRAAAK
...WITH AN EDGE THIN ENOUGH TO FIND THE FISSURES...
KRAAK
SHTIIIING

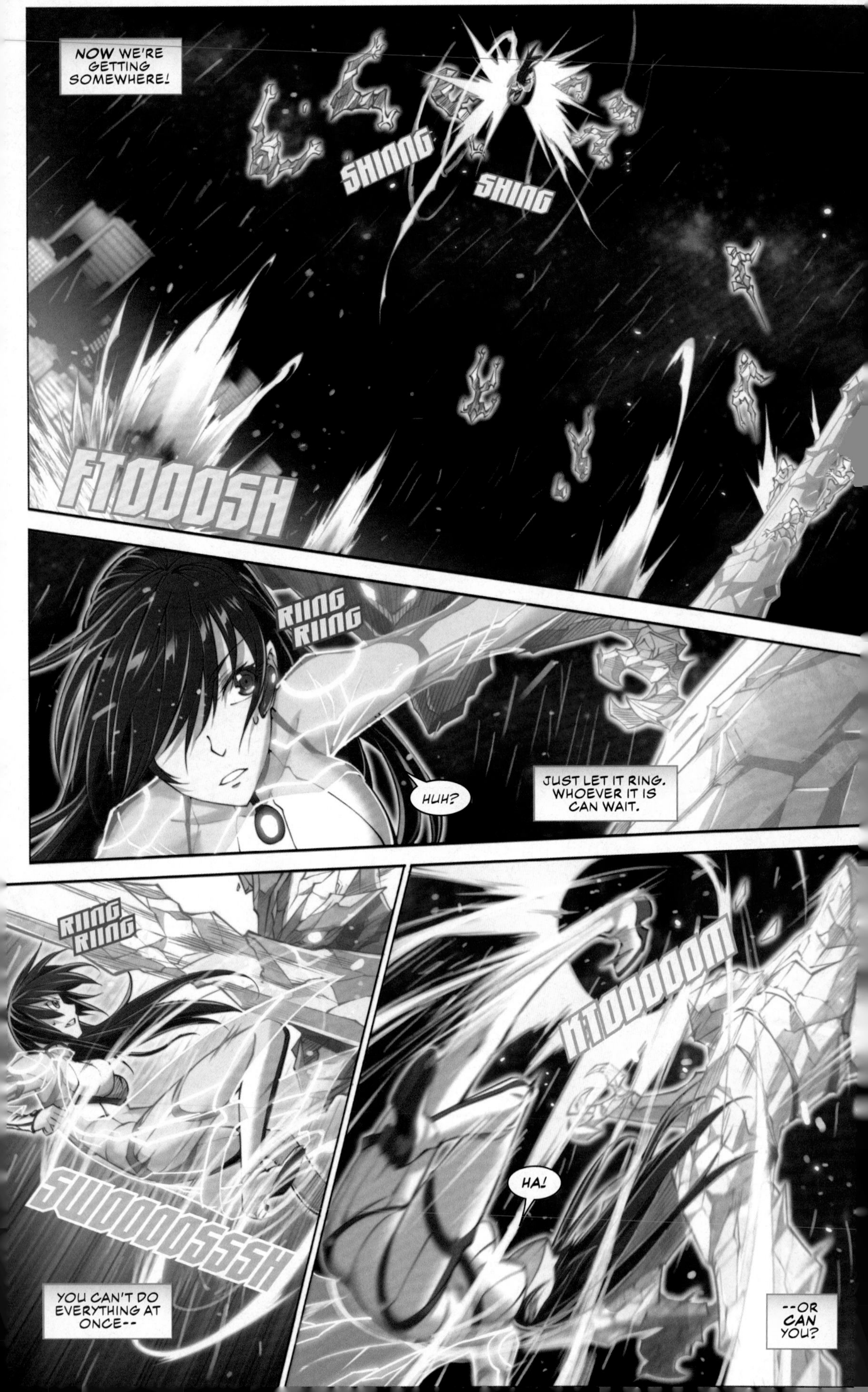

NOW WE'RE GETTING SOMEWHERE!
SHINNG
SHING
FTOOOSH
RIING RIING
HUH?
JUST LET IT RING. WHOEVER IT IS CAN WAIT.
RIING RIING
SWOOOSSSH
YOU CAN'T DO EVERYTHING AT ONCE--
KTOOOOOM
HA!
--OR CAN YOU?

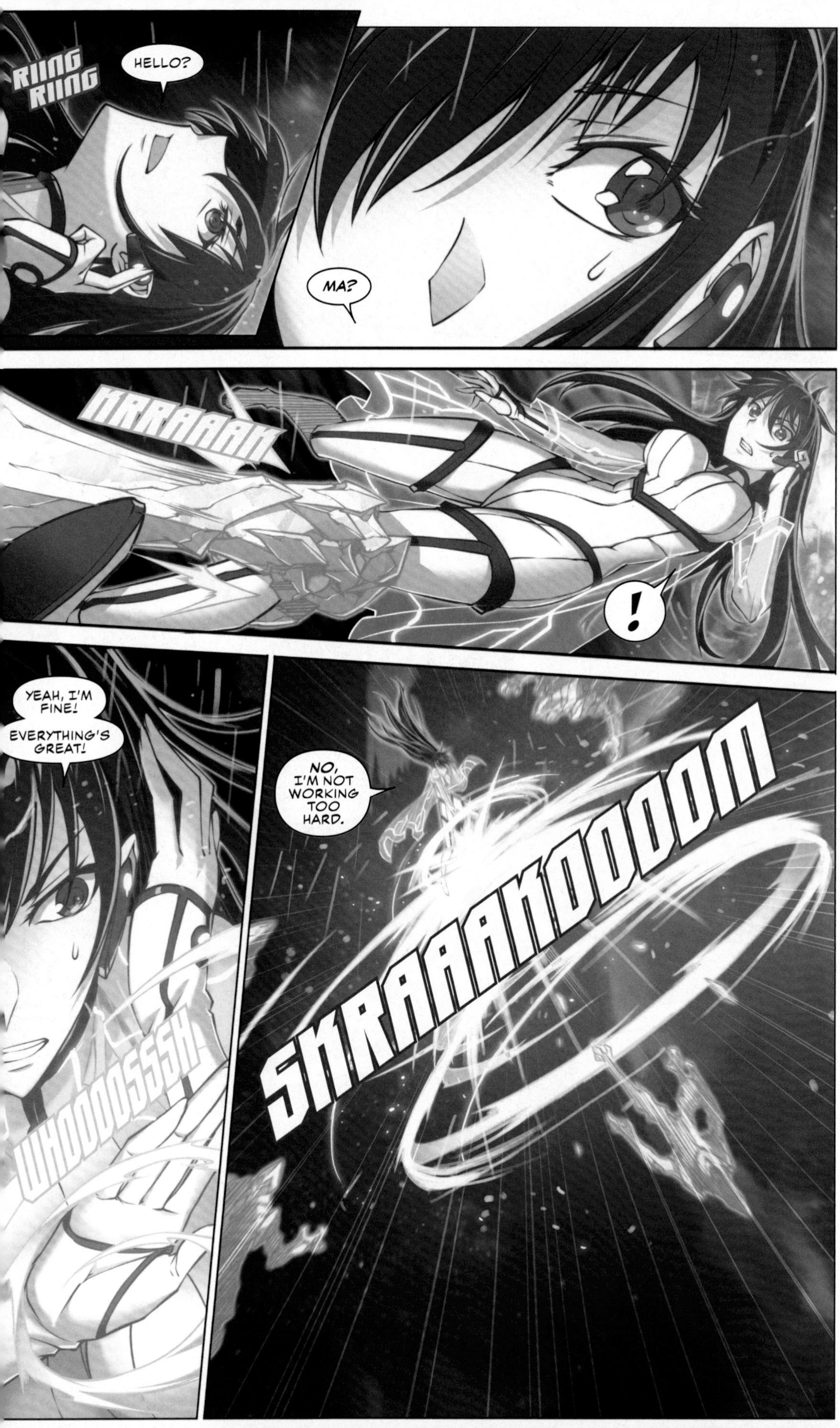
RIIING RIIING
HELLO?
MA?
KRRAAAK
!
YEAH, I'M FINE!
EVERYTHING'S GREAT!
NO, I'M NOT WORKING TOO HARD.
SKRAAAKOOOOM
WHOOOOSSSH

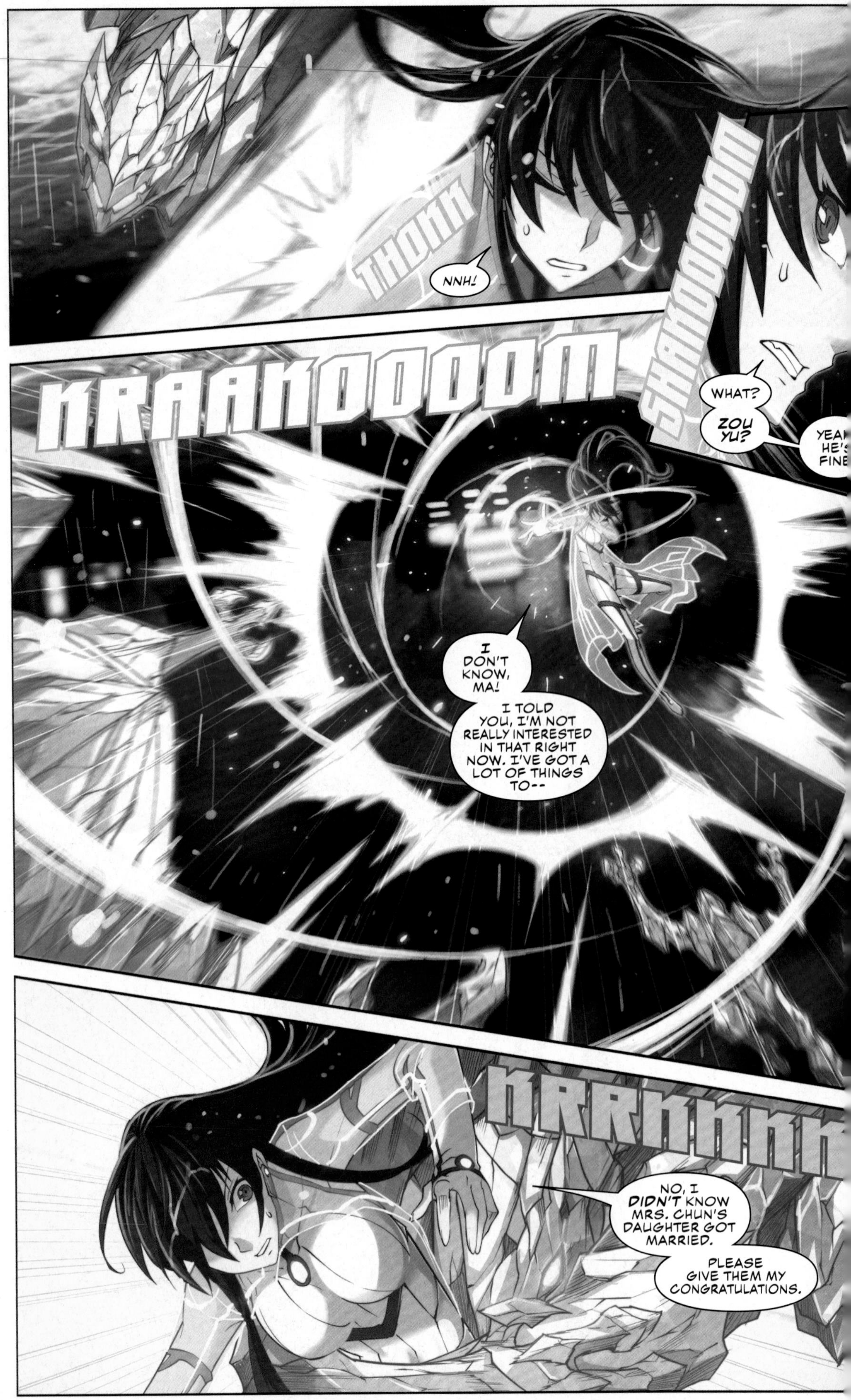
THONK
NNH!
SHABOOOOOOM
WHAT?
ZOU YU?
YEA HE'S FINE
KRAAKOOOOOM
I DON'T KNOW, MA!
I TOLD YOU, I'M NOT REALLY INTERESTED IN THAT RIGHT NOW. I'VE GOT A LOT OF THINGS TO--
KRRKKKKK
NO, I DIDN'T KNOW MRS. CHUN'S DAUGHTER GOT MARRIED.
PLEASE GIVE THEM MY CONGRATULATIONS.

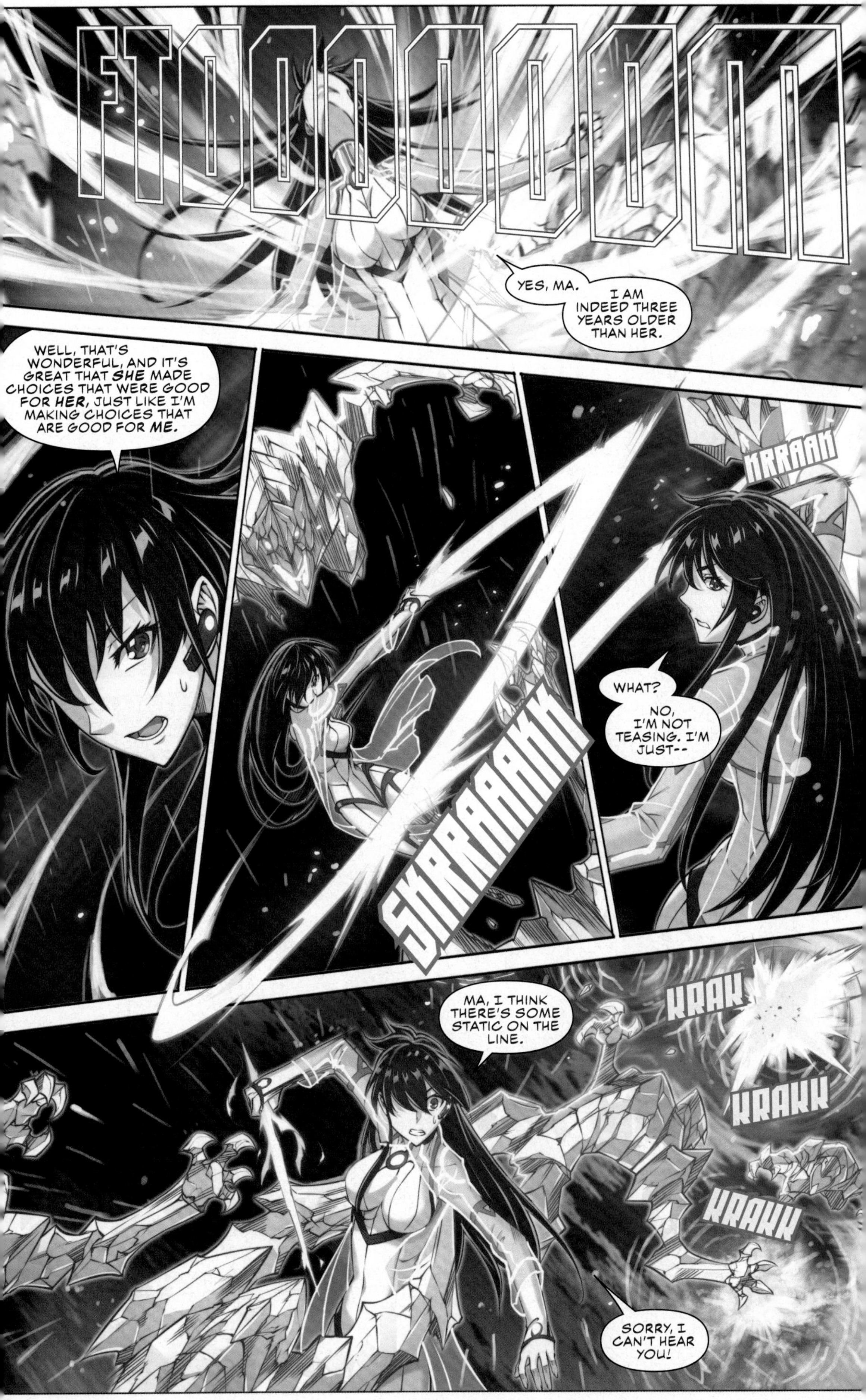
FTOOOOOOM
YES, MA.
I AM INDEED THREE YEARS OLDER THAN HER.
WELL, THAT'S WONDERFUL, AND IT'S GREAT THAT **SHE** MADE CHOICES THAT WERE GOOD FOR **HER**, JUST LIKE I'M MAKING CHOICES THAT ARE GOOD FOR **ME.**
SKRRAAAKK
KRRAAK
WHAT?
NO, I'M NOT TEASING. I'M JUST--
MA, I THINK THERE'S SOME STATIC ON THE LINE.
KRAK
KRAKK
KRAKK
SORRY, I CAN'T HEAR YOU!

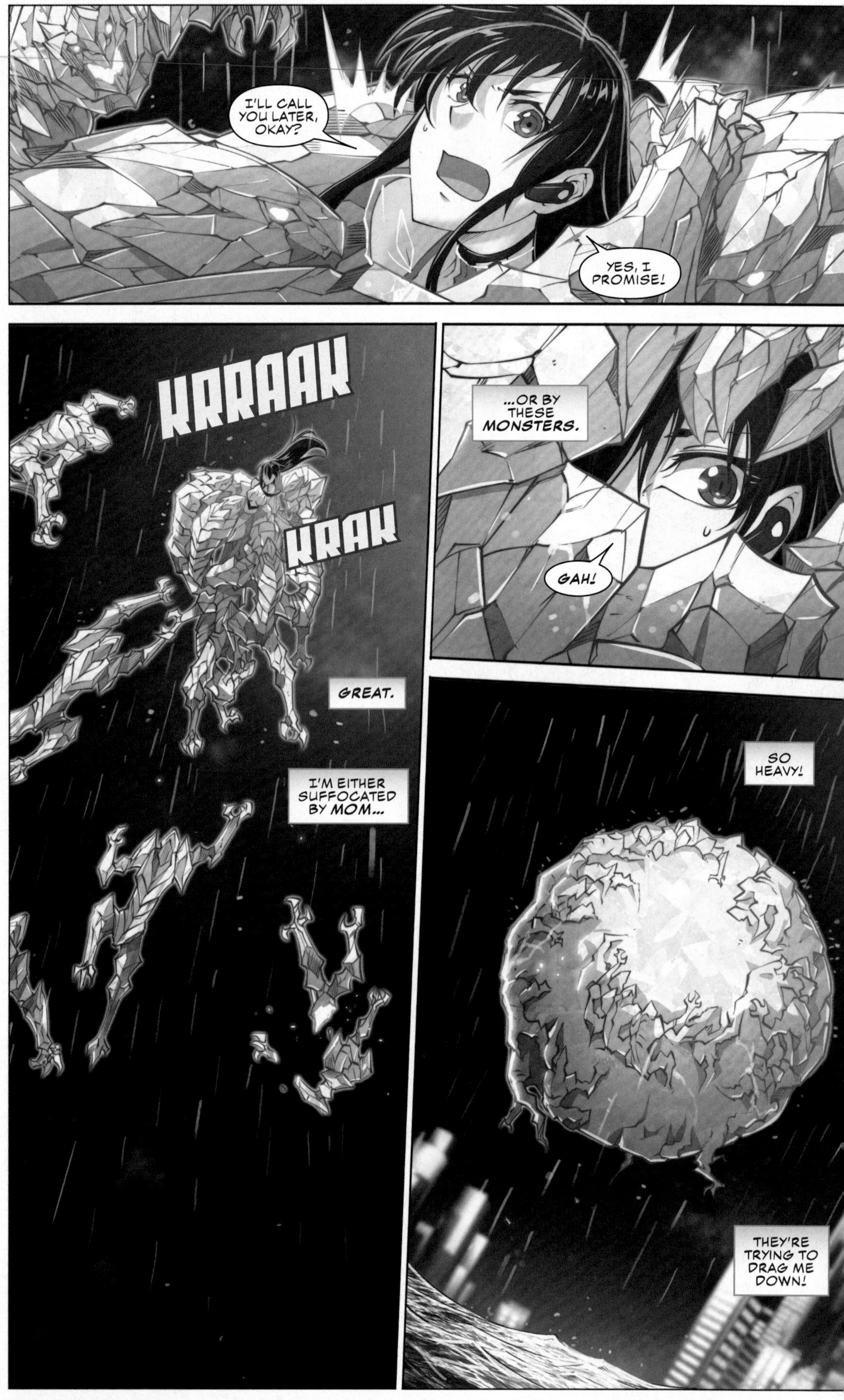
I'LL CALL YOU LATER, OKAY?
YES, I PROMISE!
KRRAAK
KRAK
GREAT.
I'M EITHER SUFFOCATED BY MOM...
...OR BY THESE MONSTERS.
GAH!
SO HEAVY!
THEY'RE TRYING TO DRAG ME DOWN!

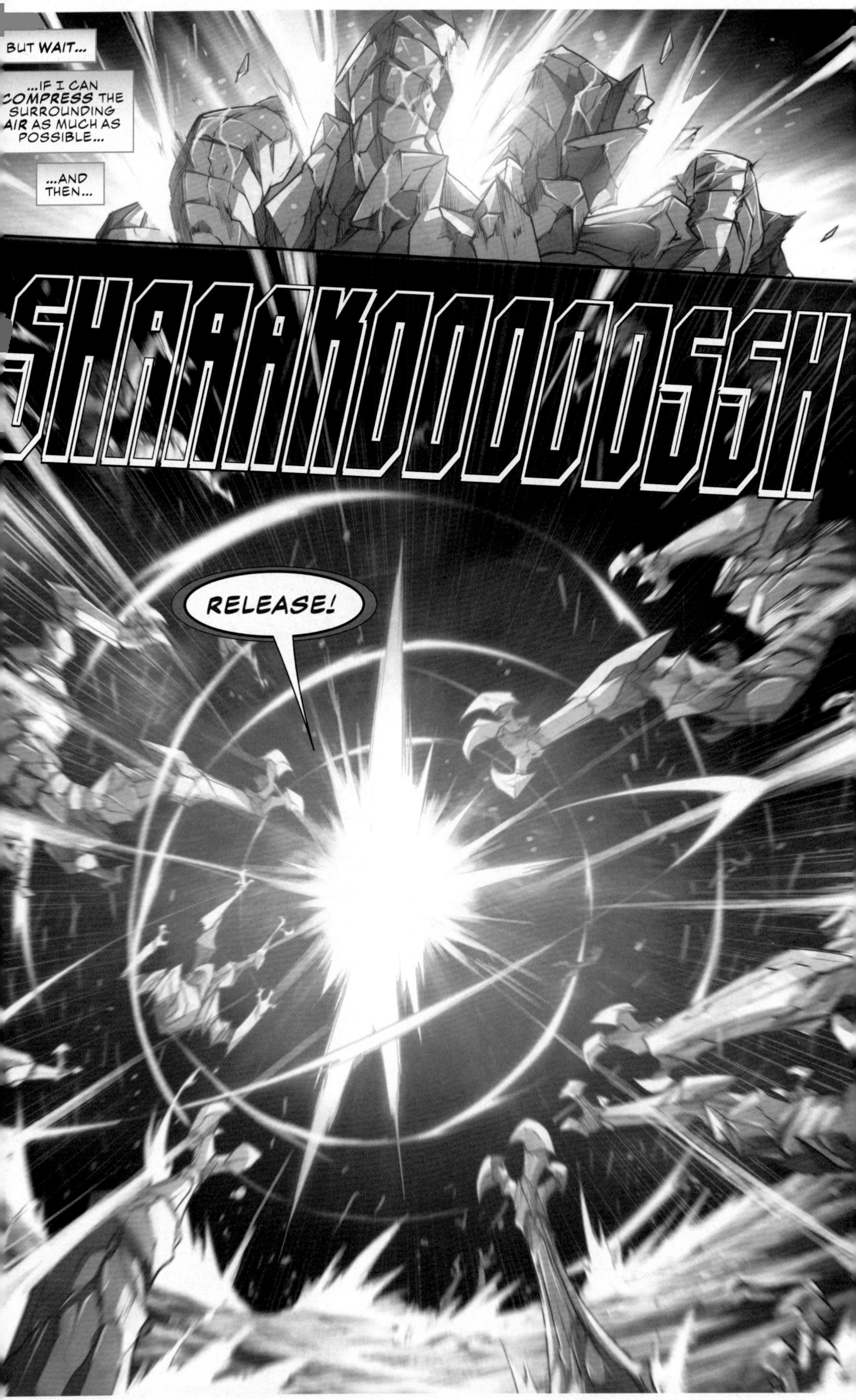
BUT WAIT...
...IF I CAN COMPRESS THE SURROUNDING AIR AS MUCH AS POSSIBLE...
...AND THEN...
SHAAAKOOOOOOSSH
RELEASE!

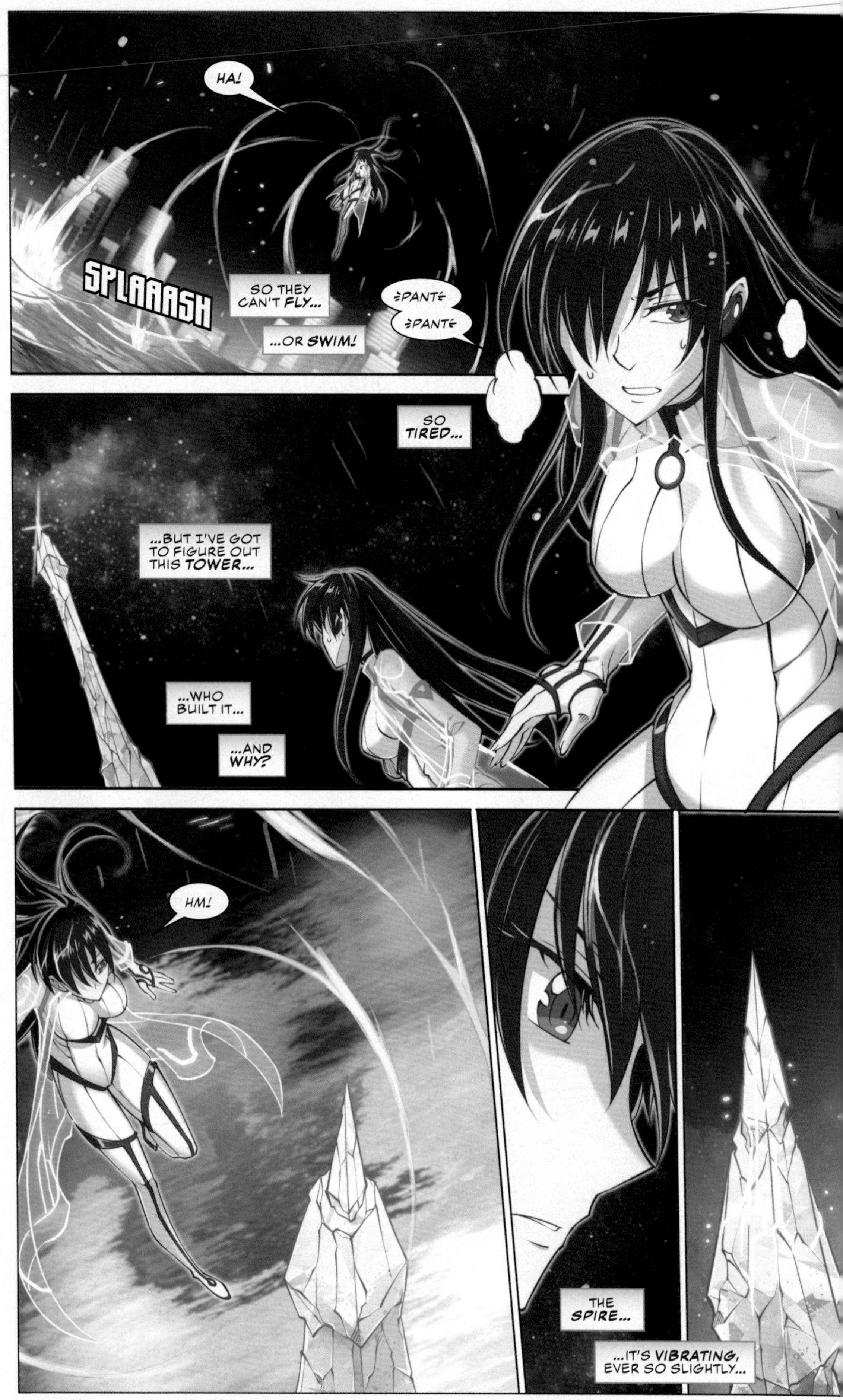
HA!
SPLAAASH
SO THEY CAN'T FLY...
...OR SWIM!
PANT
PANT
SO TIRED...
...BUT I'VE GOT TO FIGURE OUT THIS TOWER...
...WHO BUILT IT...
...AND WHY?
HM!
THE SPIRE...
...IT'S VIBRATING, EVER SO SLIGHTLY...

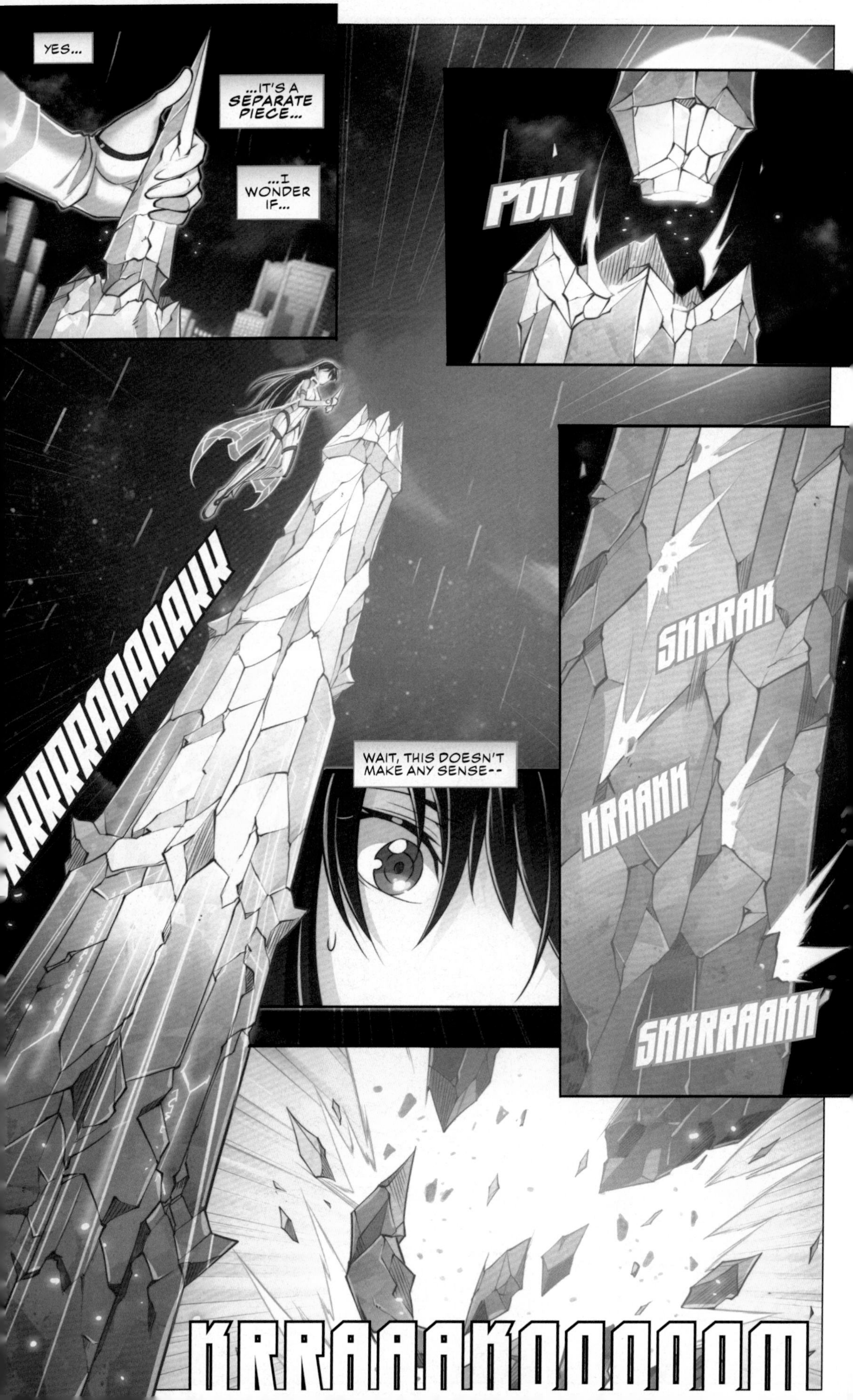
YES...
...IT'S A SEPARATE PIECE...
...I WONDER IF...
POK
KRRRAAAAAAKK
WAIT, THIS DOESN'T MAKE ANY SENSE--
SKRRAK
KRAAKK
SKRRAAKK
KRRAAAKOOOOOOM

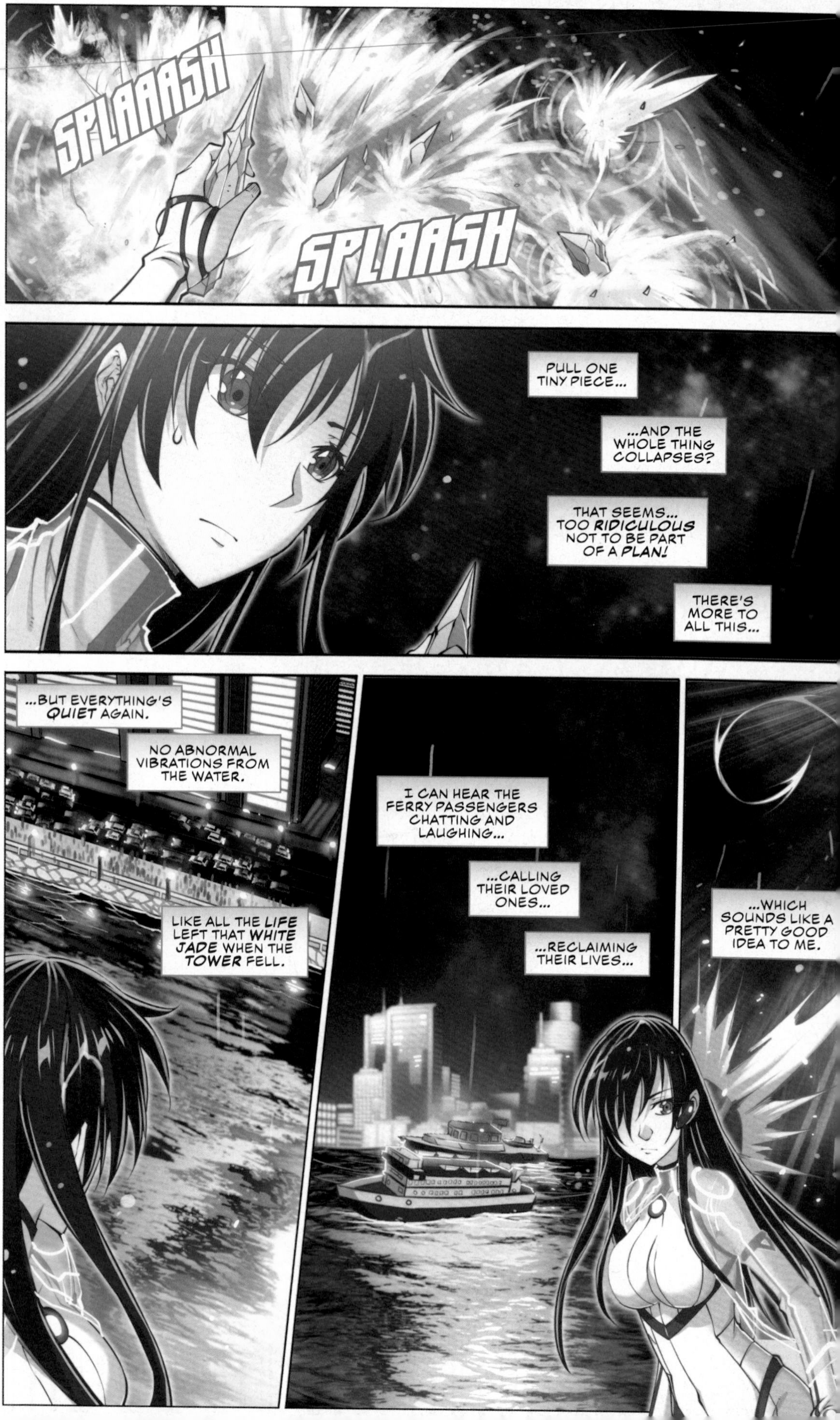
SPLAAASH
SPLAASH
PULL ONE TINY PIECE...
...AND THE WHOLE THING COLLAPSES?
THAT SEEMS... TOO RIDICULOUS NOT TO BE PART OF A PLAN!
THERE'S MORE TO ALL THIS...
...BUT EVERYTHING'S QUIET AGAIN.
NO ABNORMAL VIBRATIONS FROM THE WATER.
LIKE ALL THE LIFE LEFT THAT WHITE JADE WHEN THE TOWER FELL.
I CAN HEAR THE FERRY PASSENGERS CHATTING AND LAUGHING...
...CALLING THEIR LOVED ONES...
...RECLAIMING THEIR LIVES...
...WHICH SOUNDS LIKE A PRETTY GOOD IDEA TO ME.

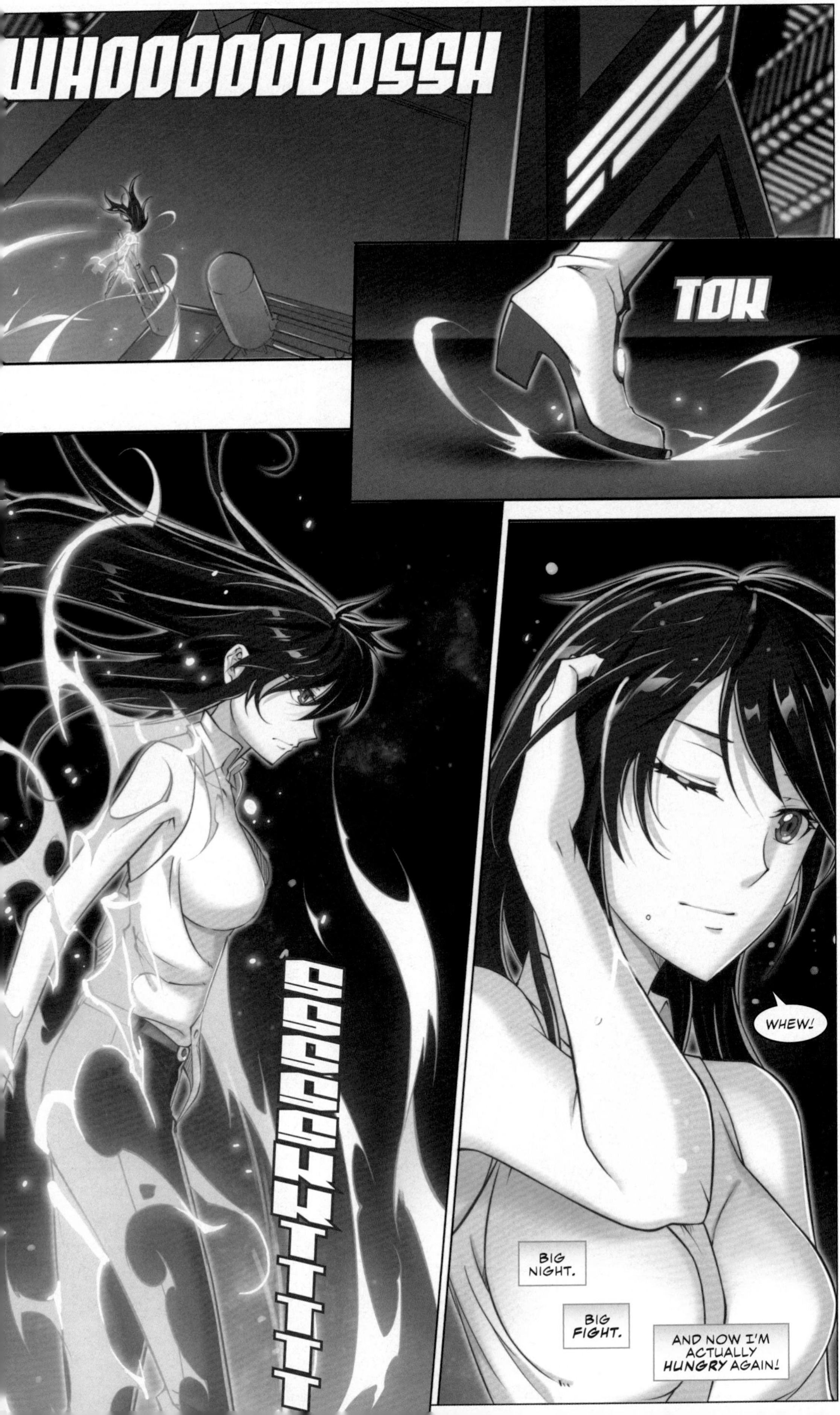
WHOOOOOOOSSH
TOK
SSSSSHTTTTTT
WHEW!
BIG NIGHT.
BIG FIGHT.
AND NOW I'M ACTUALLY HUNGRY AGAIN!

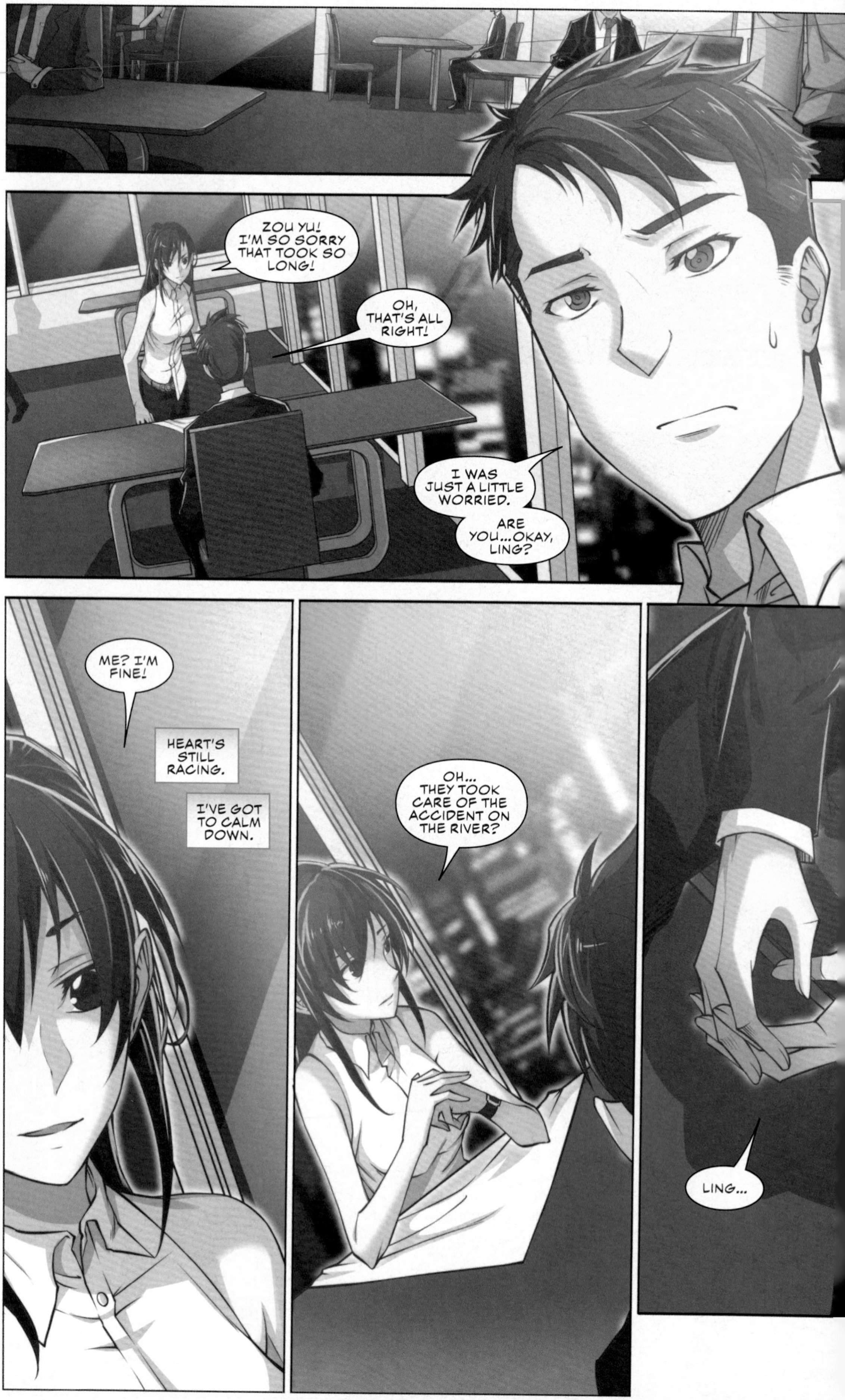
ZOU YU! I'M SO SORRY THAT TOOK SO LONG!
OH, THAT'S ALL RIGHT!
I WAS JUST A LITTLE WORRIED.
ARE YOU...OKAY, LING?
ME? I'M FINE!
HEART'S STILL RACING.
I'VE GOT TO CALM DOWN.
OH... THEY TOOK CARE OF THE ACCIDENT ON THE RIVER?
LING...

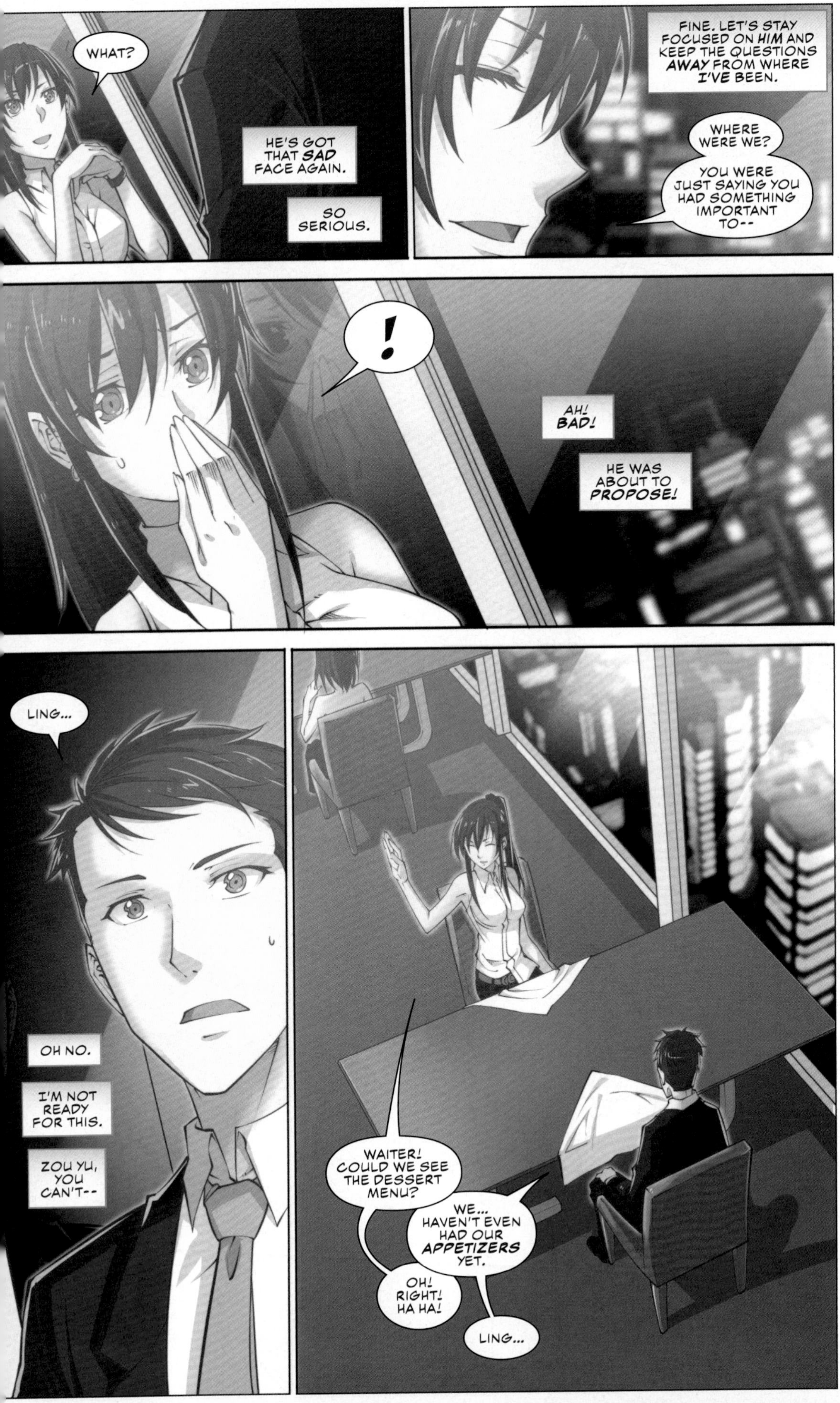
WHAT?
HE'S GOT THAT SAD FACE AGAIN.
SO SERIOUS.
FINE. LET'S STAY FOCUSED ON HIM AND KEEP THE QUESTIONS AWAY FROM WHERE I'VE BEEN.
WHERE WERE WE?
YOU WERE JUST SAYING YOU HAD SOMETHING IMPORTANT TO--
!
AH! BAD!
HE WAS ABOUT TO PROPOSE!
LING...
OH NO.
I'M NOT READY FOR THIS.
ZOU YU, YOU CAN'T--
WAITER! COULD WE SEE THE DESSERT MENU?
WE... HAVEN'T EVEN HAD OUR APPETIZERS YET.
OH! RIGHT! HA HA!
LING...

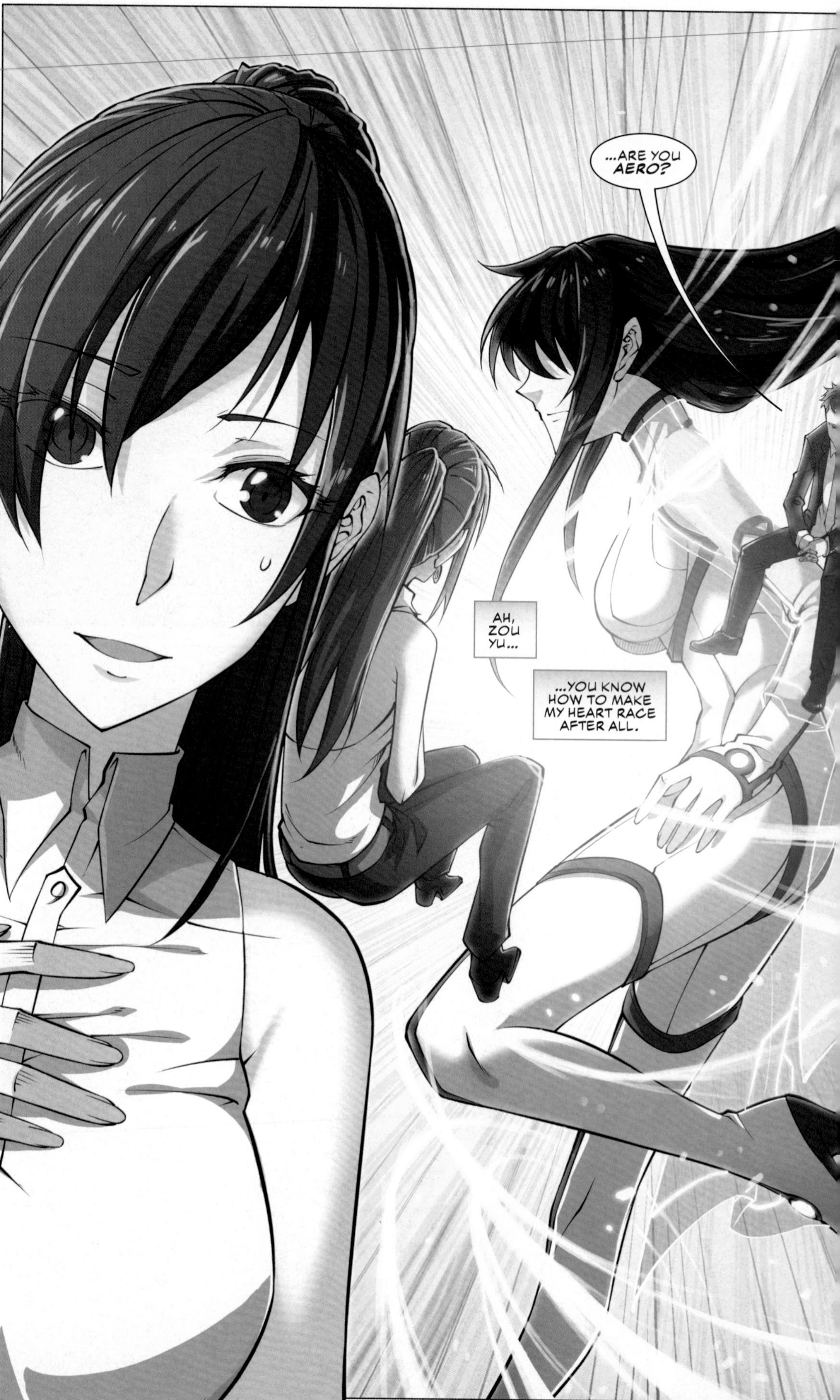
...ARE YOU AERO?
AH, ZOU YU...
...YOU KNOW HOW TO MAKE MY HEART RACE AFTER ALL.

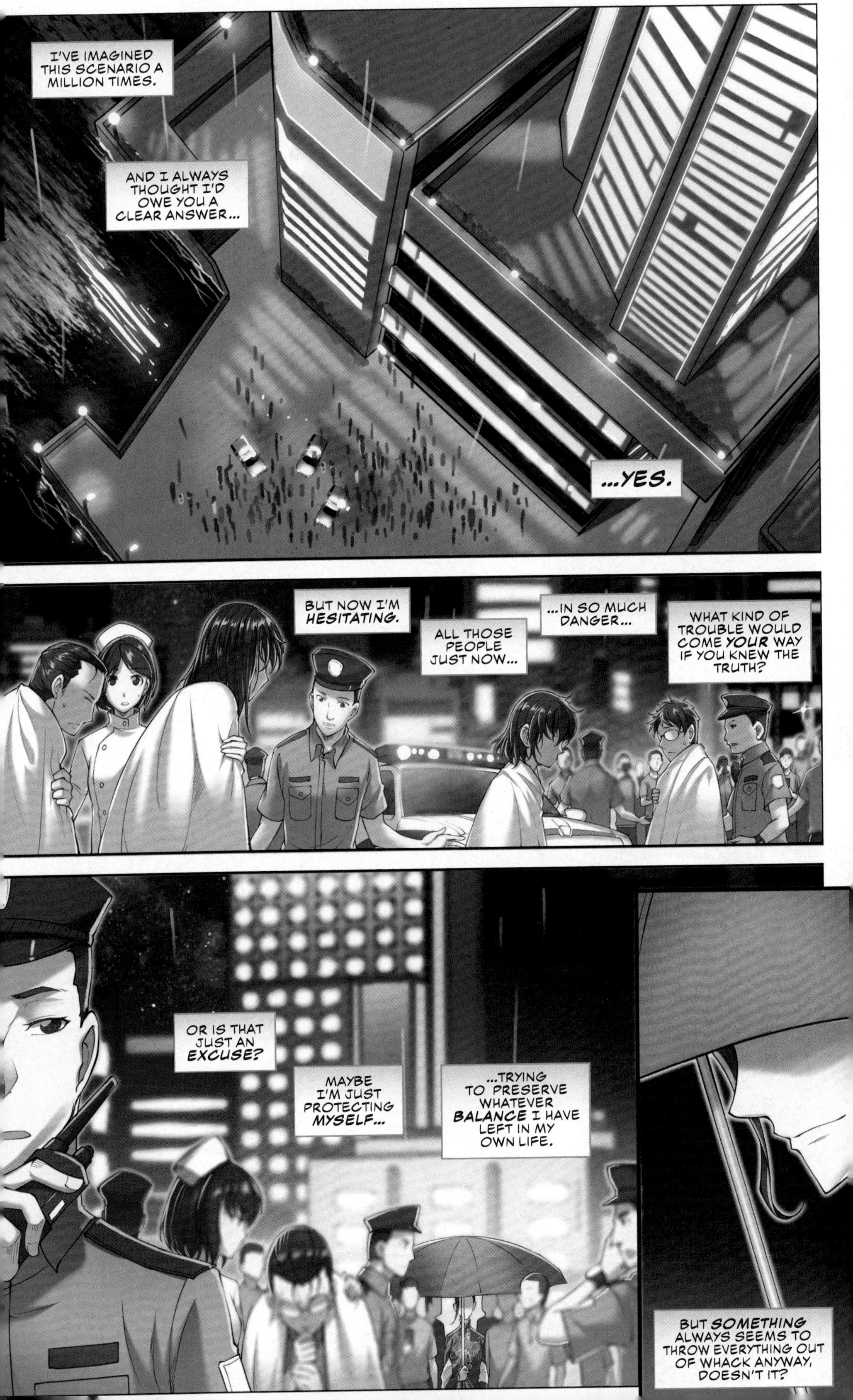

I'VE IMAGINED THIS SCENARIO A MILLION TIMES.
AND I ALWAYS THOUGHT I'D OWE YOU A CLEAR ANSWER...
...YES.
BUT NOW I'M HESITATING.
ALL THOSE PEOPLE JUST NOW...
...IN SO MUCH DANGER...
WHAT KIND OF TROUBLE WOULD COME YOUR WAY IF YOU KNEW THE TRUTH?
OR IS THAT JUST AN EXCUSE?
MAYBE I'M JUST PROTECTING MYSELF...
...TRYING TO PRESERVE WHATEVER BALANCE I HAVE LEFT IN MY OWN LIFE.
BUT SOMETHING ALWAYS SEEMS TO THROW EVERYTHING OUT OF WHACK ANYWAY, DOESN'T IT?

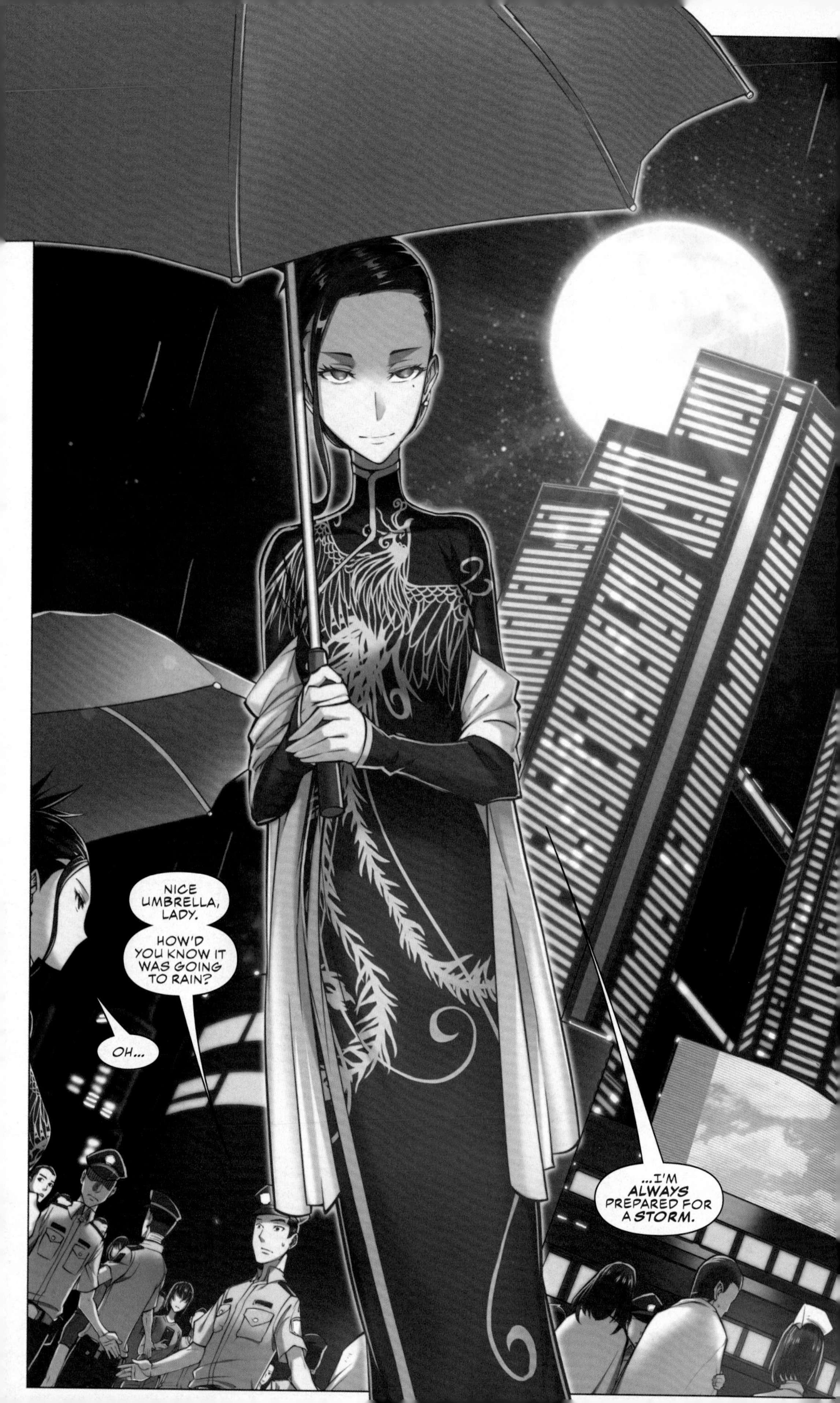
NICE UMBRELLA, LADY.
HOW'D YOU KNOW IT WAS GOING TO RAIN?
OH...
...I'M ALWAYS PREPARED FOR A STORM.

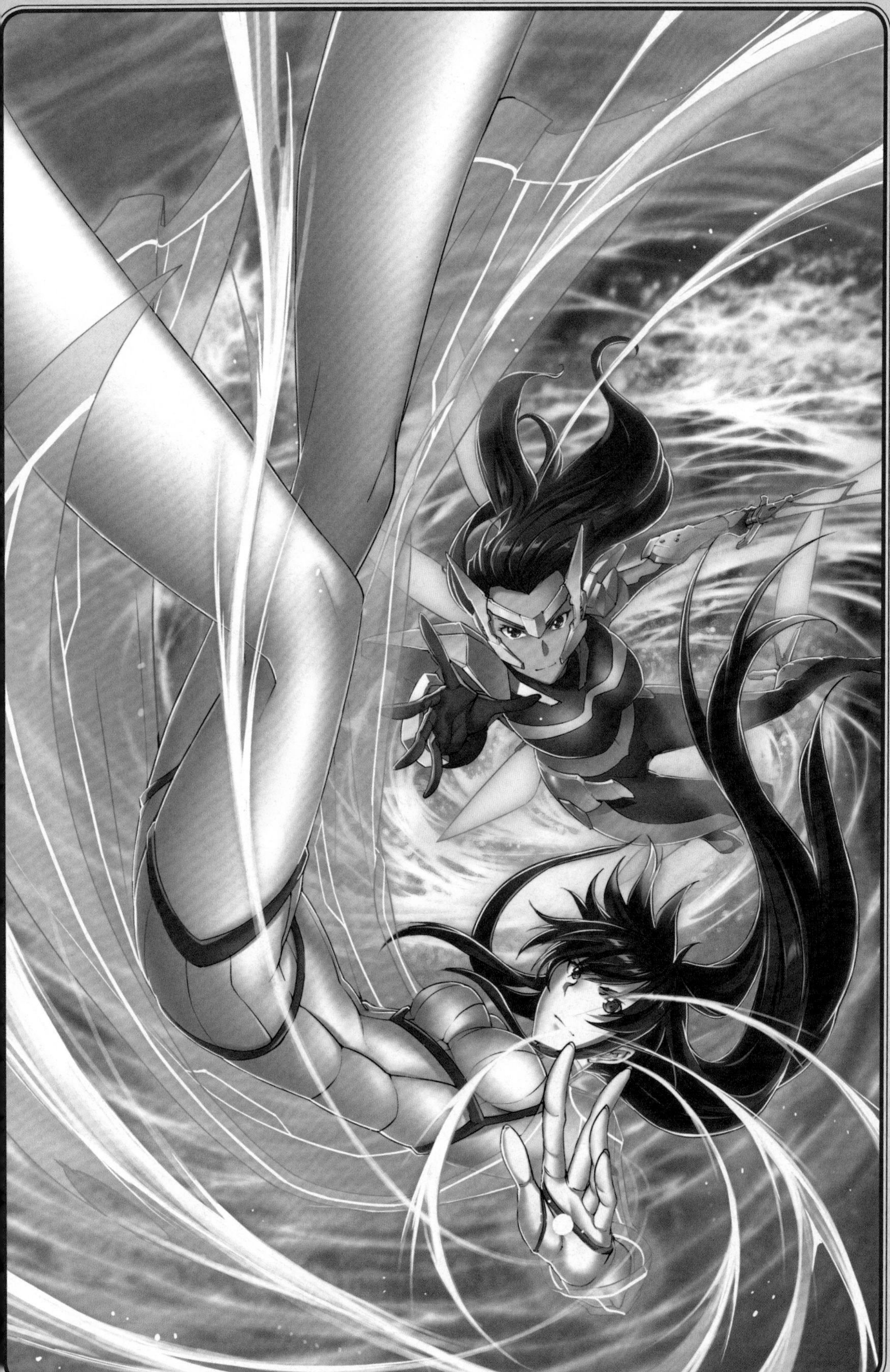

6 Madame Huang

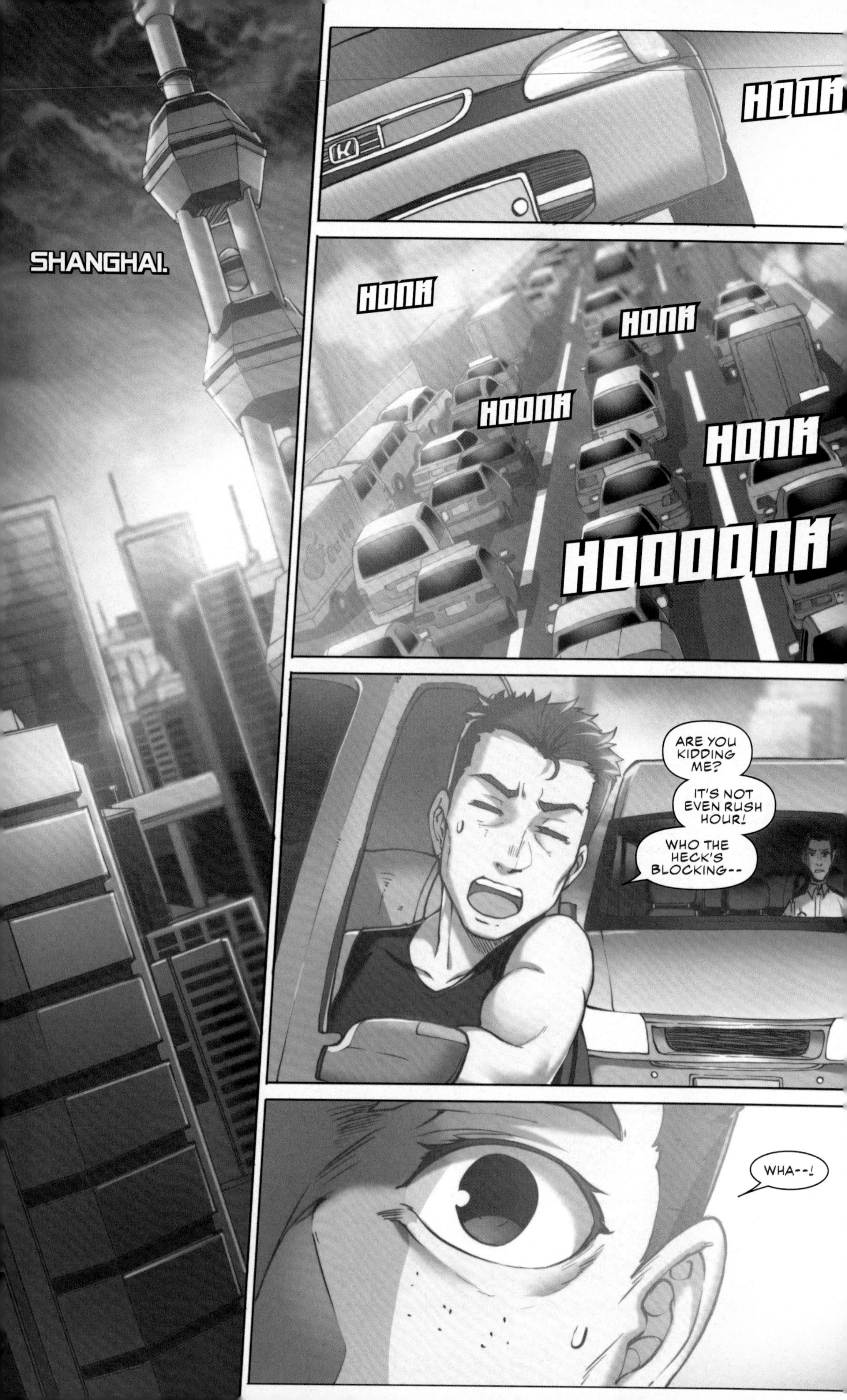
SHANGHAI.
HONK
HONK
HONK
HOONK
HONK
HOOOONK
ARE YOU KIDDING ME?
IT'S NOT EVEN RUSH HOUR!
WHO THE HECK'S BLOCKING--
WHA--!

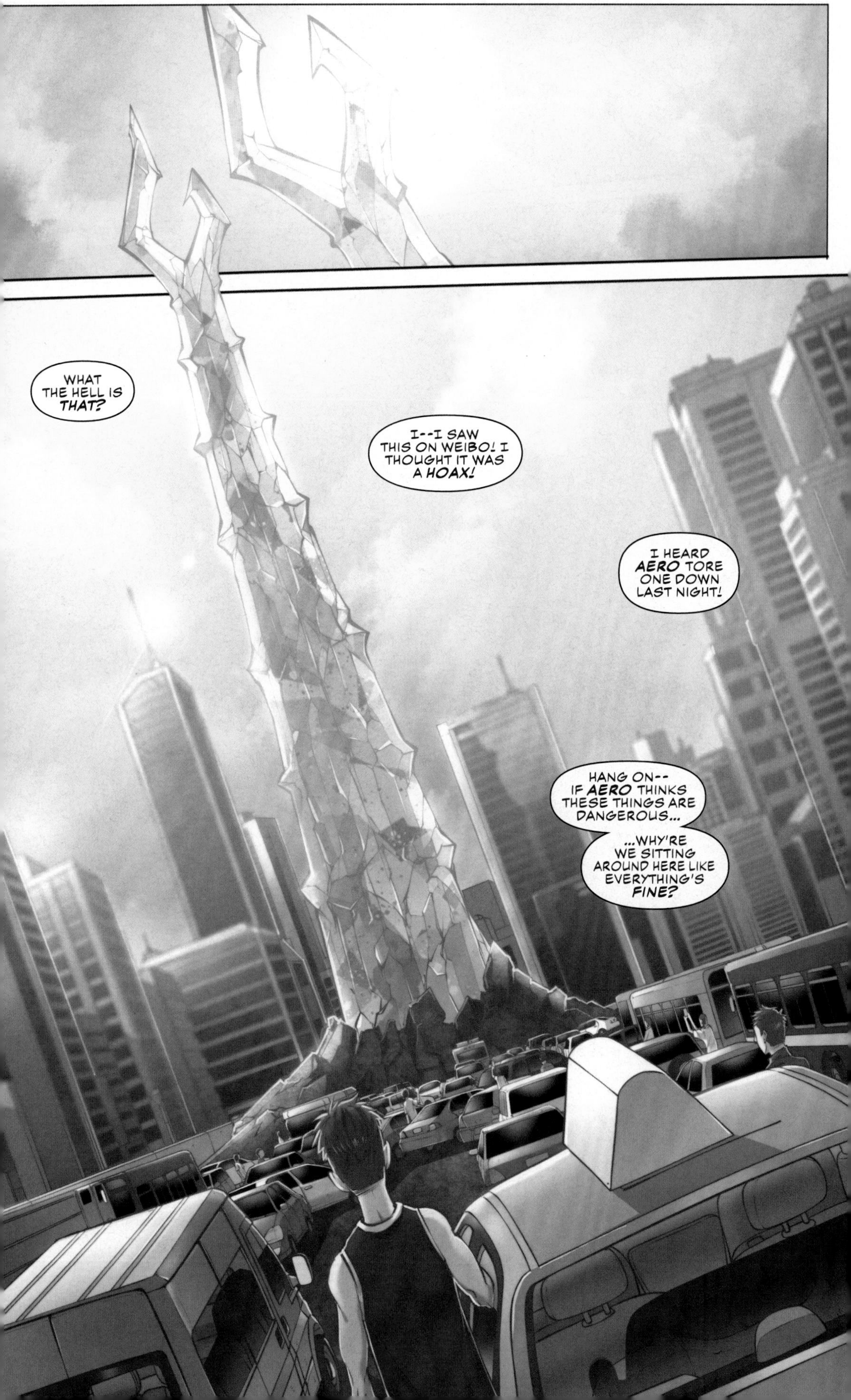
WHAT THE HELL IS THAT?
I--I SAW THIS ON WEIBO! I THOUGHT IT WAS A HOAX!
I HEARD AERO TORE ONE DOWN LAST NIGHT!
HANG ON-- IF AERO THINKS THESE THINGS ARE DANGEROUS...
...WHY'RE WE SITTING AROUND HERE LIKE EVERYTHING'S FINE?

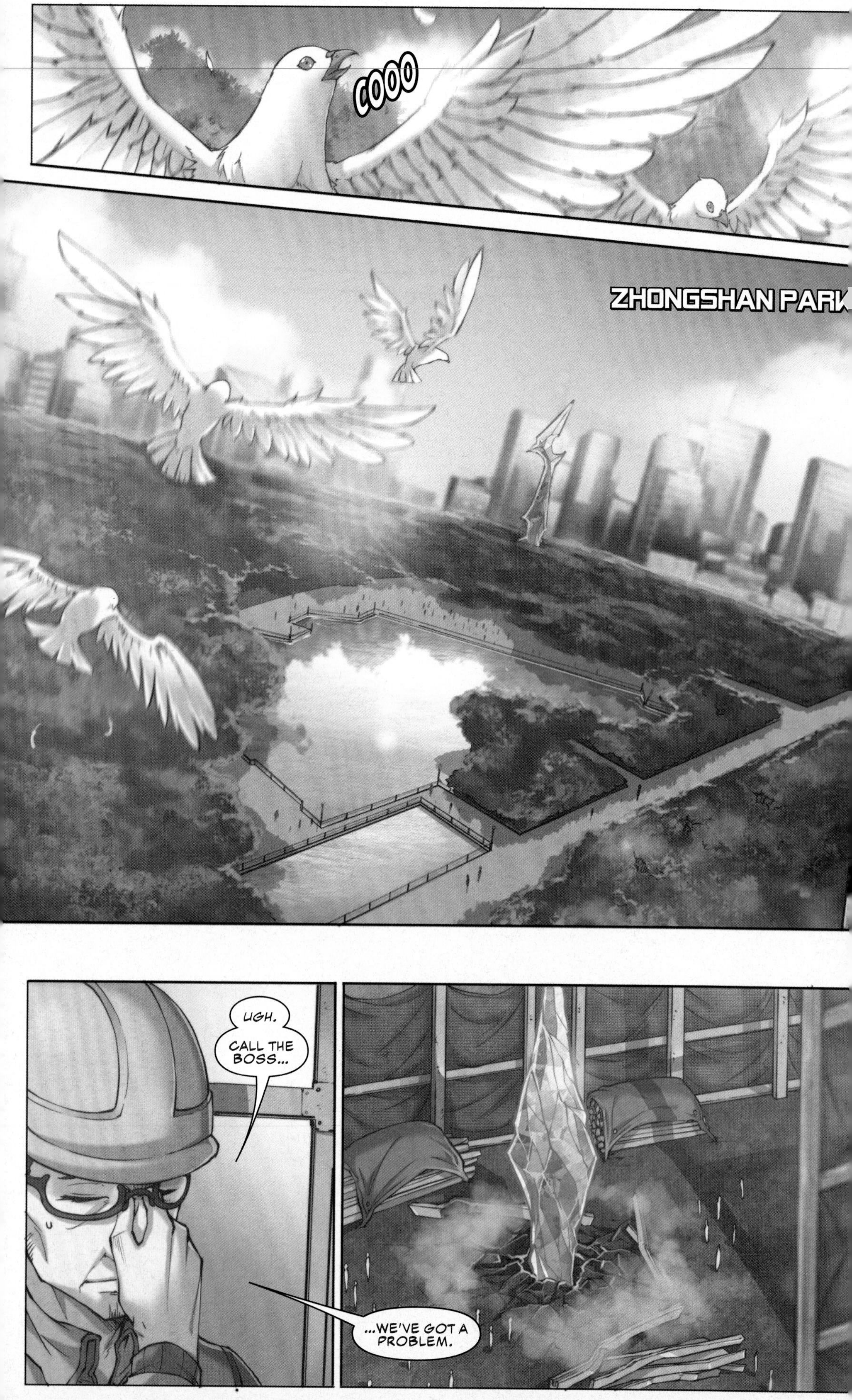
COOO
ZHONGSHAN PARK
UGH.
CALL THE BOSS...
...WE'VE GOT A PROBLEM.

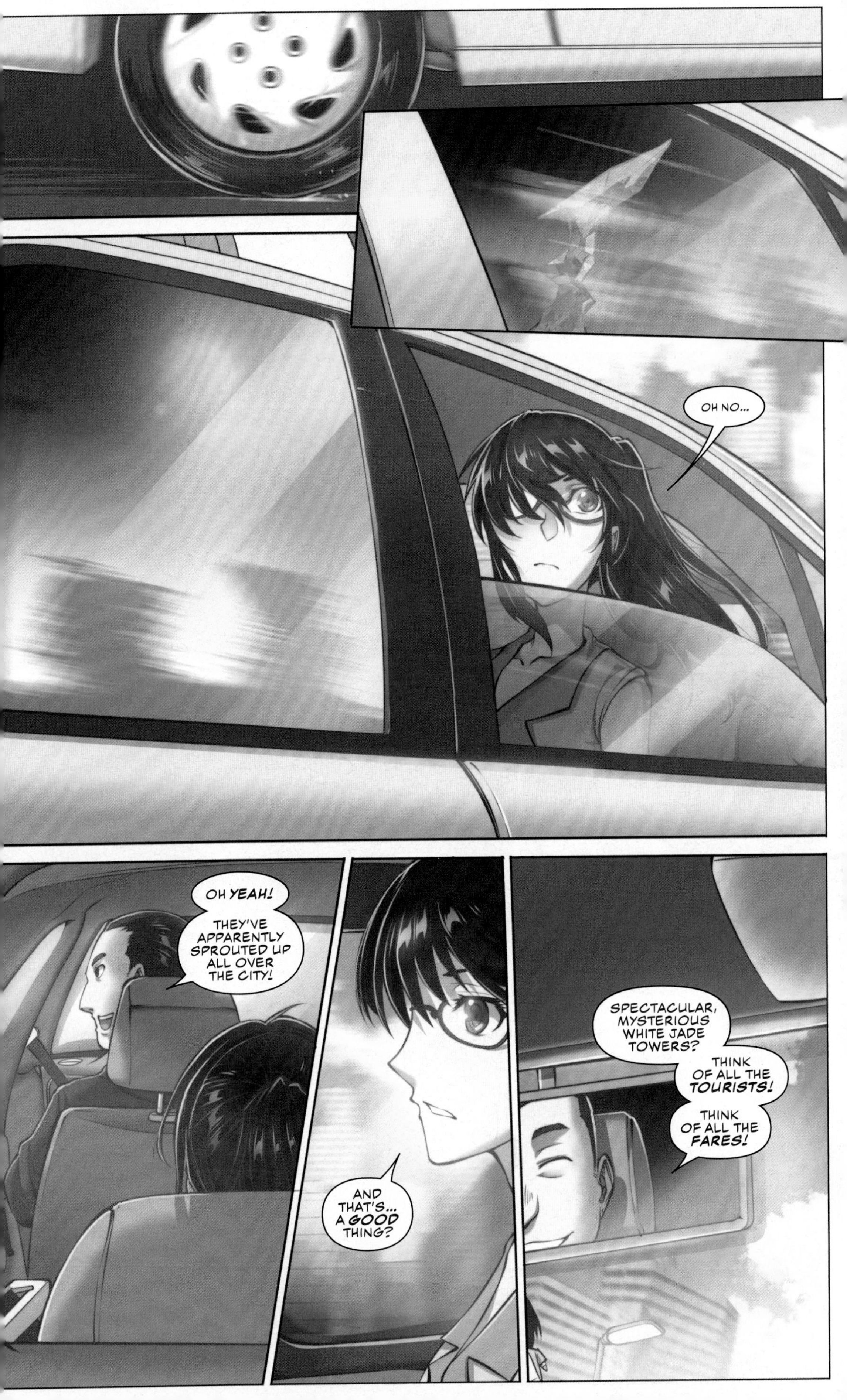
OH NO...
OH YEAH!
THEY'VE APPARENTLY SPROUTED UP ALL OVER THE CITY!
AND THAT'S... A GOOD THING?
SPECTACULAR, MYSTERIOUS WHITE JADE TOWERS?
THINK OF ALL THE TOURISTS!
THINK OF ALL THE FARES!

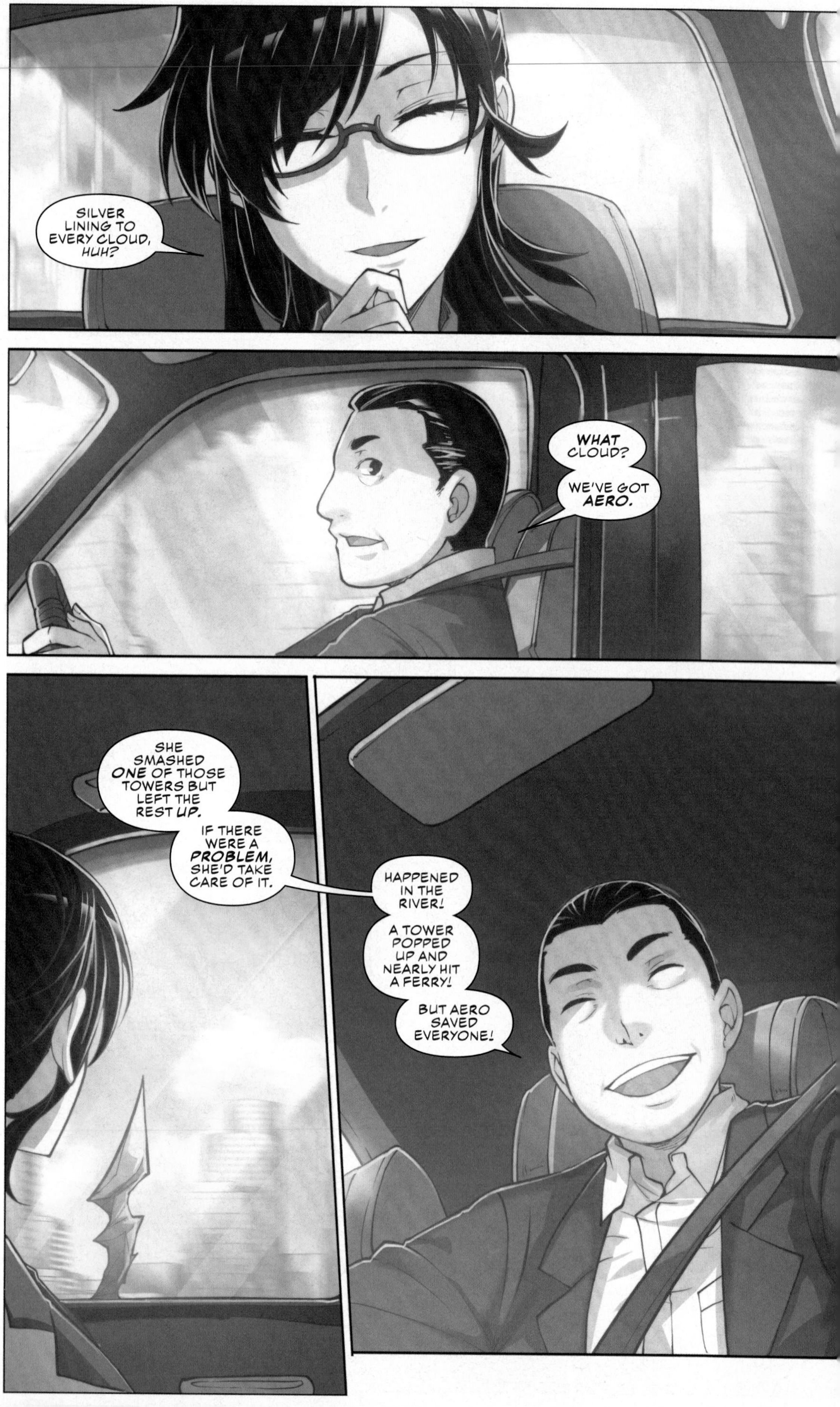
SILVER LINING TO EVERY CLOUD, HUH?
WHAT CLOUD?
WE'VE GOT AERO.
SHE SMASHED ONE OF THOSE TOWERS BUT LEFT THE REST UP.
IF THERE WERE A PROBLEM, SHE'D TAKE CARE OF IT.
HAPPENED IN THE RIVER!
A TOWER POPPED UP AND NEARLY HIT A FERRY!
BUT AERO SAVED EVERYONE!

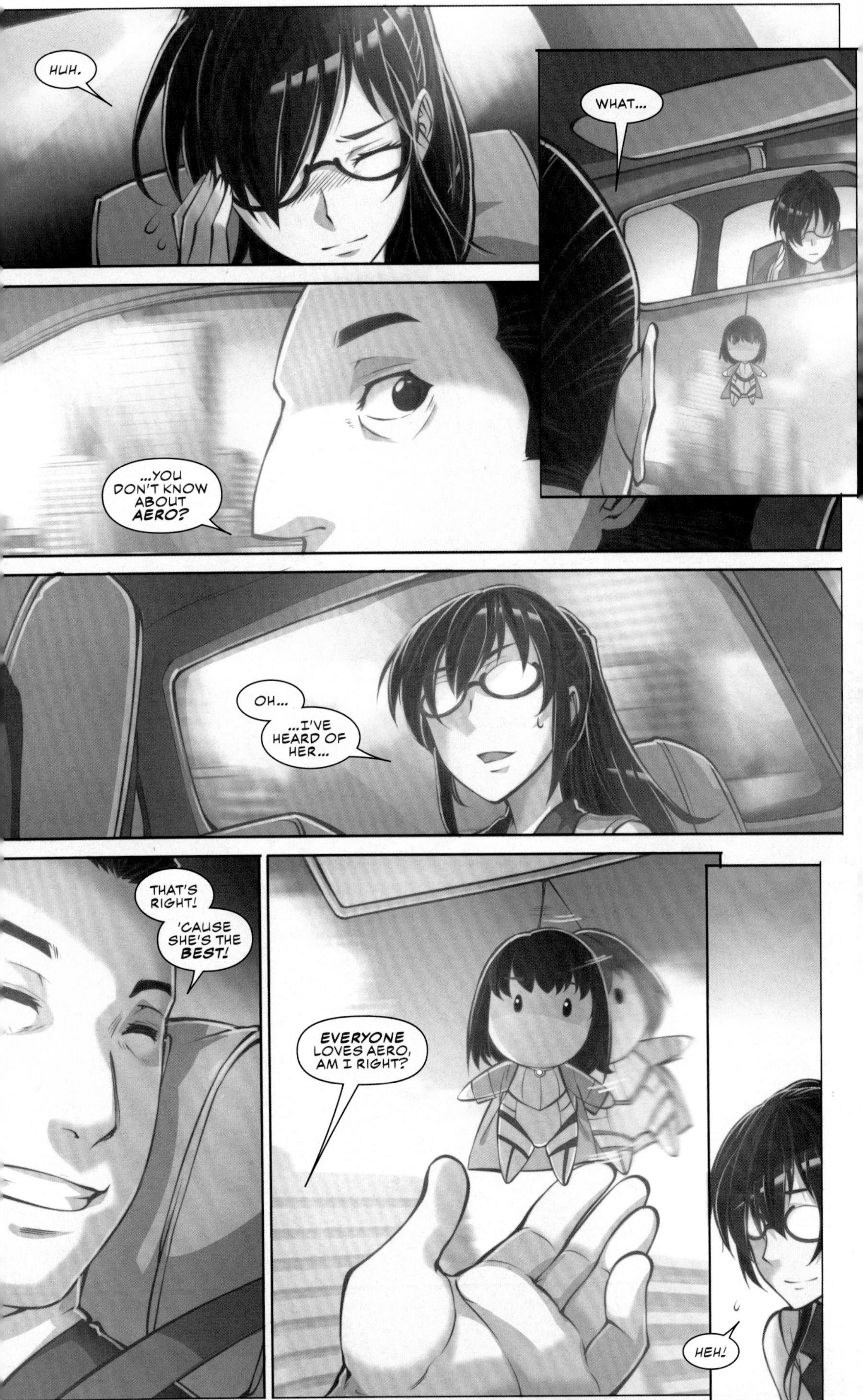
HUH.
WHAT...
...YOU DON'T KNOW ABOUT AERO?
OH...
...I'VE HEARD OF HER...
THAT'S RIGHT!
'CAUSE SHE'S THE BEST!
EVERYONE LOVES AERO, AM I RIGHT?
HEH!

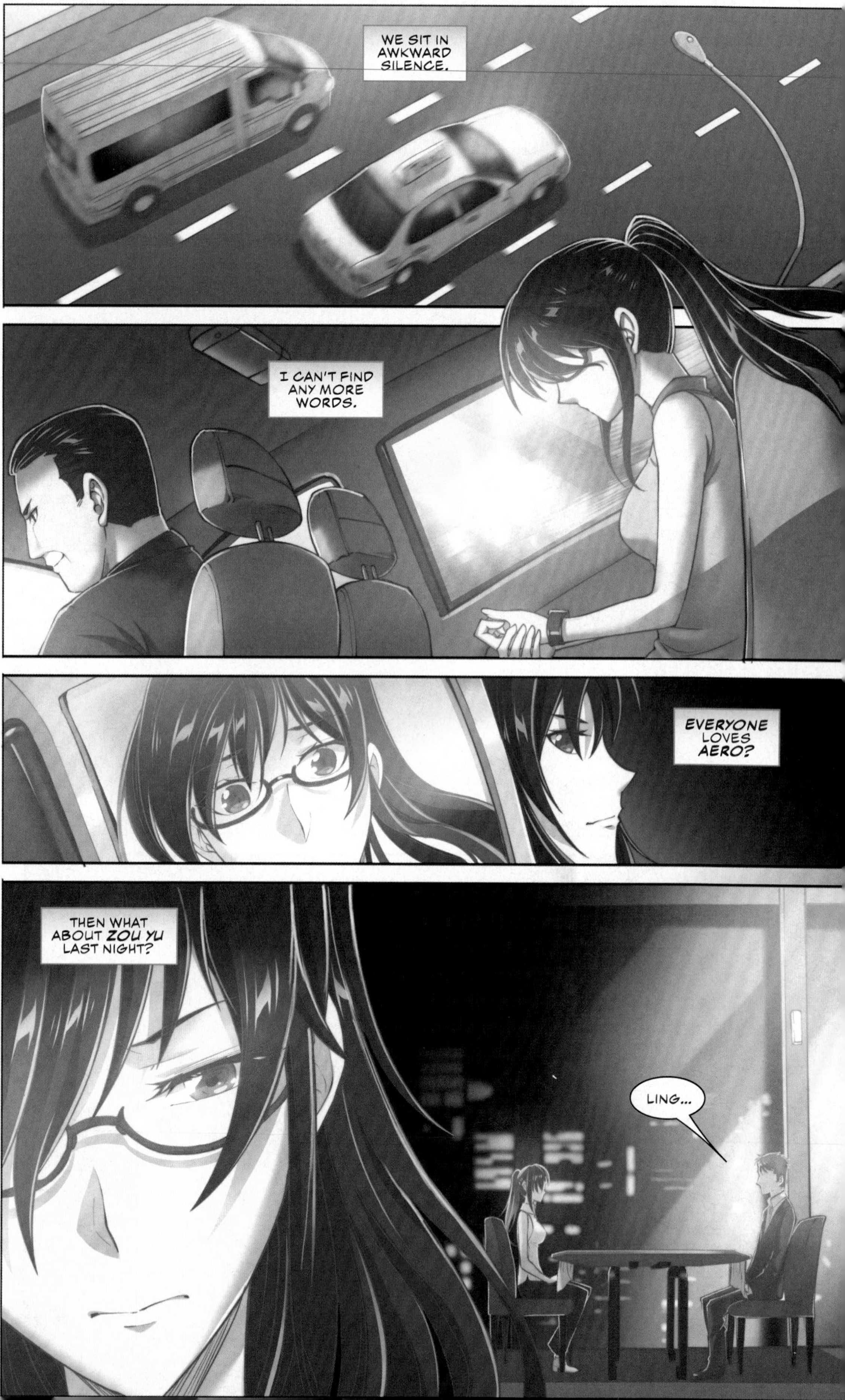
WE SIT IN AWKWARD SILENCE.
I CAN'T FIND ANY MORE WORDS.
EVERYONE LOVES AERO?
THEN WHAT ABOUT ZOU YU LAST NIGHT?
LING...

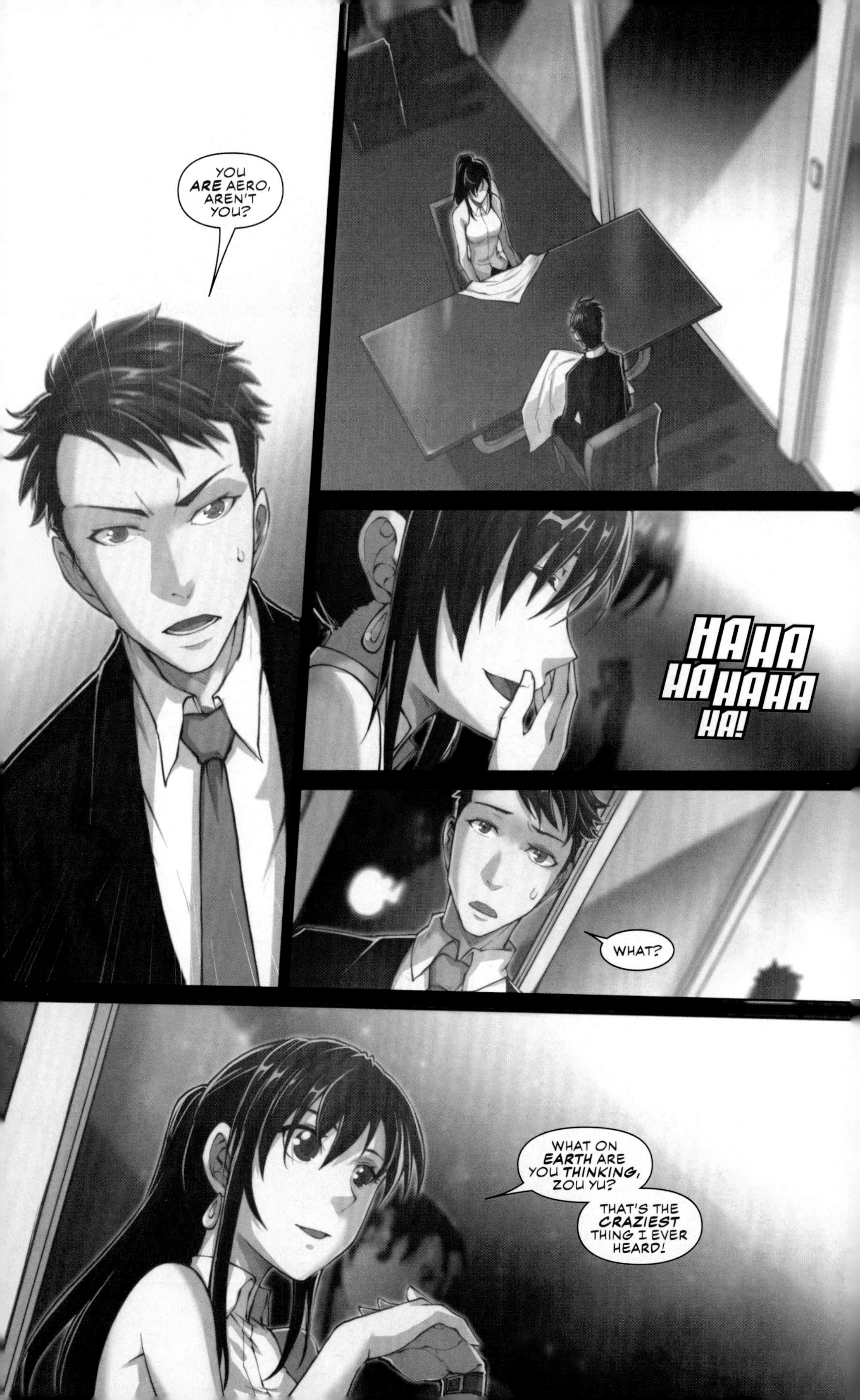
YOU ARE AERO, AREN'T YOU?
HA HA HA HA HA HA HA!
WHAT?
WHAT ON EARTH ARE YOU THINKING, ZOU YU?
THAT'S THE CRAZIEST THING I EVER HEARD!

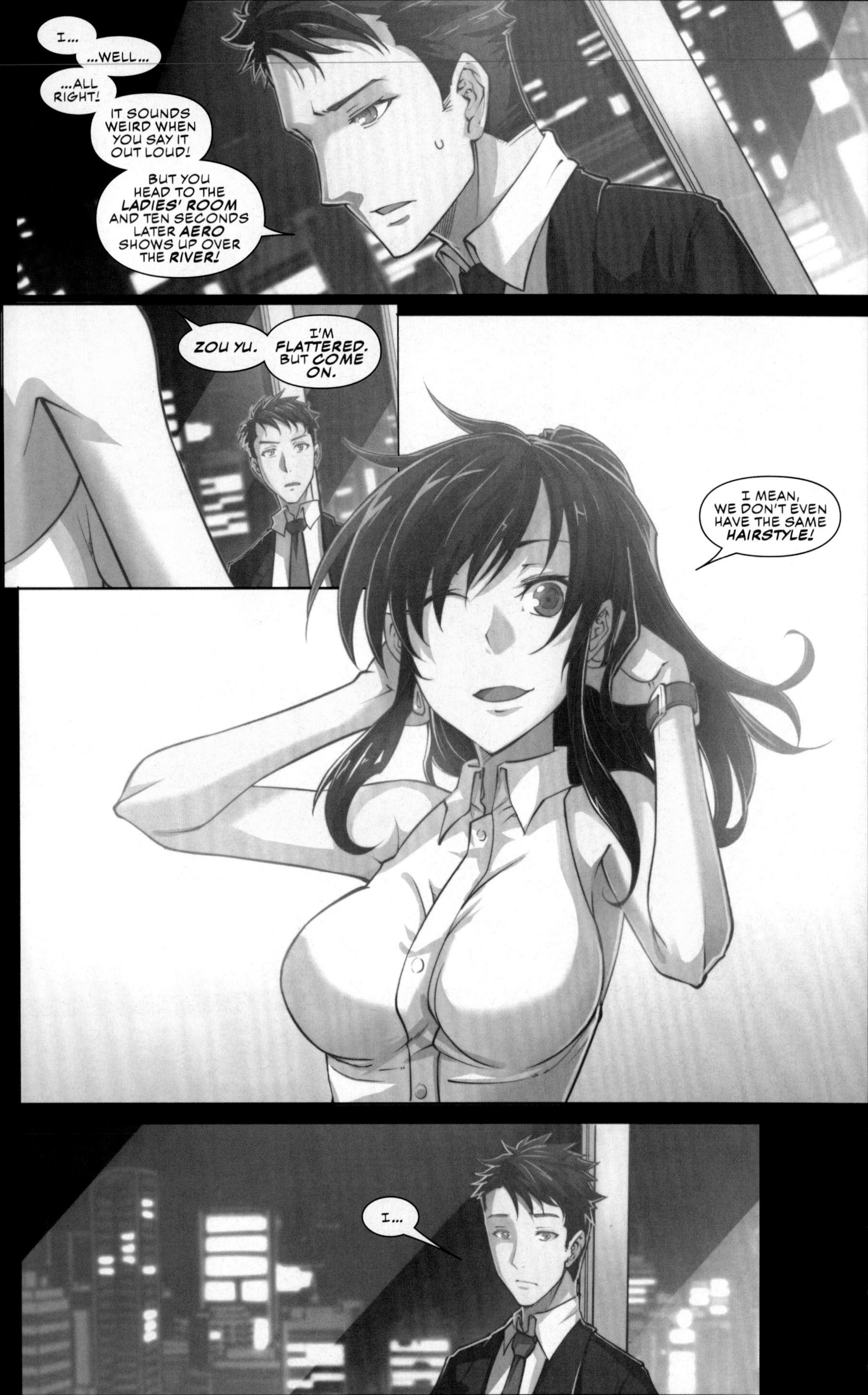
I...
...WELL...
...ALL RIGHT!
IT SOUNDS WEIRD WHEN YOU SAY IT OUT LOUD!
BUT YOU HEAD TO THE LADIES' ROOM AND TEN SECONDS LATER AERO SHOWS UP OVER THE RIVER!
ZOU YU.
I'M FLATTERED. BUT COME ON.
I MEAN, WE DON'T EVEN HAVE THE SAME HAIRSTYLE!
I...

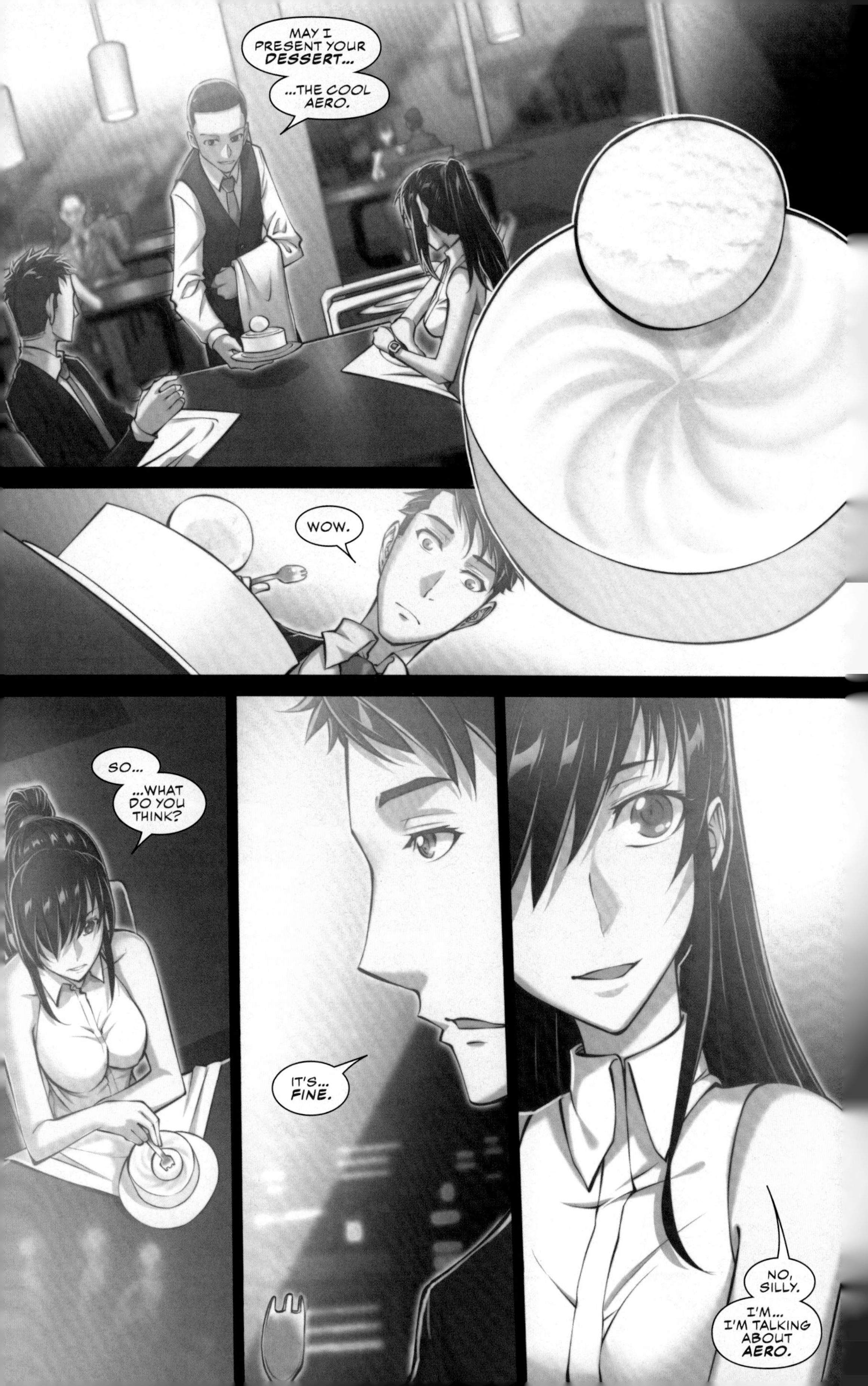
MAY I PRESENT YOUR DESSERT...
...THE COOL AERO.
WOW.
SO...
...WHAT DO YOU THINK?
IT'S... FINE.
NO, SILLY.
I'M... I'M TALKING ABOUT AERO.

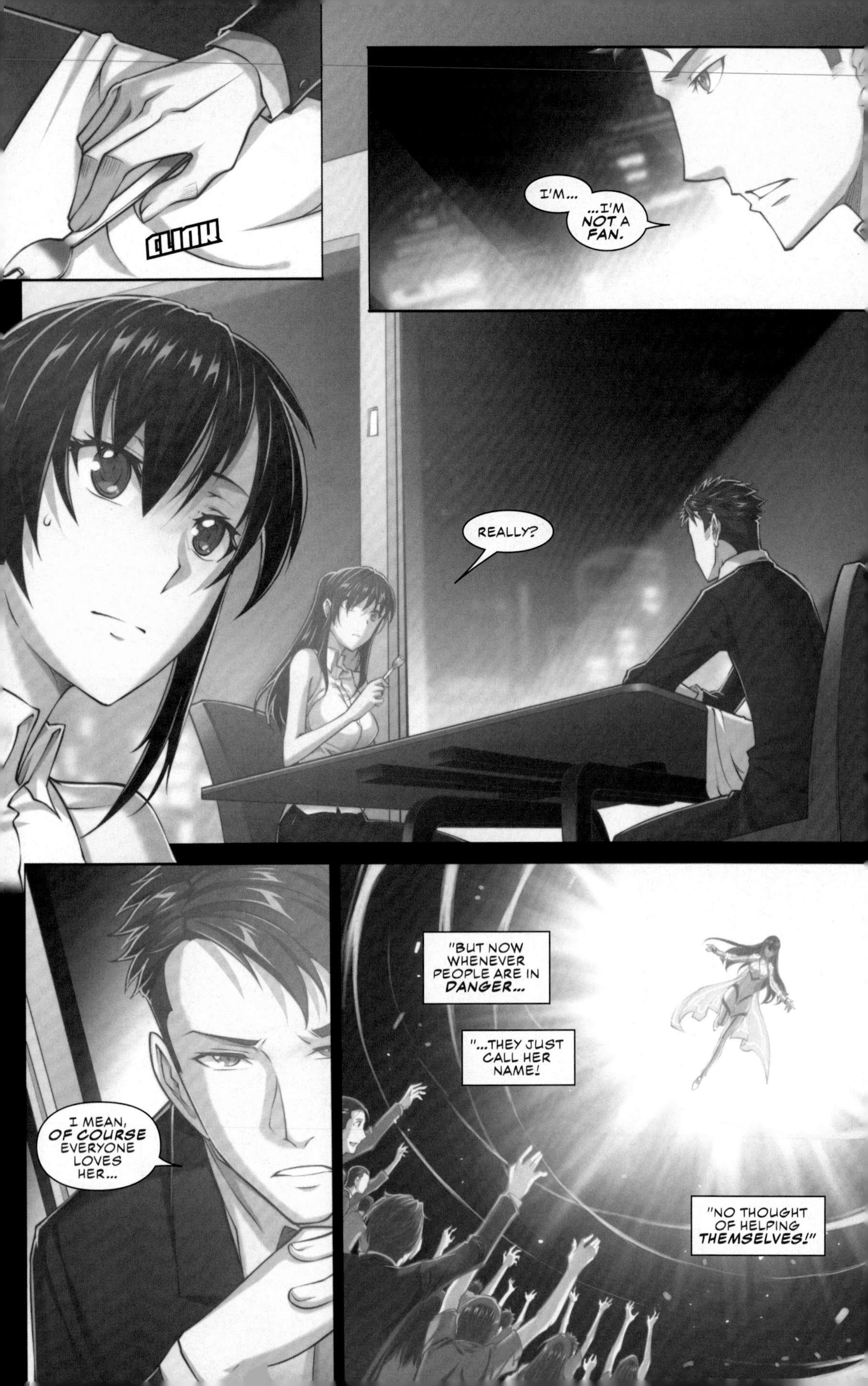
CLINK
I'M...
...I'M NOT A FAN.
REALLY?
I MEAN, OF COURSE EVERYONE LOVES HER...
"BUT NOW WHENEVER PEOPLE ARE IN DANGER...
"...THEY JUST CALL HER NAME!
"NO THOUGHT OF HELPING THEMSELVES!"

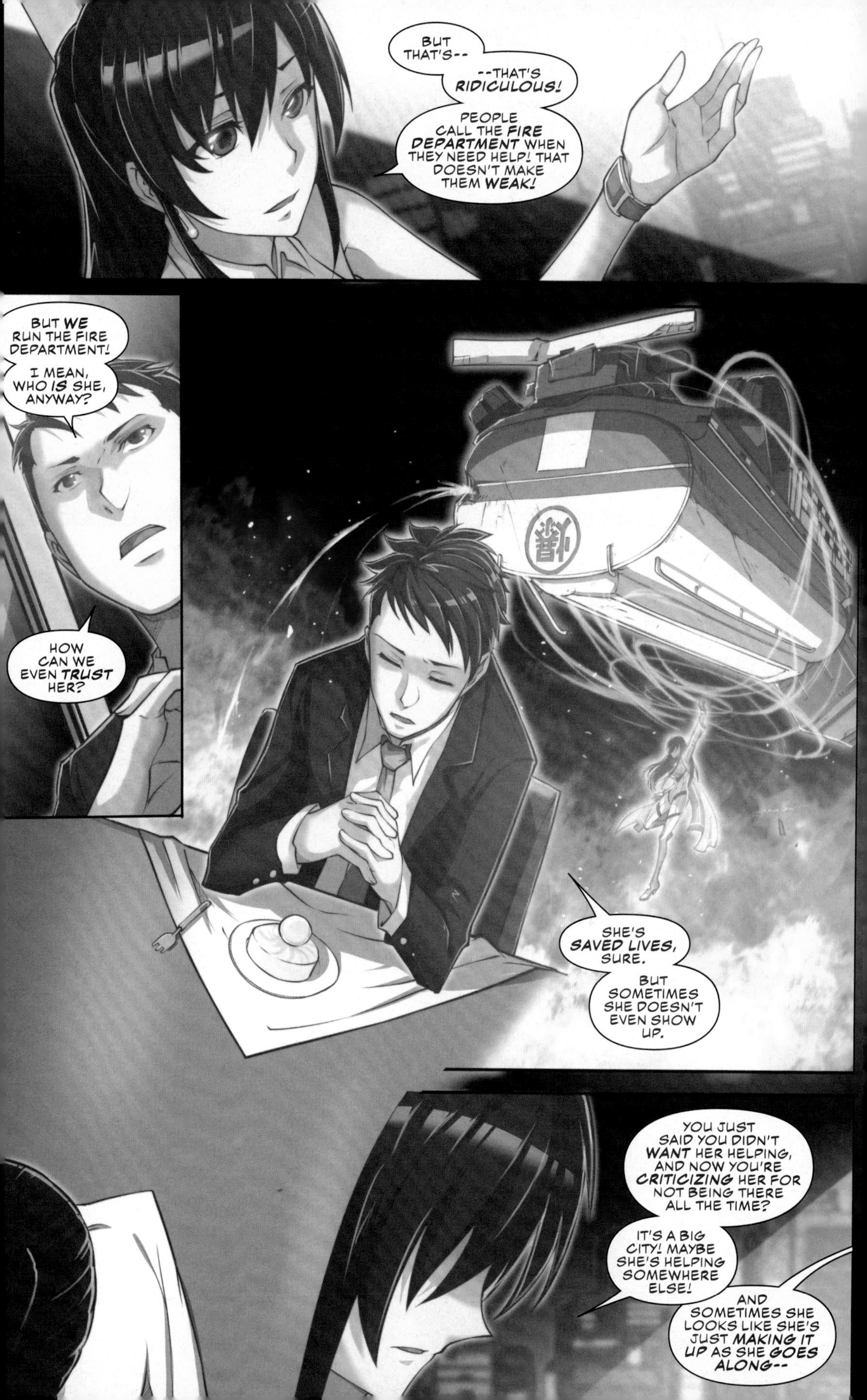
BUT THAT'S--
--THAT'S RIDICULOUS!
PEOPLE CALL THE FIRE DEPARTMENT WHEN THEY NEED HELP! THAT DOESN'T MAKE THEM WEAK!
BUT WE RUN THE FIRE DEPARTMENT!
I MEAN, WHO IS SHE, ANYWAY?
HOW CAN WE EVEN TRUST HER?
SHE'S SAVED LIVES, SURE.
BUT SOMETIMES SHE DOESN'T EVEN SHOW UP.
YOU JUST SAID YOU DIDN'T WANT HER HELPING, AND NOW YOU'RE CRITICIZING HER FOR NOT BEING THERE ALL THE TIME?
IT'S A BIG CITY! MAYBE SHE'S HELPING SOMEWHERE ELSE!
AND SOMETIMES SHE LOOKS LIKE SHE'S JUST MAKING IT UP AS SHE GOES ALONG--

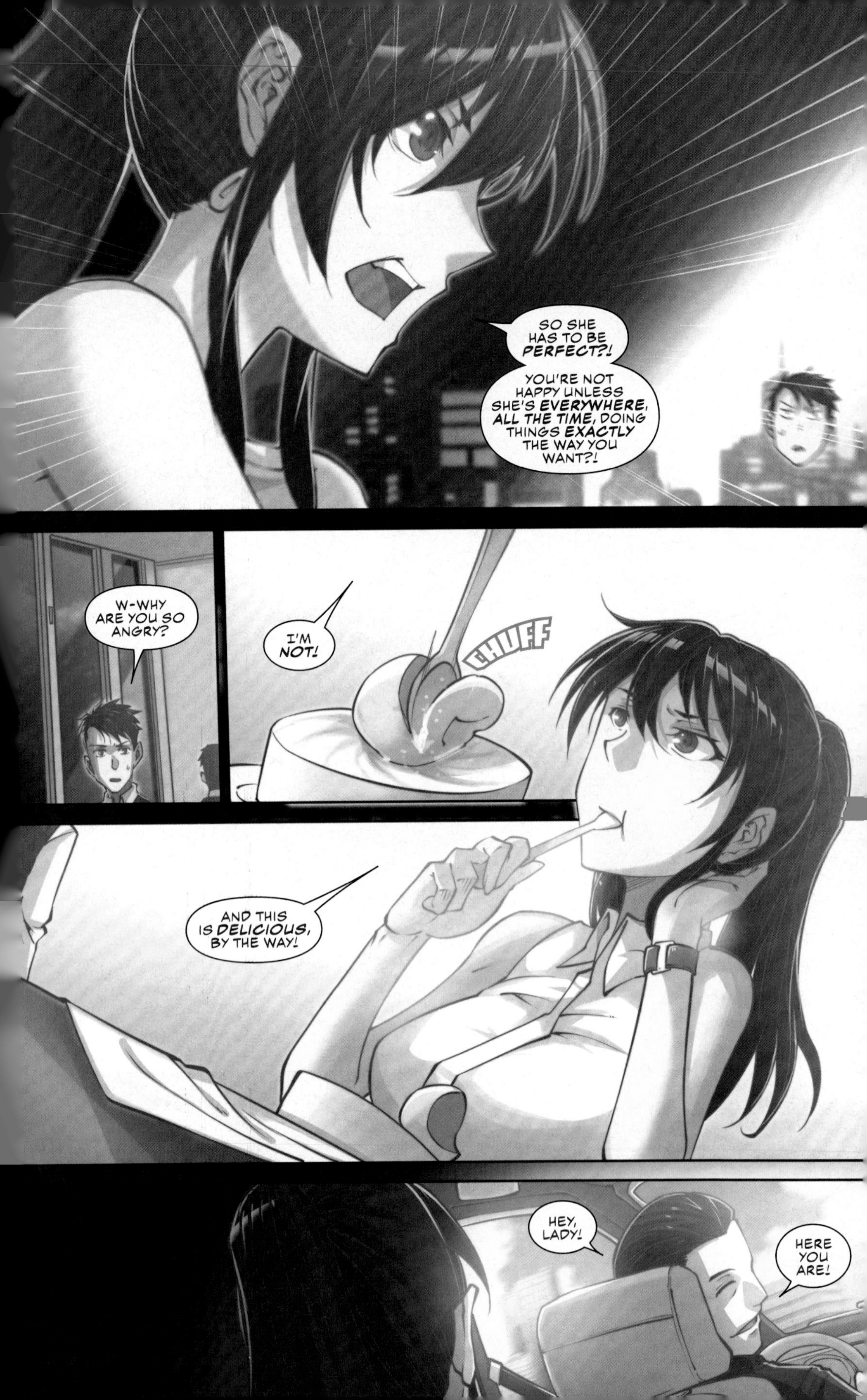
SO SHE HAS TO BE PERFECT?!
YOU'RE NOT HAPPY UNLESS SHE'S EVERYWHERE, ALL THE TIME, DOING THINGS EXACTLY THE WAY YOU WANT?!
W-WHY ARE YOU SO ANGRY?
I'M NOT!
CHUFF
AND THIS IS DELICIOUS, BY THE WAY!
HEY, LADY!
HERE YOU ARE!

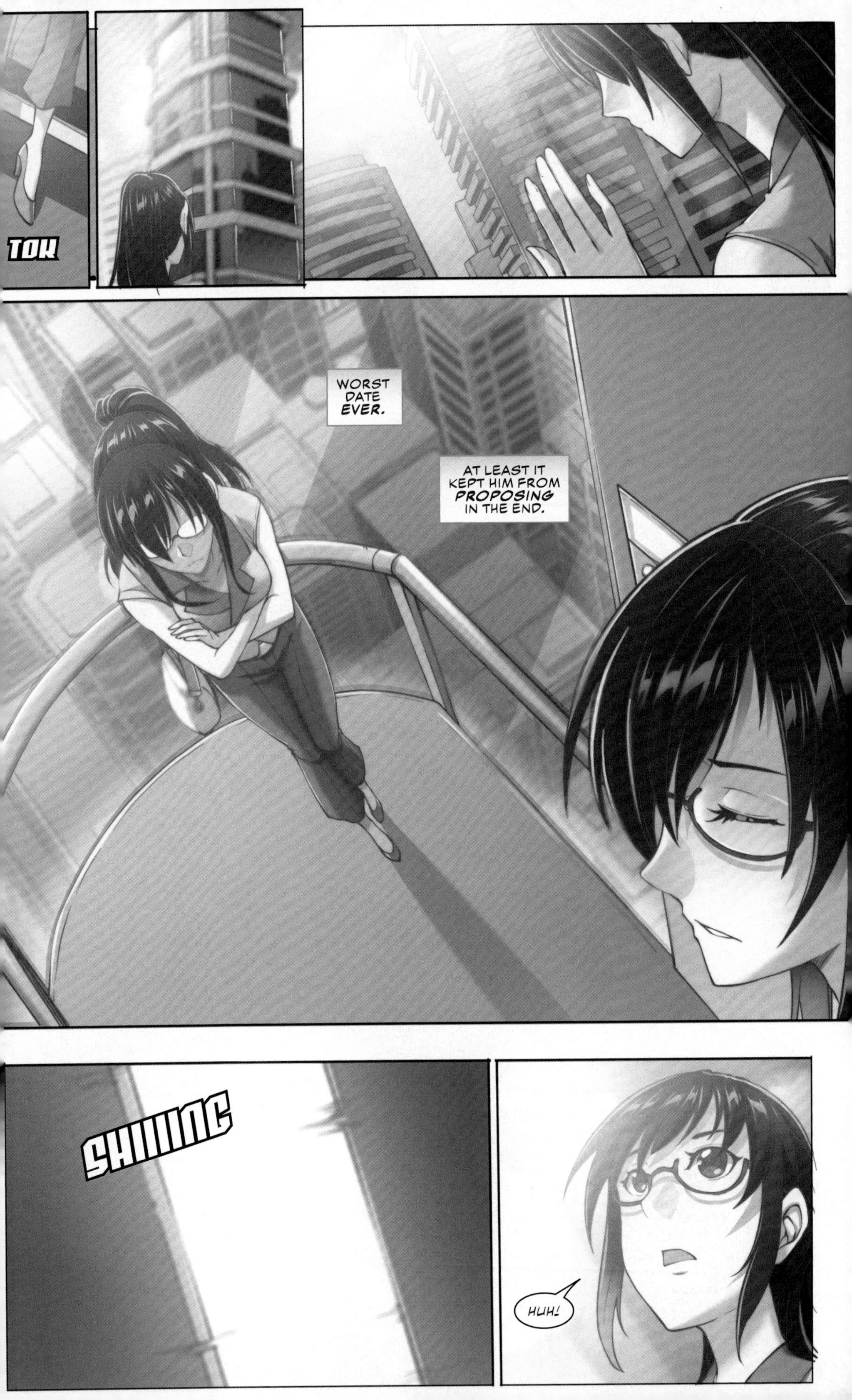
TOK
WORST DATE EVER.
AT LEAST IT KEPT HIM FROM PROPOSING IN THE END.
SHIIIING
HUH!

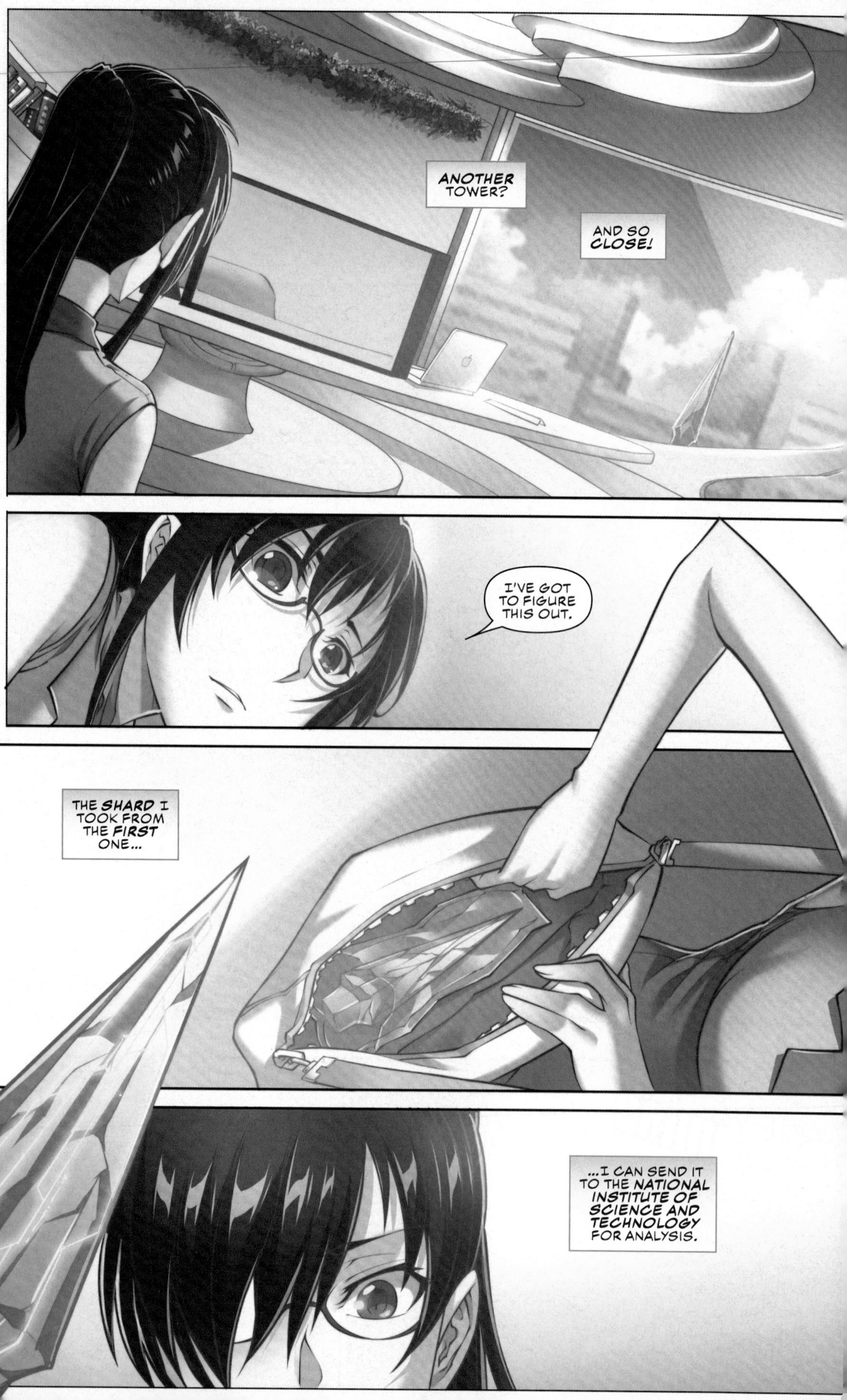
ANOTHER TOWER?
AND SO CLOSE!
I'VE GOT TO FIGURE THIS OUT.
THE SHARD I TOOK FROM THE FIRST ONE...
...I CAN SEND IT TO THE NATIONAL INSTITUTE OF SCIENCE AND TECHNOLOGY FOR ANALYSIS.

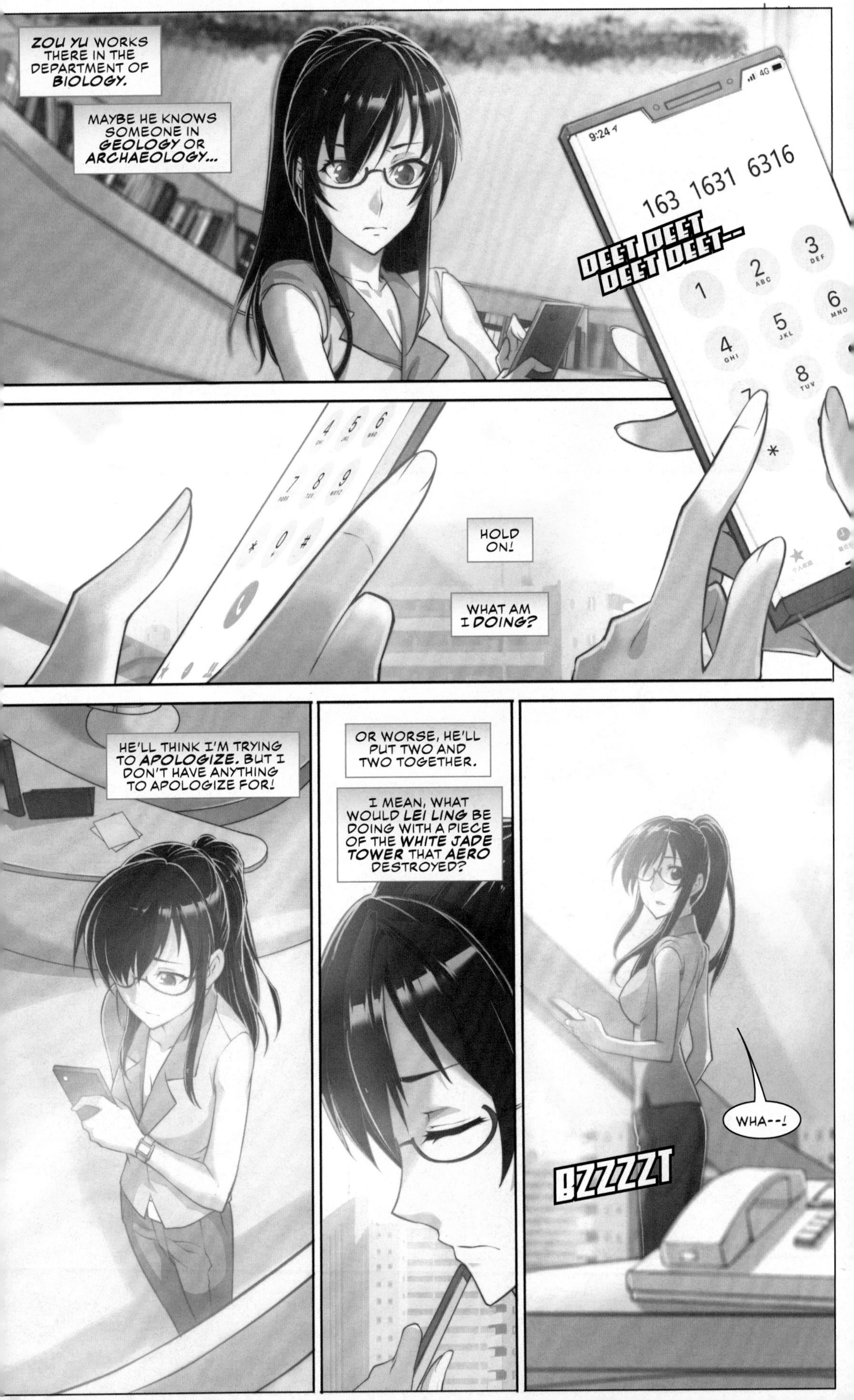
ZOU YU WORKS THERE IN THE DEPARTMENT OF BIOLOGY.
MAYBE HE KNOWS SOMEONE IN GEOLOGY OR ARCHAEOLOGY...
163 1631 6316
DEET DEET DEET DEET--
HOLD ON!
WHAT AM I DOING?
HE'LL THINK I'M TRYING TO APOLOGIZE. BUT I DON'T HAVE ANYTHING TO APOLOGIZE FOR!
OR WORSE, HE'LL PUT TWO AND TWO TOGETHER.
I MEAN, WHAT WOULD LEI LING BE DOING WITH A PIECE OF THE WHITE JADE TOWER THAT AERO DESTROYED?
BZZZZT
WHA--!

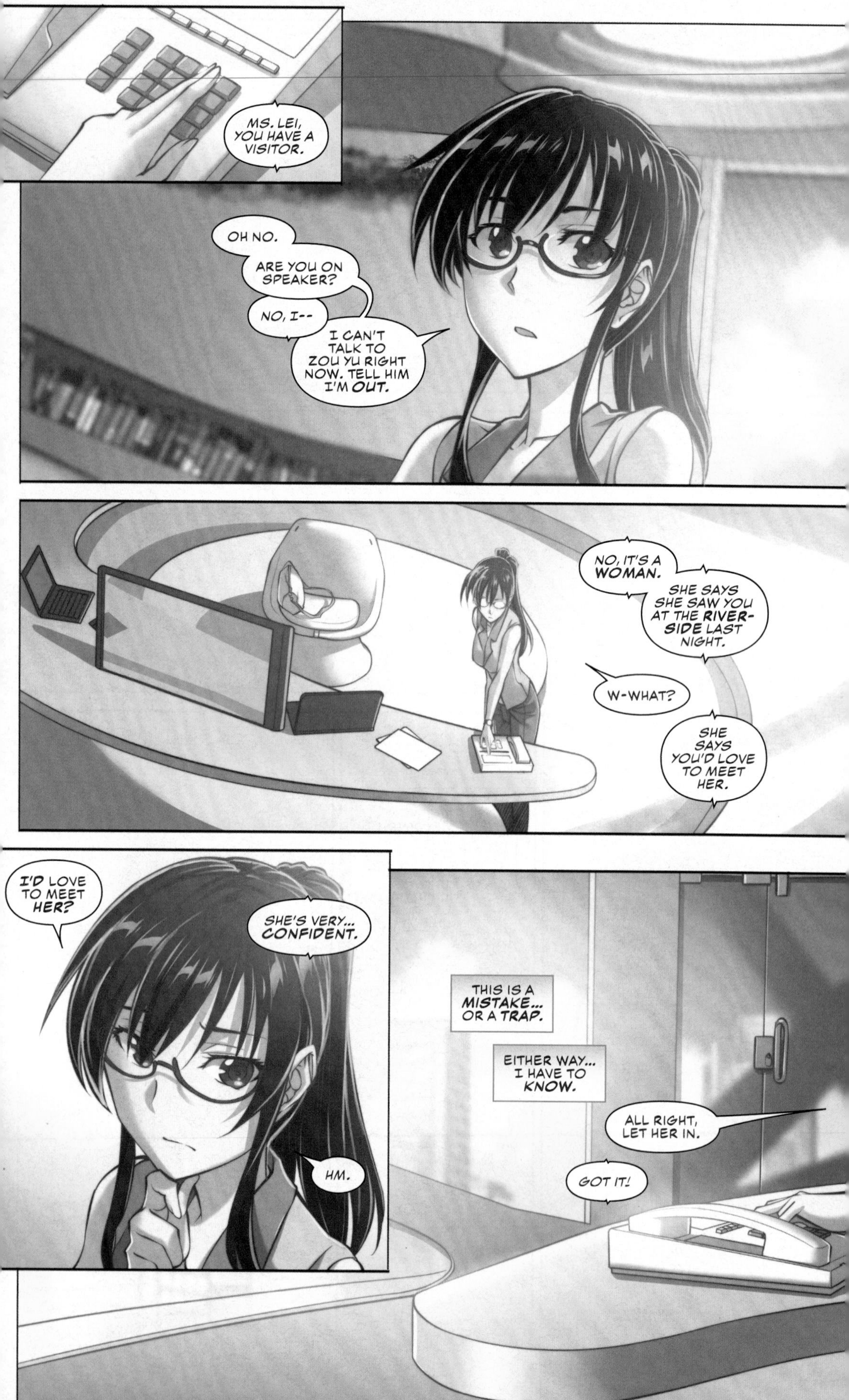
MS. LEI, YOU HAVE A VISITOR.
OH NO.
ARE YOU ON SPEAKER?
NO, I--
I CAN'T TALK TO ZOU YU RIGHT NOW. TELL HIM I'M OUT.
NO, IT'S A WOMAN.
SHE SAYS SHE SAW YOU AT THE RIVERSIDE LAST NIGHT.
W-WHAT?
SHE SAYS YOU'D LOVE TO MEET HER.
I'D LOVE TO MEET HER?
SHE'S VERY... CONFIDENT.
HM.
THIS IS A MISTAKE... OR A TRAP.
EITHER WAY... I HAVE TO KNOW.
ALL RIGHT, LET HER IN.
GOT IT!

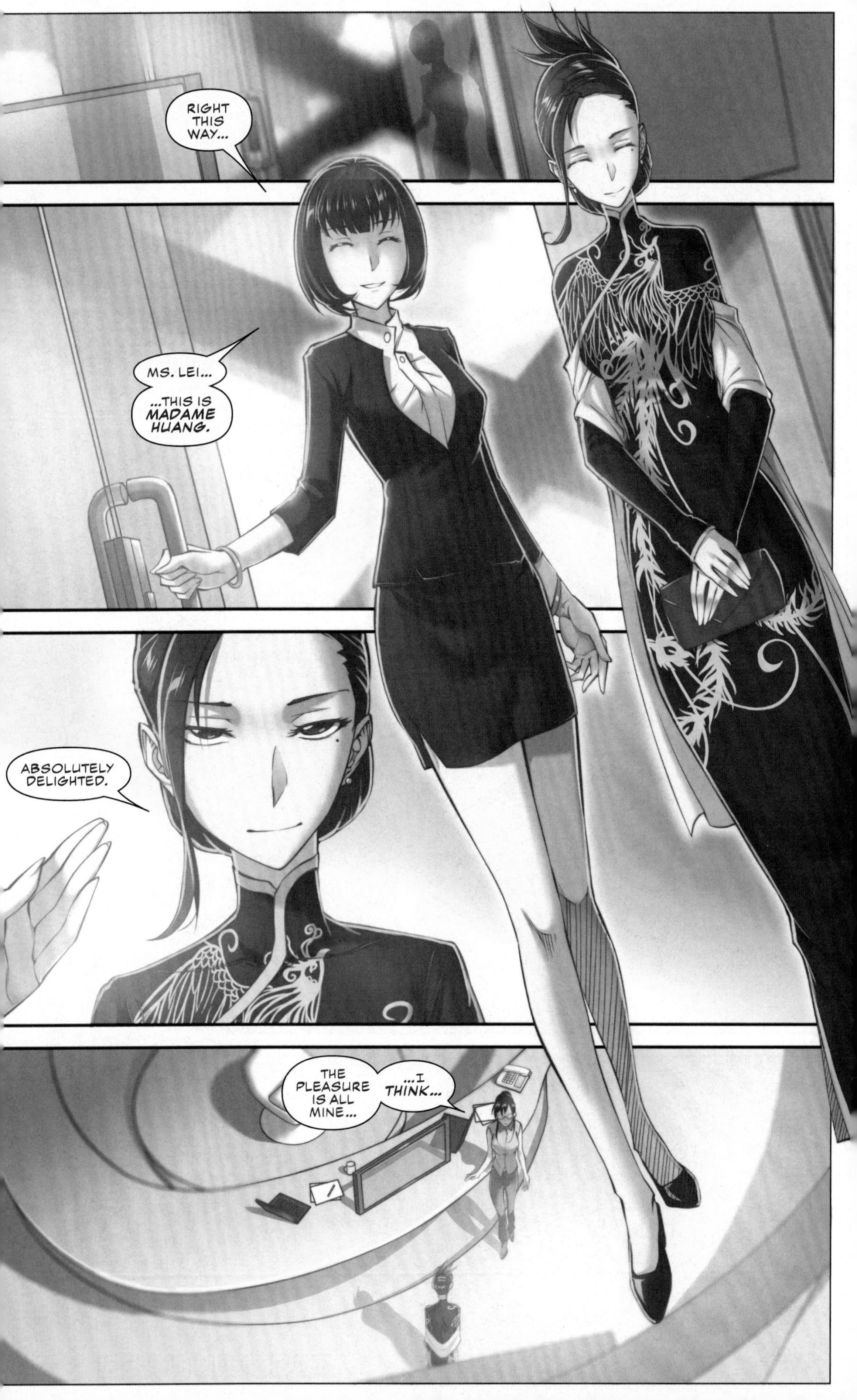
RIGHT THIS WAY...
MS. LEI...
...THIS IS MADAME HUANG.
ABSOLUTELY DELIGHTED.
THE PLEASURE IS ALL MINE...
...I THINK...

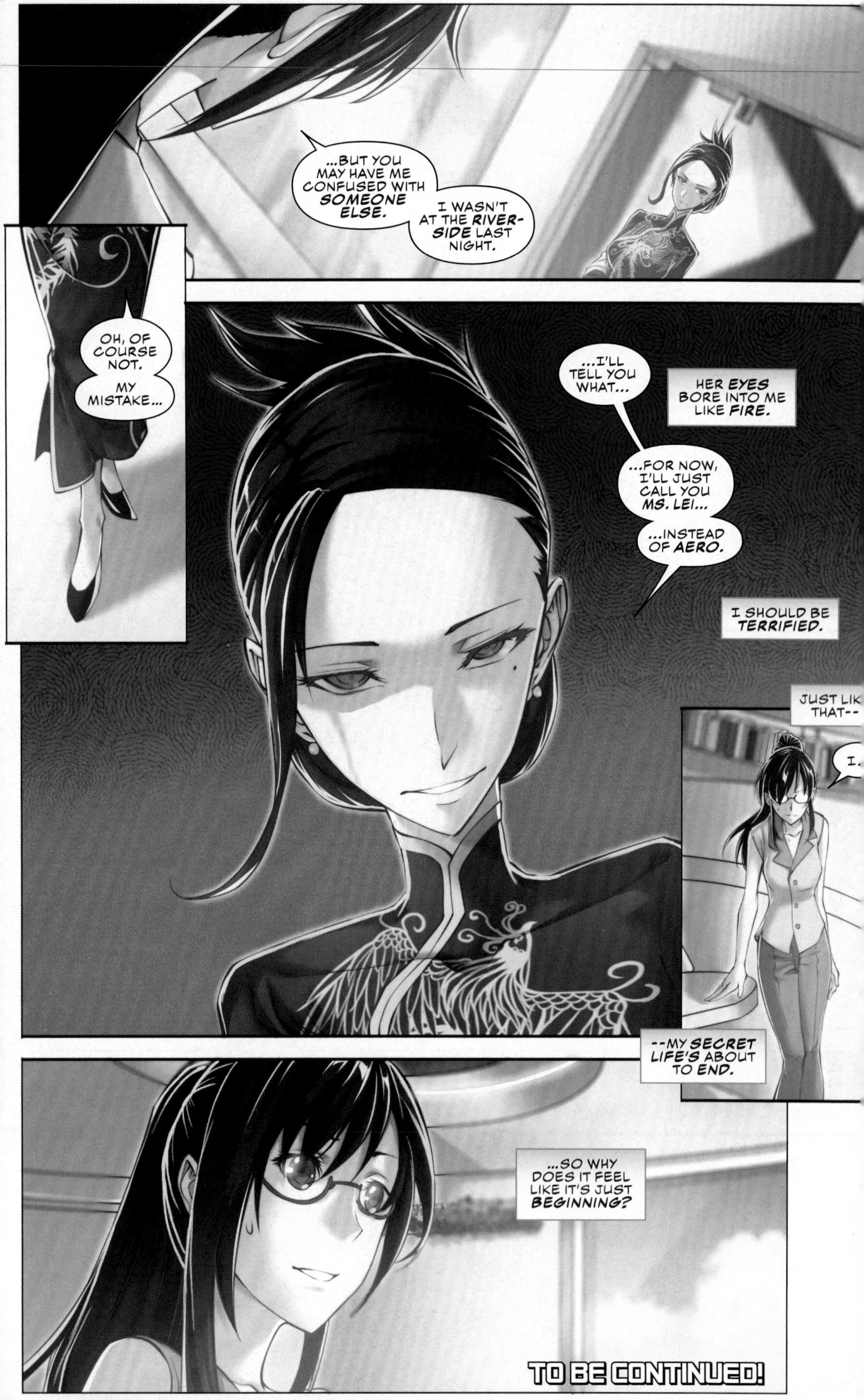
...BUT YOU MAY HAVE ME CONFUSED WITH SOMEONE ELSE.
I WASN'T AT THE RIVER-SIDE LAST NIGHT.
OH, OF COURSE NOT.
MY MISTAKE...
...I'LL TELL YOU WHAT...
HER EYES BORE INTO ME LIKE FIRE.
...FOR NOW, I'LL JUST CALL YOU MS. LEI...
...INSTEAD OF AERO.
I SHOULD BE TERRIFIED.
JUST LIK THAT--
I.
--MY SECRET LIFE'S ABOUT TO END.
...SO WHY DOES IT FEEL LIKE IT'S JUST BEGINNING?
TO BE CONTINUED!

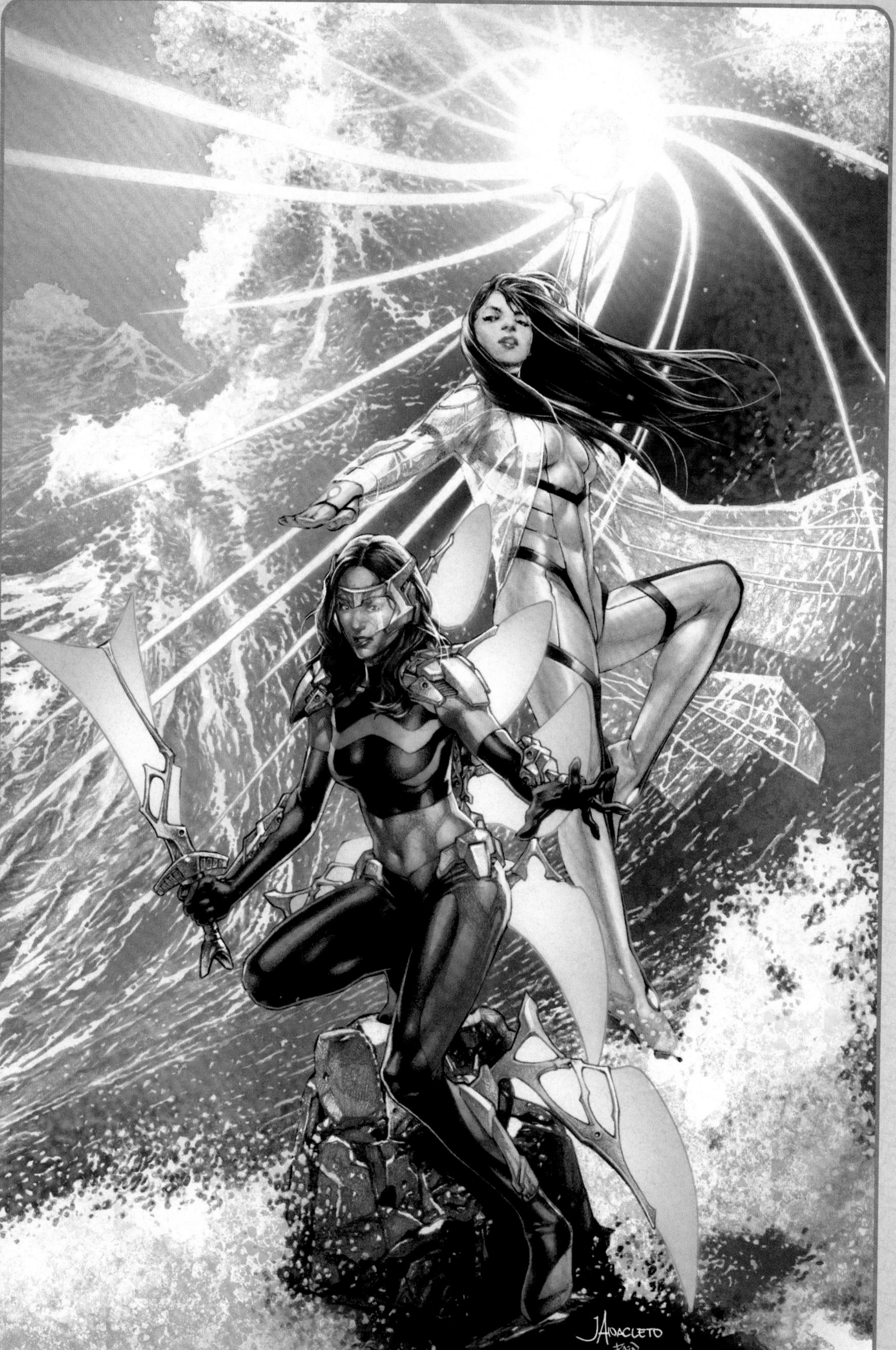

Jay Anacleto & **Rain Beredo**

1 variant

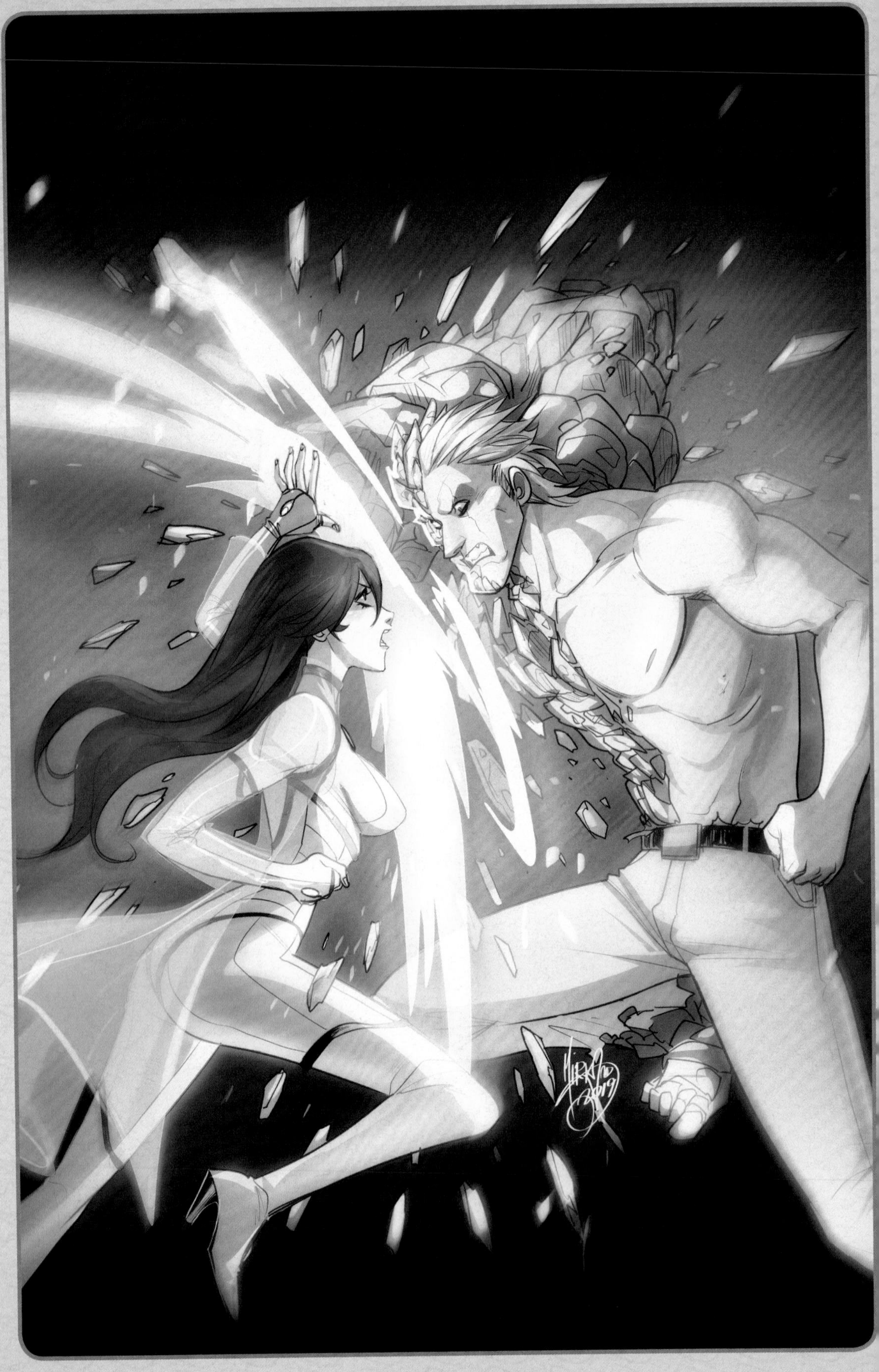

Mirka Andolfo

1 variant

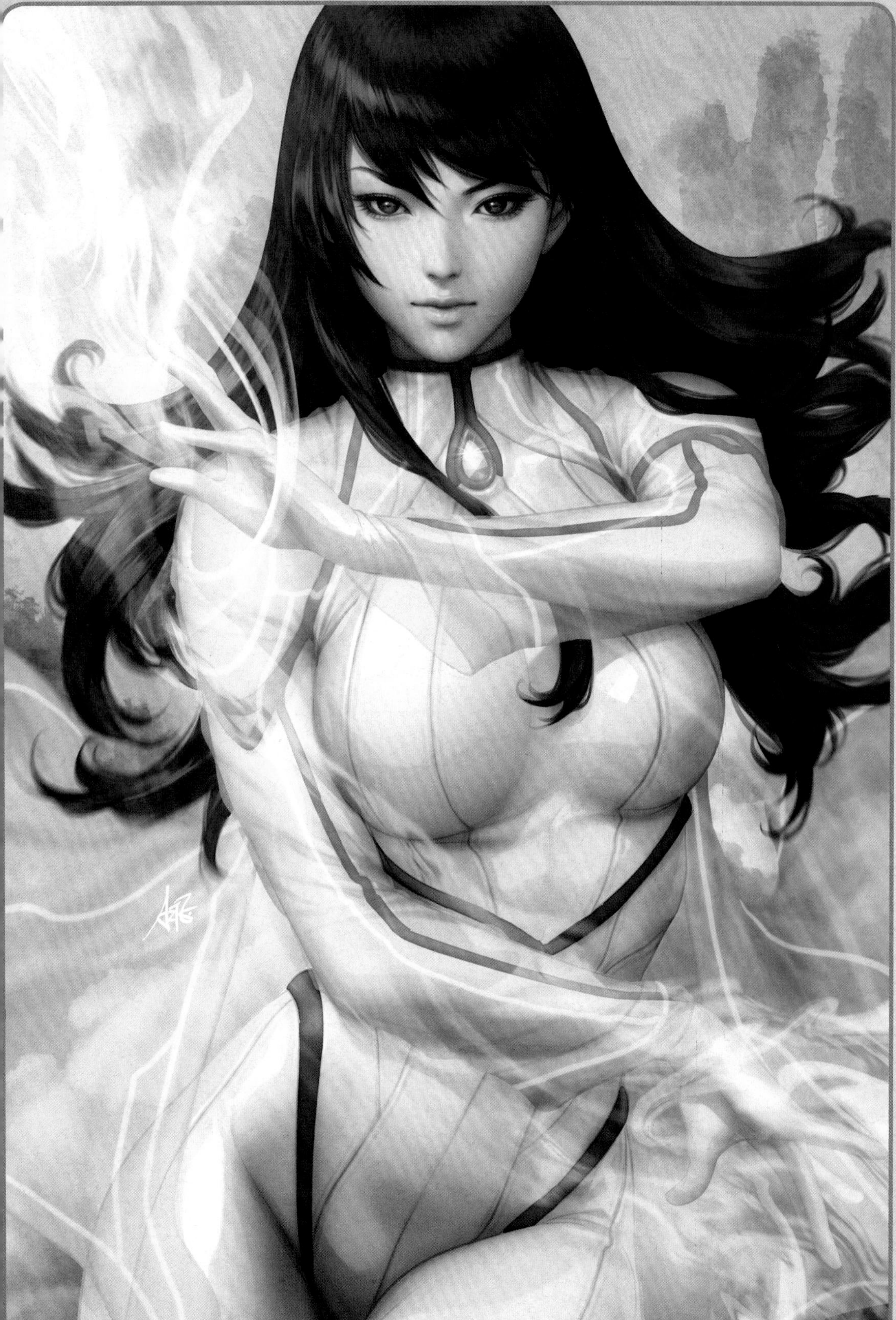

Stanley "Artgerm" Lau

1 variant

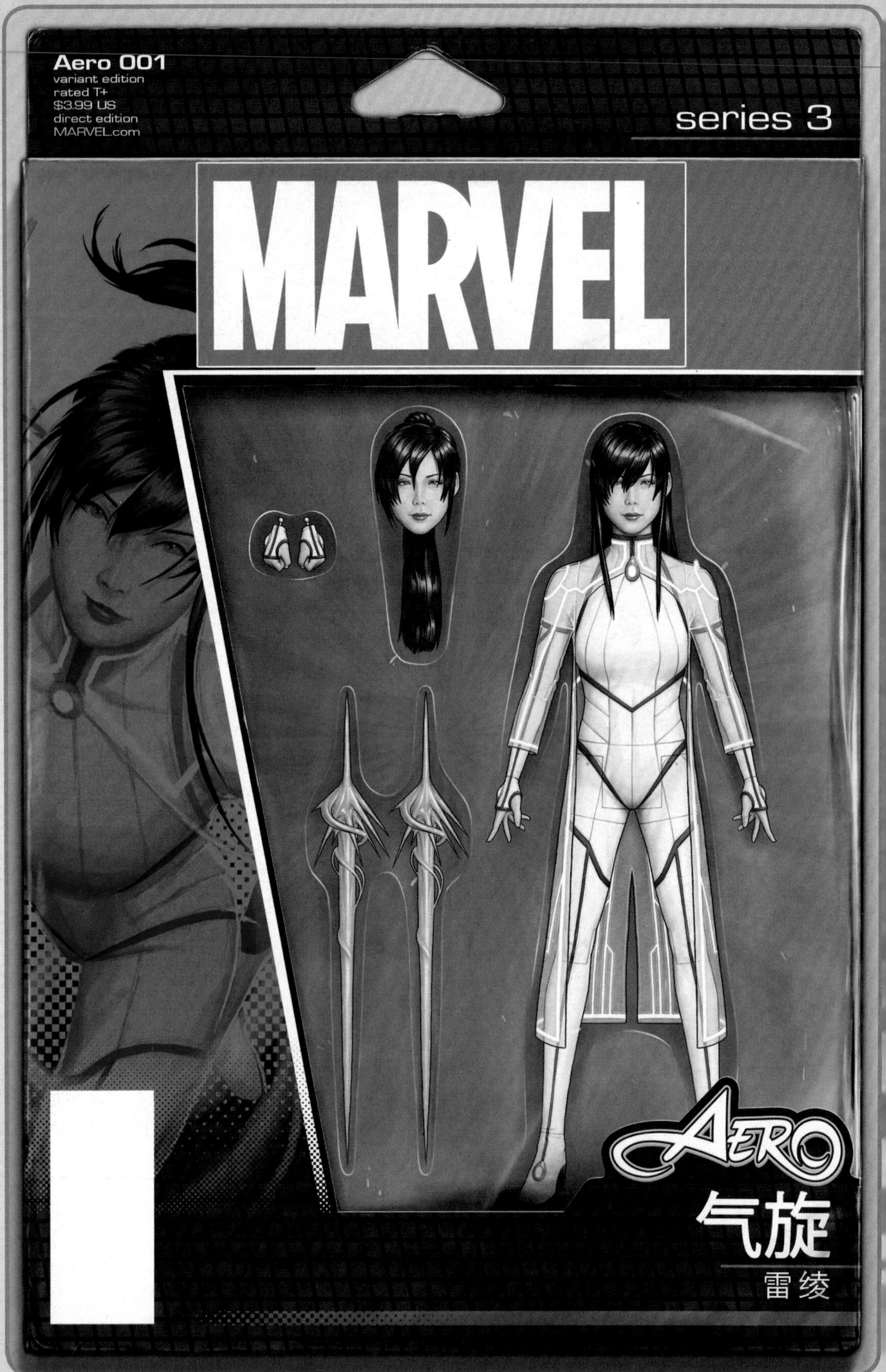
Aero 001
variant edition
rated T+
$3.99 US
direct edition
MARVEL.com
series 3
MARVEL
AERO
气旋
雷绫

John Tyler Christopher
1 action figure variant

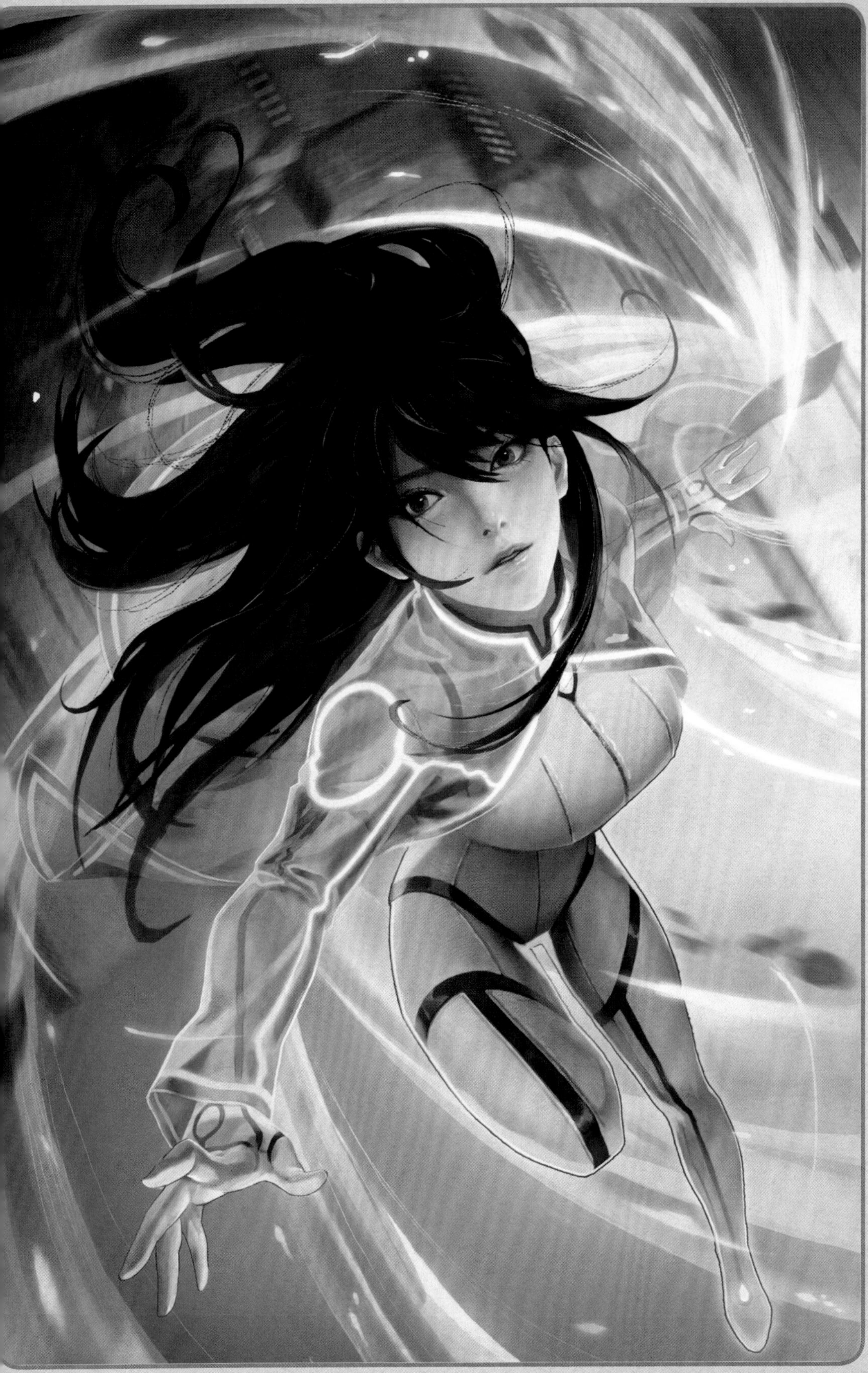

Coax
2 variant

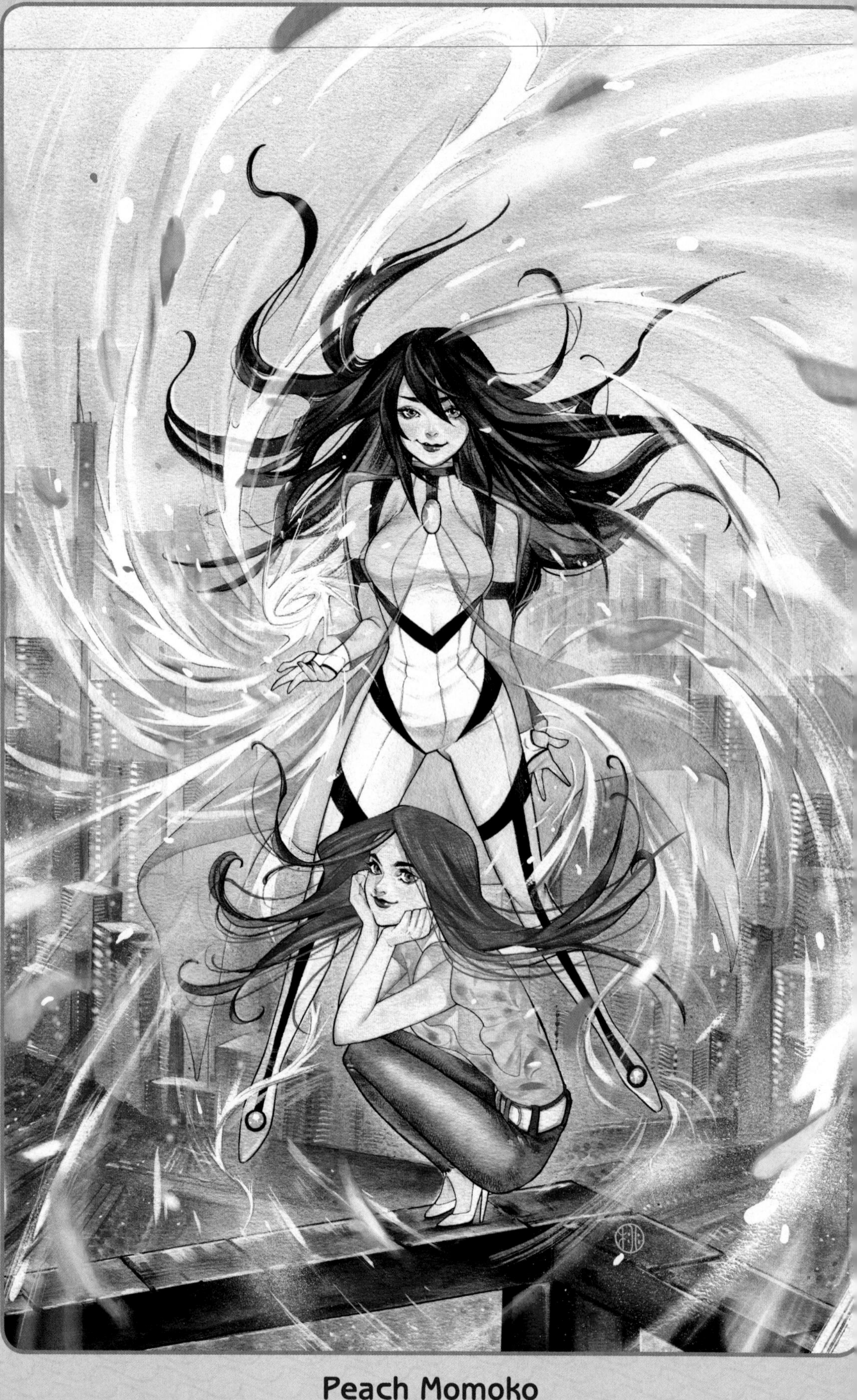

Peach Momoko

4 Mary Jane variant

Character Designs by

Keng

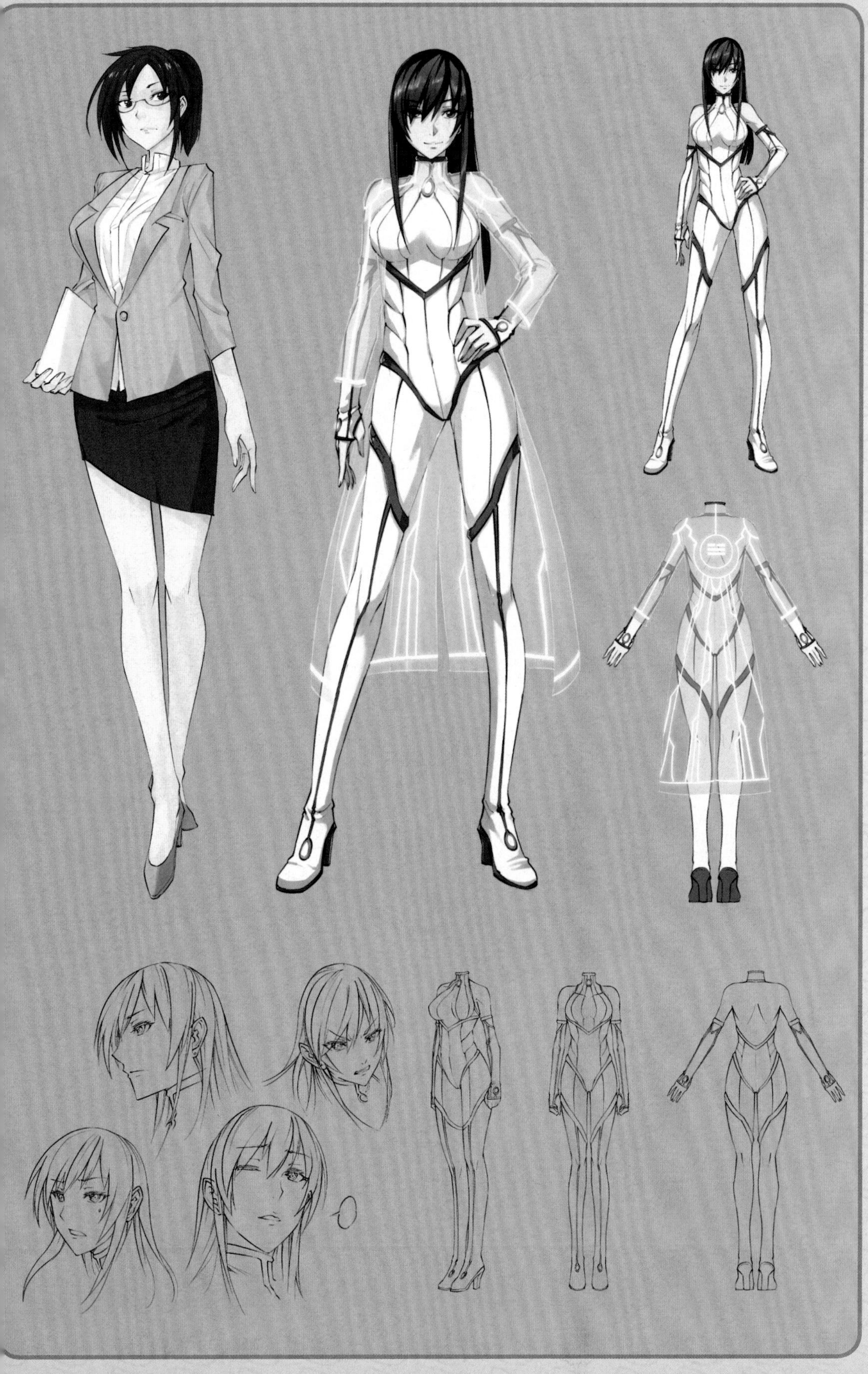

Character Designs by

Keng

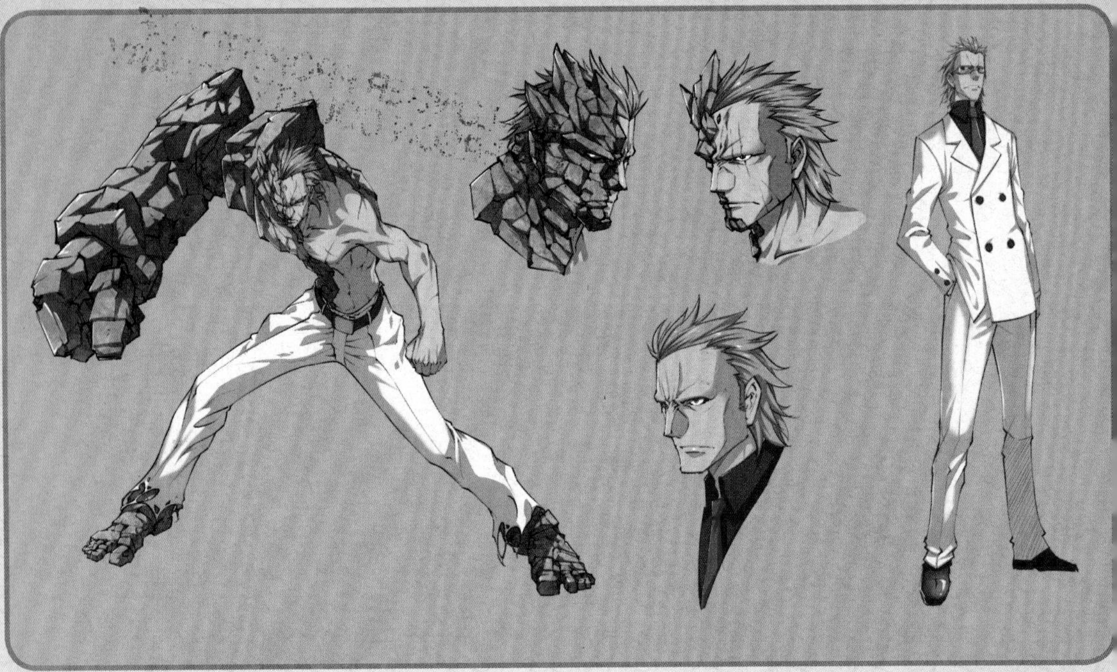

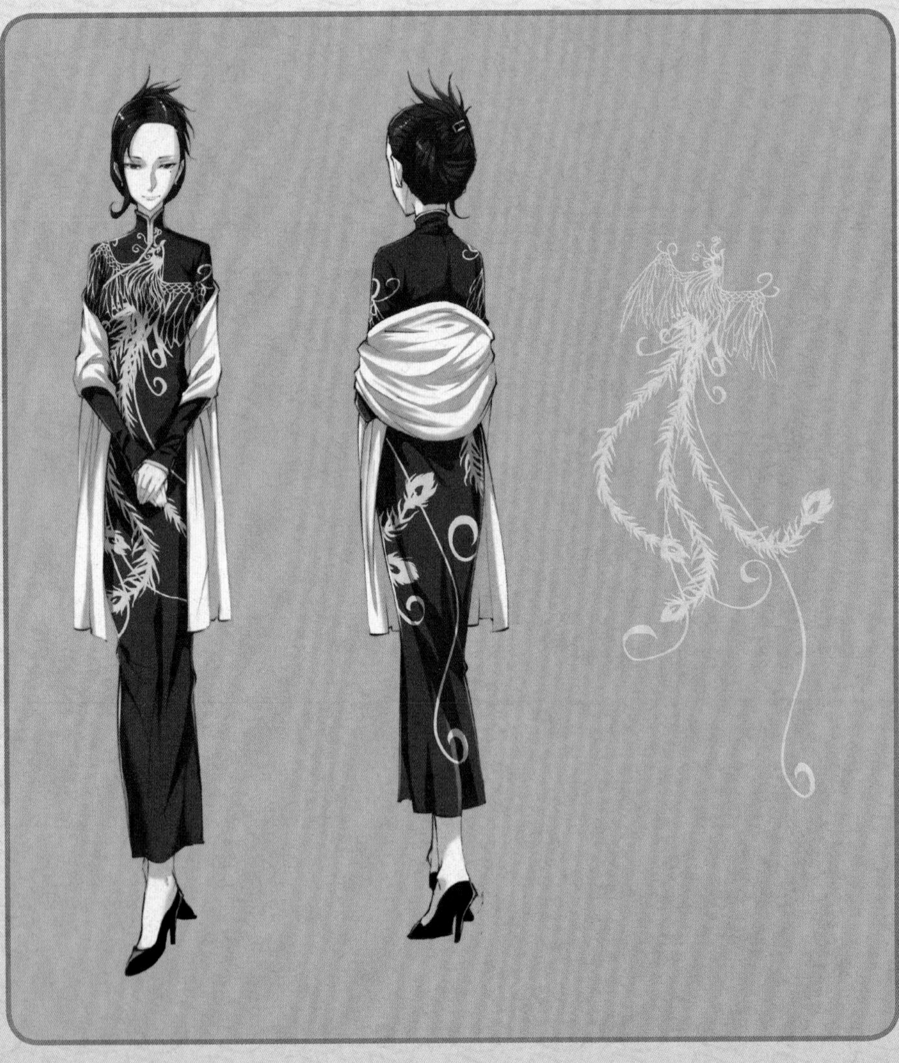